D1066024

DISCIPLINING LOVE

DISCIPLINING LOVE

Austen and the Modern Man

Michael Kramp

THE OHIO STATE UNIVERSITY PRESS
Columbus

Copyright © 2007 by The Ohio State University.
All rights reserved.

Library of Congress Cataloging-in-Publication Data
Kramp, Michael.
Disciplining love : Austen and the modern man / Michael Kramp.
p. cm.
Includes bibliographical references and index.
ISBN-13: 978–0–8142–1046–8 (alk. paper)
ISBN-13: 978–0–8142–9126–9 (cd-rom)
1. Austen, Jane, 1775–1817—Criticism and interpretation. 2. Austen, Jane,
1775–1817—Characters—Men. 3. Austen, Jane, 1775–1817—Influence.
4. Masculinity in literature. 5. Men in literature. I. Title.
PR4037.K73 2007
823.'7—dc22
2006031386

Cover design by James Baumann.
Text design by Jennifer Shoffey Forsythe.
Type set in Adobe Minion.
Printed by Thomson-Shore, Inc..

The paper used in this publication meets the minimum requirements of
the American National Standard for Information Sciences—Permanence of
Paper for Printed Library Materials. ANSI Z39.48–1992.

9 8 7 6 5 4 3 2 1

To Joseph Francis Swan and Dorothy Kramp—
whose importance to this work I am still learning to appreciate

CONTENTS

◄○►

PREFACE

—◄○►—

We are living at an important and fruitful moment now, for it is clear to men that the images of adult manhood given by the popular culture are worn out; a man can no longer depend on them. By the time a man is thirty-five he knows that the images of the right man, the tough man, the true man which he received in high school do not work in life. Such a man is open to new visions of what a man is or could be. (Bly ix)

We have a unique opportunity today, the chance to stand up, be counted, and give men who have chosen a different road an alternative before it's too late. . . . Christian men all over our nation and around the world are suffering because they feel they are on a losing streak and they can't break the pattern. The Adversary has us where he wants us—feeling defeated. It need not be that way. (McCartney 11–13)

Austen, the Late-Millennial Moment, and the Modern Man

Mythopoeticism and the Promise Keepers responded to what they announced as a critical time for men. The leaders of these late-millennial men's movements, Robert Bly and Bill McCartney, delineated the difficulties ostensibly experienced by American males of the 1990s, and outlined strategies to reaffirm masculine identity as stable, integral to larger hegemonic social structures, and vital to the security of the nation. These groups indicted the transformation of the American family, the proliferation of working women, and the atrophy of traditional male social and sexual roles for what they dubbed a crisis of masculinity. Bly's and McCartney's visions for rejuvenated maleness differed, but both advocated the practice of homosocial rituals in which men gathered with other men—and removed from women—to remind each other of proper male identity and activity. The success of these popular men's movements coincided with Jane Austen's mid-1990s cultural revival, in which films, television series, cookbooks, calendars, and other oddities helped to reenergize Austen's enduring appeal—an appeal that has received considerable attention from Austen critics, fans, and devotees.[1] While Bly and the Promise Keepers responded to what they saw as a crisis

moment for men by encouraging homosocial practices designed to reestablish strong hegemonic structures, Austen's late-millennial vogue showed how
the cultural authority of heterosexual men could be maintained without
evangelical meetings or Iron John ceremonies. Indeed, the late-twentieth-
century revisions of Austen's work showcased the model of modern masculinity that emerged alongside the development of the Western nation in the
years following the French Revolution; and the filmic updates of Austen's
narratives depicted such men as attractive and romantic individuals.

The reappearance and lure of Austen's men in the wake of the crisis
announced by the late-twentieth-century men's movements suggests the
value of her fictional world, and specifically her male characters and their
model of masculinity, to the amelioration of social concerns about men. Her
men are not the virile wild men imagined by Bly, nor are they the devoted
family men who attended McCartney's large Promise Keepers' gatherings.
My project aims to study the masculinity modeled by the men of Austen's
novels—men who attempt to achieve sexual and social security amid the
insecurity of the post-Revolutionary period. The men of her tales respond
to diverse and conflicting cultural standards for male identity and behavior generated by England's volatile discursive response to the Revolution.
They are well-managed men who are capable of becoming active members
of the modern English nation because they monitor their desires. Despite
the romantic draw of the men in the late-millennial filmic versions of
Austen's tales, my readings of her novels will demonstrate that her men are
appealing and effective modern men precisely because they regulate their
susceptibility to amorous emotions. Devoney Looser, in her assessment of
Austen's relevance to mid-1990s men's movements, questions: "Are Austen's
heroes appealing because they are in some sense 'new' to us; because they
harken back to older versions of masculinity; or because they are—like her
women—some sort of hybrid of the two?" (164). I will argue that Austen's
men are attractive to late-millennial American culture because they embody
a well-disciplined masculinity that allows them to maintain their participation in hegemonic and heterosexual social structures, such as marriage and
family, without isolating themselves from women.

Men's collectives such as Bly's Mythopoeticism and the Promise Keepers
attempted to rebuild such hegemonic and heterosexual social structures by
reminding men of their supposedly distinct sexual and social responsibilities.
These movements charged that contemporary men had lost their cultural
identity, function, and direction;[2] Bly and the Promise Keepers, like many
other pundits and critics of masculinity, offered plans for repairing men that
required what Michael A. Messner describes as "spiritually based homosocial

rituals through which [men] can collectively recapture a lost or strayed 'true manhood'" (17).[3] These men's groups wanted to stabilize sex-based identity and function as fixed and oppositional, and this project generated a vast cultural following. Michael Kimmel and Michael Kaufman note that "millions of men have been forced to grapple with what it means to be a man," and they conclude that these "men are searching, looking for a new sense of meaning" that movements such as Mythopoeticism and the Promise Keepers were ready to provide (283). Bly's *Iron John: A Book About Men* (1990) encouraged men to embrace their intrinsic manliness—in opposition to intrinsic womanliness—and to dismiss diluted or complicated models of masculinity that might subdue male potency; the Promise Keepers, likewise, urged confused or troubled men to recall the gender stability inherent in what Messner calls "biblical essentialism." Messner explains that the "Promise Keepers' discourse relies on little or no scientific justification or basis for its essentialist beliefs"; rather, biblical essentialism is "based on faith" and "allows Promise Keepers' discourse about women to be couched in terms of 'respect' for women (in their proper places as mothers, wives, and emotional caretakers of house and home)" (30). The 1990s men's movements insisted that men are fundamentally different from women, and they charged men to embrace such differences as vital to their sexual identities and social functions.

While these men's movements reacted to what they saw as a crisis in masculinity, the updates of Austen's narratives reminded us that crises of masculinity are nothing new, and the successful period-piece films provided American culture with an efficient strategy for easing anxieties about contemporary men without banishing them from women. The long-standing appeal of Austen's narratives has been due to the charm of her characters, their manners, and their society; more specifically, Austen's tales have remained attractive because they supposedly show us men and women who engage in romantic relationships devoid of angst or crisis in a world free of conflict, controversy, and uncertainty.[4] Henry Grunwald wrote of the several Austen films:

> Many teenagers say that they are attracted by the elegant houses and what they believe to have been a gentler and more humane way of life. Other observers argue that these films convey a controlled passion that is more sensuous than the crass sexual exhibitions of so many current movies. . . . As for me, watching each of the Austen productions, I was struck by the good manners and the correct English—language representing manners of the mind. The contrast with the vulgarity of most other films and much of daily life brought me a sense of relief, of being in an oasis. (A16)

Grunwald's comments on the 1990s Austen films illustrate the millennial conception of the novelist's work as a repository of a well-organized society clearly distinct from the present. The organization of her characters was also observed by late-twentieth-century American audiences. Ellen Goodman explored America's obsession with Austen's men and women and concluded "that what makes the characters appealing and exotic to us is that they are so full of restraints and/or constraints" (A23). The self-regulation of Austen's men and women mirrors their ostensibly structured society that critics admire. And it is noteworthy that the sexual restraint and social stability that Goodman and Grunwald value in the Austen recreations is quite similar to the stability—both social and sexual—that Bly and the Promise Keepers attempted to provide men through their manifestoes. American culture of the 1990s was enamored of both the discipline of Austen's heterosexual romances and the sex-based dichotomy of the men's movements: both appeared to offer a return to hegemonic social and sexual structures as a simple strategy for ridding modernity of its complexity. Ultimately, the social/sexual subjectivity modeled by Austen's men is at once more attractive and more useful to society; her men do not need homosexual rites to amend their insecurities, and their relations with women promote the biological and cultural reproduction of the nation.

I am not suggesting that the Austen vogue of the late twentieth century responds to, corrects, or perpetuates the men's movements of the same period; I believe that Austen's late-millennial reappearance helped American culture to recall a model of masculinity that was vital to the resolution of a previous social and sexual crisis. The men of Austen's novels become contributing members of English society in the years following the French Revolution, the era in which the emerging modern nation develops its organizing civic structures. These male figures of Austen's corpus are examples of what have become a prototype of modern masculinity and a vital component of the heterosexual hegemony that the late-millennial men's movements sought to preserve. Kimmel and Kaufman explain that the men's movements of the 1990s vocalized "the cry of anguish of privileged American men, men who [felt] lost in a world in which the ideologies of individualism and manly virtue are out of sync with the realities of urban, industrialized, secular society" (263). The late-twentieth-century man, according to Kimmel and Kaufman, was no longer able to make sense of his sexuality in an altered world, and the men's movements gave such uncertainty a voice and a home. Austen's corpus, however, offers uncertain modern men a solution; her works show how post-Revolutionary men resolved their insecurities and gained access to the modern nation and its social structures by placating cultural desires for proper masculinity and managing their desires. The filmic updates of Austen depicted attractive heterosexual men who did not need to retreat from women to be functional social and sexual subjects. The Austen films portrayed men who were at once pleasant and safe; in addition, these men upheld the hegemonic quality of patriarchal structures such as family and marriage without appearing separatist or tyrannical. My study invites us to reconsider the simultaneity of the popular men's movements and Austen's late-millennial vogue as a way of assessing the social value of her men, but my book is fundamentally a reading of Austen's novels. My goal is to demonstrate the enduring cultural utility of Austen's men, and I am specifically interested in how the disciplined masculinity modeled by her men helps to resolve social and sexual crises and promote social order.

ACKNOWLEDGMENTS

◄○►

This book is the product of a longstanding obsession with the work of Jane Austen, and thus I know that I owe debts of gratitude to far more people than I am able to remember here. Thanks are due to my many colleagues and friends who have read all or parts of the manuscript, and in particular to Erin Jordan, Ann Little, Brian Luskey, Mark Berrettini, and Tom Bredehoft. I would also like to express my sincere gratitude to Devoney Looser for her helpful suggestions and advice on this project. For her tireless and precise work as a research assistant, thanks to Amy Otis. I am also extremely grateful to my many teachers over the years who have encouraged me to continue writing and thinking. I especially wish to thank Virginia Hyde, Albert J. Rivero, Debbie Lee, Ronald J. Bieganowski, S. J., Shawn Michelle Smith, Claudia L. Johnson, Tim Machan, John Ehrstine, Nicholas Kiessling, John D. McCabe, Victor Villanueva, Joan Burbick, Alex Hammond, and Michael F. McCanles. Special thanks are due to Carol Siegel—especially for her ceaseless commitment to intellectualism.

Thanks to my family, and especially my parents, for their love and support. I would also like to thank Joseph Conwell, S.J., and Jane Rinehart, who long ago showed me the importance of this work; perhaps I was paying more attention than I knew.

I am very appreciative of the financial support of the University of Northern Colorado Office of the Provost and the Sponsored Programs and Academic Research Center for providing financial support to help fund research for this project.

My special thanks to Sandy Crooms, my editor at The Ohio State University Press, for making the publication process a joy for me. I would also like to thank Maggie Diehl and her staff for their precise copyediting.

Thanks to Jackson and Nicholas, for reminding me of the ever-impending hope of youthful masculinity. And finally, my dearest gratitude to Rita, who consistently shows me that love need not be disciplined.

Part of chapter 7, "Imagining Malleable Masculinity and Radical Nomadism in *Persuasion*," and part of the conclusion appeared in *Rhizomes* 2 (2001), 5–30. For their permission to reprint that material here, I thank the journal's editors, Ann Kibbey and Carol Siegel.

Love, Social/Sexual
Organization, and Austen

◄○►

Remember the country and the age in which we live. Remember that we are English, that we are Christians. Consult your own understanding, your own sense of the probable, your own observation of what is passing around you. (Henry Tilney, in Northanger Abbey *159)*

So unlike what a man should be! — None of that upright integrity, that strict adherence to truth and principle, that disdain of trick and littleness, which a man should display in every transaction of his life. (Emma Woodhouse, in Emma *360)*

In Henry Tilney's charge to Catharine Morland, he implies that this land and time are safe and ordered. In Emma Woodhouse's expression of disgust with the behavior of Frank Churchill, she identifies his actions as unmanly. Her aversion, likewise, presumes that there is *a* proper way for a man to act in society that all males ought to know. These comments of Austen's characters remind us of her concern with the identity of the English nation and its men. Austen's corpus dramatizes England's transformation into a modern nation, and an integral element of this process is the modernization of English men. She depicts men who achieve the social and sexual propriety referenced by Emma Woodhouse despite the cultural turmoil engendered by England's response to the French Revolution—turmoil that Henry Tilney does not acknowledge. Austen's men respond to a variety of cultural directives for proper masculinity, and they acclimate themselves to the needs of a changing society, but they must carefully regulate their proclivity to sexual desires to ensure their prolonged stability.

Austen's novels do not portray a society attempting to forbid men from engaging in sexual activity; rather, Austen's tales present a modernizing nation that attempts to regulate how its men stylize and fashion themselves as sexualized subjects. Michel Foucault points out that "sexual behavior is not, as is too often assumed, a superimposition of, on the one hand, desires that derive from natural instincts, and, on the other hand, of permissive or restrictive laws that tell us what we should or shouldn't do." He concludes that "sexual behavior is more than that. It is also the consciousness one has of what one is doing, what one makes of the experience, and the value one attaches to it" ("Sexual Choice, Social Act" 141–42). I will treat the issues of sexuality, sexual desire, and love within Austen's texts not as natural instincts that must be either satisfied or repressed, but as matters of social conduct and cultural consciousness that are crafted, maintained, and adjusted. Austen repeatedly represents men who monitor their sexualities as part of their larger civic duty, and their self-management allows them to participate more fully in a modernizing culture.

As I discuss in my opening chapter, the English society that emerged in the years following the French Revolution specifically instructed men how to prevent emotion from endangering their civic identities. Early-nineteenth-century England actively sought strategies to curb the passionate behavior of men associated with the radical experiment in France, and England was especially nervous about men's susceptibility to love and sexual desire. Austen's works consistently illustrate this important dialectic between the individual's sexuality and the security of the national community. Austen specifically notes the social complications and consequences involved in sexual desire, love relations, and marriage, and she likewise demonstrates how civic duties affect the pursuit of desire and romance. Throughout my argument, I will use the term social/sexual subjectivity to denote this complex interrelation between the social statuses and sexualities of Austen's men. I want to emphasize how the late-eighteenth-century cultural discourses that I discuss in my first chapter were concerned with *both* the construction of a modern English nation and the formation of a disciplined modern man.

Austen's corpus is a useful cultural site to study how men of a modernizing nation respond to cultural anxieties about masculinity. Her narratives depict men who monitor their amorous emotions while maintaining romantic relationships with women; these relationships, however, are inevitably marked by the order amenable to a society in transition rather than the volatile unpredictability of love. Gilles Deleuze and Félix Guattari provokingly inquire, "What does it mean to love somebody," and they conclude:

> It is always to seize that person in a mass, extract him or her from a group, however small, in which he or she participates, whether it be through the family only or through something else; then to find that person's own packs, the multiplicities he or she encloses within himself or herself which may be of an entirely different nature. To join them to mine, to make them penetrate mine, and for me to penetrate the other person's. Heavenly nuptials, multi-

plicities of multiplicities. Every love is an exercise in depersonalization. . . .
(*Thousand Plateaus* 35)

For Deleuze and Guattari, love destroys the singularity and security of the
individual and compels each lover to embrace the diversity and complexity
in both the self and the other; love engenders lines of flight or new kinds
of relationships between the diverse and mobile packs that constitute the
lovers. Such love prevents men and women from embracing the specific
and singular roles that both the post-Revolutionary English nation and the
late-millennial men's movements assigned to citizens to establish gender
clarity and ordered civilizations. For Deleuze and Guattari, "being-lover"
and "being-loved" allow individuals to pursue fluid emotion, pleasurable
sensation, and subjectivities marked by flexibility. They ultimately announce
that we should "use love and consciousness to abolish subjectification"; they
see the potential of love to subvert the ordering forces of modern civilization
that subject us/make us subject to disciplined modes of sexuality (*Thousand
Plateaus* 134).[1] The male figures of Austen's corpus are, however, strongly
urged to become regulated social/sexual subjects in order to provide the civic
and cultural leadership required to stabilize the modern English nation. The
literary and political discourses of the 1790s establish distinct desires for
appropriate English maleness, and each of these models requires the proper
man to maintain a singular, static, and well-managed sexuality that does
not entail self-banishment from women; Austen's work offers us portraits
of men who relinquish the "heavenly nuptials" and powerful desire theorized by Deleuze and Guattari in favor of a disciplined model of modern
love endorsed by post-Revolutionary England.[2] This modern love solidifies
stable individual identities for men and women, and, by ensuring strict gender polarity, it ultimately helps to justify and maintain hegemonic structures
that support modern patriarchy.

Austen, Love, and Marriage

The issues of love, sexuality, and marriage have, of course, received considerable attention in Austen scholarship, and the centrality of these features in
her work has helped to promote her enduring appeal.[3] Austen's late-twentieth-century revival illustrated how her supposed documentation of gender
and social propriety has remained extremely attractive to American consum-
ers. Austen's ostensible authority on gender, marriage, and love, however, has
historically focused upon women. Eve Kosofsky Sedgwick, in a later manifestation of her infamous 1989 MLA conference presentation, noted that

"Austen criticism is notable mostly, not just for its timidity and banality, but for its unresting exaction of the spectacle of a Girl Being Taught a Lesson" ("Jane Austen and the Masturbating Girl" 315). Sedgwick's characterization of Austen scholarship as a practice in disciplining vivacious young women reflects a lengthy tradition of "marriage" criticism that Claudia Johnson discusses in her influential essay, "Austen Cults and Cultures."[4] Austen criticism continues to insist upon the educational value of her corpus for young women, and the late-millennial Austen craze reminded us of this reputed applicability of the writer's stories. Natalie Tyler, in her wonderfully entertaining handbook *The Friendly Jane Austen* (1999), reveals the longevity of this cultural belief in Austen's panoramic authority on both women's lives and their progression toward marriage.[5] Tyler presents Austen as an advisor who offers helpful counsel to troubled individuals, and she specifically upholds the valuable marital advice in Austen's works. Tyler adds that "the marriage plot compels Austen's heroines to learn how to read human character. . . . Hence it is also an education plot" (59). This popular conception of her tales as guidebooks for young women's effective marriage preparation has prompted numerous critics in the years following Austen's Hollywood successes to explore the role of the writer and her tales in expounding the cultural narrative of heteronormativity.[6] And her contemporary cultural clout as a heterosexual romance advisor has encouraged scholars to sustain both the "Girl-Being-Taught-A-Lesson" model of criticism *and* the focus on the narratives' marriage plots; however, Austen criticism remains notably silent on the sexuality and behavior of the heterosexual male lover.[7]

Instead, the critical penchant to view Austen's corpus as a marital training ground for young women has led to a scholarly focus on the female subject.[8] Important feminist and female-centered treatments of Austen throughout the 1980s—including Sandra M. Gilbert and Susan Gubar's *The Madwoman in the Attic* (1979), LeRoy W. Smith's *Jane Austen and the Drama of Woman* (1983), Margaret Kirkham's *Jane Austen, Feminism and Fiction* (1983), Mary Poovey's *The Proper Lady and the Woman Writer* (1984), and John Hardy's *Jane Austen's Heroines: Intimacy in Human Relationships* (1984)—established a vital new arena in Austen criticism by advancing sophisticated arguments about the depiction of women and femininity in the six novels.[9] These early feminist critics provided detailed explorations of femininity and women's social lives in Austen's texts. Their works, nonetheless, often isolated Austen's representations of female characters, effectively disregarding the symbiotic and complex processes of gender formation in Austen's narratives; moreover, this concentration on her portrayal of the heroine has traditionally theorized (either implicitly or explicitly) a simple and static man who is the opposite and/or oppressor of women. The critical emphasis on Austen's marriage plots has thus encouraged many to read her corpus as a collection of tales documenting a woman's search not for love or a lover, but for a stable and stabilizing husband.

The young woman's marital quest, according to this standard approach of Austen criticism, involves various lessons the heroine must learn as she matures and accepts her own social/sexual limitations. This critical supposition depends upon a conception of masculinity as fixed and static; the ideal man for each heroine is presumably somewhere within the narrative, and if she learns the requisite lessons, she will find *her* man—who is simply waiting to be found. Laura Tracy claims that Austen portrays exactly such autonomous and self-determining men; she argues that "one of Austen's sub-themes about men in her work [is] that they cannot be changed by women"; she concludes that "Austen implied that men in Western culture are created to be independent subjects—heroes of their own lives" (157). This traditional reading of Austen, which casts each woman's idealized man as a secure and independent figure, is strongly rooted in Freudian notions of Oedipal development that presuppose the masculine subject as an always-already complete and fully formed sexual subject. In *Sexuality and the Psychology of Love,* Freud outlines the different challenges faced by men and women throughout their Oedipal developments. He theorizes that men must successfully progress beyond these trials to achieve sexual and social maturity, but he bemoans that "the majority of men are . . . far behind the masculine ideal" (193). Freud's notion of a "masculine ideal" that men supposedly seek has remained important to the field of masculinity studies and integral to the success of the late-millennial popular men's movements.[10] Kaja Silverman's widely anthologized study, *Male Subjectivity at the Margins* (1992), may have epitomized this Freudian influence as she explored the struggles and failures of modern men to reach the apex of masculinity—the same struggles and failures that prompted many men's interest in Bly's mythopoetic manifesto and Promise Keepers' gatherings. This Freudian theory of masculinity effectively bifurcates men—that is, each man is either an ideal male sexual subject, or he is lacking.[11]

Freud's conception of men and masculinity is reductive, and it is specifically ineffective for studying Austen's fictional representation of gendered identity. The men of Austen's corpus, rather than attempting to imitate a single and stable paragon of masculinity, must negotiate numerous intertwined and contradictory standards for proper maleness that are always inflected by national concerns and perpetually debated and revised. Claudia L. Johnson accurately expresses the complexity of Austen's male characters when she announces that "we will miss what is distinctive about Austen's achievement if we assume that masculine self-definitions were givens rather than qualities under reconstruction" (*Equivocal Beings* 199). The developing English nation does not offer Austen's men a single and static system for male sexual development à la Freud; the literary and political discourses of the 1790s debate various models of masculinity and male social identity. Deleuze and Guattari, in their response to Freud, take up precisely this point, explaining that modern societies "make a habit of feeding on the contradictions they give rise to, on the crises they provoke, on the anxieties they *engender*" (*Anti-Oedipus* 151). The post-Revolutionary cultural disorder creates such a contradictory situation for England's men, and Freud's prominent theory of sexuality cannot negotiate this complexity. Angus McLaren points out that "Freud's famous question 'What do women want?' has garnered a good deal of indignant attention," but as McLaren reminds us, "few have observed that he did not ask 'What do men want?,' the assumption being that everyone knew" (3). My treatment of Austen allows for a reexamination of the emergent model of Western masculinity, and I demonstrate that post-Revolutionary men's desires—and perhaps more importantly, post-Revolutionary society's desires for men—were neither certain nor static.

Modern Man and the Aesthetic of Existence

Austen's corpus provides us with a unique opportunity to study masculinity and male sexual development for three primary reasons: (1) it coincides with profound historical changes in Western conceptions of men and maleness; (2) it demonstrates the important dialectical process of gender formation; and (3) it portrays men who have become cultural icons of masculinity. Joseph A. Kestner rightly notes that "the formation of modern ideologies of masculinity occurred precisely at the time of Austen's formation as a novelist" (147). Austen's texts depict modern men who attempt to achieve new and changing standards for proper male sexual identity, and she emphasizes how this process is affected by numerous discourses and events, including the transformation of English society, the reconfiguration of its class structure, and the social/sexual formation of women. To consider the complexity of these various cultural concerns to which Austen's men respond, I employ Foucault's notion of the aesthetic of existence that he develops in the second and third volumes of *The History of Sexuality*. Foucault's work offers a flexible understanding of sexualized subjectivity that allows me to theorize the impact of diverse socially produced qualifications for appropriate maleness without neglecting the individual's interaction with these cultural forces. Foucault indicates that the deployment and regulation of sexuality involves an ethics or aesthetics of existence that he discusses as an "elaboration of a form of relation to self that enables an individual to fashion himself into a subject of ethical conduct" (*Use of Pleasure* 251).[12] He explains that the subject's ethics involve "the kind of relationship you ought to have with yourself . . . which determines how the individual is supposed to constitute himself as a moral subject of his own actions" ("On the Genealogy" 263).[13] England's cultural debates of the 1790s delineate various and conflicting standards for proper masculinity that the men of Austen's fiction must negotiate as they fashion themselves as sexual and national subjects; Austen's tales reveal that these men's efforts repeatedly compel them to relinquish their identities as lovers and discipline their sexual desire. While Freud's theory of an idealized masculinity invites critics to read Austen's corpus as a manual for young women in quest of Mr. Right, Foucault's theory of the aesthetic of existence allows us to examine—within the context of England's late-eighteenth-century discussions—how and why Austen's male characters form their social/sexual subjectivities.

Austen's men craft disciplined social/sexual identities that enable them to satisfy a variety of cultural desires for proper masculinity, and this model of male sexuality is integral to the development of the modern English nation throughout the nineteenth century. Austen's men learn to become stable subjects who are then able to participate in hegemonic heterosexual structures like marriage and family; moreover, the regulation of their desires masks their complexity and prevents any destabilizations. Austen's novels illustrate an efficient model of love and desire that serves the state and its systems of cultural reproduction. Her portrayal of the heterosexual romance narrative is undeniably marked by such concerns of national stability and social rehabilitation, and her corpus offers us multiple portraits of men who opt to pursue the ordered rationality of secure/securing love rather than the messiness and complications of sexual desire. This strategy for male sexual formation has become the dominant model of Western masculinity that is reinforced whenever the hackneyed "crisis of masculinity" resurfaces.

In Deleuze's brilliant "Letter to a Harsh Critic," he explains that "non-oedipal love is pretty hard work," and he points out that the majority of modern lovers are hesitant to expose themselves "to love and desire" and instead revert to "the whining need to be loved that leads everyone to the psychoanalyst" (10). This "whining need" fueled the successes of the mid-1990s men's movements, and it likely helped to entice moviegoers to the filmic adaptations of Austen's tales in search of a simpler time when love supposedly "worked." The propinquity of the late-millennial men's move-ments and the Austen cultural revival, however, ultimately reminds us of the incipience of our efficient and effective model of disciplined modern love. Non-Oedipal love, as Deleuze notes, is risky and even arduous, and Austen's novels illustrate that as the modern English nation recovers from the radical tumult of the French Revolution, it could not allow its men to assume such perilous and laborious tasks that might distract them from the business of ordering the state.

Austen Criticism and Masculinity

Despite Freud's sustained influence in the study of sexual development, theorists of masculinity finally succeeded in questioning and destabilizing the long-standing assumption of a fixed and natural male figure during the same mid-1990s period that experienced Austen's Hollywood vogue and the rise of popular men's movements. R. W. Connell's *Masculinities* (1995), Robyn Wiegman's *American Anatomies: Theorizing Race and Gender* (1995), and Michael Kimmel's *Manhood in America: A Cultural History* (1996) all challenged the cultural and critical expectation of a static man by examining the histories of different masculinities and exploring the various processes of men's social formations; moreover, these and other theorists of masculinity emphasized the intellectual and political synergy between feminist scholar-ship and masculinity studies.[14] Wiegman explained that the deconstruction or "'unmaking,' if you will, of the category of men importantly remakes masculinity as pertinent to if not constitutive of female subjectivity, thereby rendering complex feminism's ability to negotiate the distinctions and inter-connections between sex, sexuality, and gender" ("Unmaking" 33). Connell likewise insisted that "no masculinity arises except in a system of gender relations." Connell added that "rather than attempting to define masculinity as an object (a natural character type, a behavioural average, a norm), we need to focus on the processes and relationships through which men and women conduct gendered lives" (71). The work of Connell, Wiegman, and Kimmel helped to initiate new theoretical strategies for studying the forma-tion of masculinity as a dialectical process informed by historical contexts and individual men's desires.

Although Alfred P. Ollivier wrote a master's thesis on Austen's men in 1950, Austen scholars did not begin to directly address her men until this critical reconfiguration of masculinity. The theme of the 1996 meeting of the Jane Austen Society of North America (JASNA) was "Jane Austen and Her Men," and the subsequent 1996 volume of *Persuasions* collected much of the convention attendees' work on the subject.[15] During this same mid-1990s period, scholars began to treat Austen's men as part of larger critical projects. Roger Sales's *Jane Austen and Representations of Regency England* (1994) offered an impressive reading of Austen's later works within the context of regency scandals, including the indecorous activity of prominent men such as the Prince of Wales. Sales's criticism has been particularly important in identifying new ways to historicize gender identity in Austen's tales by rethinking the relationship between her narratives and the regency crises. Johnson's *Equivocal Beings: Politics, Gender, and Sentimentality in the 1790s* (1995) provided an innovative reading of gender in the late eighteenth century, but she devoted only her Afterword to Austen. Johnson read *Emma's* Knightley as an impressive male figure capable of rehearsing earlier models of chivalric masculinity while simultaneously performing modern male duties. She argued that Knightley's humane model of masculinity "[diminished] the authority of male sentimentality, and [reimmasculated] men and women alike with a high sense of national purpose" (191). Johnson suggested that Knightley initiated a new type of English maleness that is neither anachronistic nor overly progressive; this model of masculinity, according to Johnson, "desentimentalizes and deheterosexualizes virtue, and in the process makes it accessible to women as well [as men]" (199). The critical work of Sales and Johnson demonstrated the importance of Austen's men to our larger understanding of post-Revolutionary England, and specifically illustrated the emergence of modern men alongside the development of the modern nation.

Tim Fulford's *Romanticism and Masculinity: Gender, Politics and Poetics in the Writings of Burke, Coleridge, Cobbett, Wordsworth, De Quincey and Hazlitt* (1999) has likewise been a vital contribution to the study of masculinity in early-nineteenth-century literature. Fulford added to Johnson's work by evaluating the national responses to the French Revolution and the subsequent reconfigurations of England's cultural conception of proper masculinity. Fulford argued that throughout the Romantic period, "Chivalric manhood did not die"; he asserted "it was relocated in the middle classes," and he traced this thesis through the writings of many major male writers of the period (*Romanticism and Masculinity* 9). His work encouraged a reconsideration of both the Romantic(ized) male subject and the literary representation of men in the period, and his more recent treatments of Austen's novels have been especially informative to my investigation of masculinity in her corpus.[16] And yet, this critical energy has not generated sustained critical study of Austen's male characters; rather, this interest in Austen's men seems to have culminated with the publication of Audrey Hawkridge's *Jane and Her Gentlemen: Jane Austen and the Men in Her Life and Novels* (2000).

Hawkridge's work provided a comprehensive but uncritical and ahistorical assessment of the male figures in Austen's family and fiction. While this book did offer interesting speculations on the representation of maleness in Austen's texts, Hawkridge's goal was simply to demonstrate the artistry of Austen's characterization by documenting the impact of the men in her life on the men of her stories. Hawkridge made clear that her "particular examination of Jane's world looks at the men in her family and her social circle, what she thought of them and how they affected her life. They cast their own light on the men in her works, most of whom she presents so roundly that we feel they are old friends, to admire or smile at as she intended but never to hate" (7). Hawkridge's fond appreciation for Austen's men may have concluded what appeared to be a promising new area of Austen studies. Despite the accomplishments of masculinity theorists and the work of scholars such as Sales, Johnson, and Fulford, Austen's men have not yet received the critical study necessary to delineate the cultural efficacy of her novelistic project's conceptions of masculinity.

Men, Love, and the Modern Nation

I treat Austen's novels as a collection of cultural documents that exposes both a social anxiety about masculinity *and* a social response to this anxiety. My focus throughout is to evaluate the social discipline of the male lover that Austen's work dramatizes. Austen's works have been influential in crafting Western notions of the idealized man, but it is a critical misreading to assume that Austen's tales advocate or uphold either a disciplined model of masculinity or any other ideal of maleness.[17] Instead, in my discussions of the individual novels, I consider various men's attempts to develop social/sexual subjectivities that will allow them to participate in the civic community and its hegemonic structures, and I explore the ramifications of such attempts on the men's identities as lovers. I make no effort to take up every man in Austen's corpus, and prominent figures such as Mr. Darcy, Edward Ferrars, and Henry Crawford receive only brief mention. I concentrate on men whose social/sexual subjectivities reveal important shifts in the modernizing nation's expectations for men.

England's ambitions for the modernizing nation and its men are the principal topics of my first chapter, and I briefly frame my discussion of the late-eighteenth-century discourses on nation and masculinity by considering the influence of prominent eighteenth-century courtesy books upon such public debates. The turbulent decade of the 1790s has proved fecund ground for studies of Austen, and yet treatments of her novels have largely ignored the various prescriptions of ideal manliness that emerged throughout this period. These models of maleness are produced by a nexus of literary and political texts that focused on and responded to the national crisis engendered by the French Revolution, the rising feminist movement in England and Europe, the continuing Enlightenment tradition, and the sentimental rhetoric of the late eighteenth century. The post-Revolutionary cultural documents I investigate explored plans for the future of the nation and debate the worthiness of proposals for far-reaching social reform. England's ideal of masculinity was a recurring component of these discourses, and I will specifically treat three discourses that structured the public dialogue about masculinity: the contemporary relevance of a chivalric social system, the volatile relation between the Enlightenment doctrine of rationality and the sentimental tradition, and the appropriate relations between the sexes. My goal in this chapter is to establish the historical and textual context out of which Austen's depictions of masculinity emerged. I organize my discussion of the late-eighteenth-century cultural debates around the works of Edmund Burke and Mary Wollstonecraft; I concentrate on the political and philosophical texts in the initial chapter, and I consider relevant literary works within my discussions of Austen's novels.

I then provide a selective treatment of Austen's juvenilia, and while I do not concern myself with the impact of the post-Revolutionary discourses on the male lovers of these short tales, I do note a burgeoning cultural anxiety about young men, their neglect of courtesy book guidelines, and their susceptibility to the dangers of love and sexual desire. I argue that the social/sexual subjectivity of *Northanger Abbey*'s Henry Tilney serves as Austen's fictional response to this growing concern about England's young men. Tilney's strong adherence to the doctrine of rationality protects him from the potentially overwhelming powers of love. Henry models a masculinity rooted in Jacobin principles of reason and industry; he will not allow the irrational or sublime to affect his behavior, and even his climactic decision to disobey the authority of his father and travel to the Morlands' home is based upon reason. And yet, Henry's restraint reveals his knowledge of other cultural debates on nation and masculinity, including the discourses of chivalry and Enlightenment feminism. He is a disciplined man whose structured behavior protects him against the snares of romance that entangle the young lovers of Austen's juvenilia.

The suitors of Marianne Dashwood show us more extensive examples of the dangers of love and desire. Austen casts Brandon and Willoughby as men of sensation who are schooled in the appreciation of sensory perceptions, respectful of sentiment, and liable to uncontrollable emotional outbursts. The narrator portrays these men as lovers, and she notes the severe consequences of such behavior; Brandon has taught himself to regulate his senses and manage his sensitivity, and the narrative dramatizes Willoughby's training in modern love. The long-standing reading of *Sense and Sensibility* as Marianne's epiphany that Brandon is the truly right man for her implies that there is some outstanding difference between her suitors, but I argue that Willoughby and the Colonel are essentially committed to the same model of male behavior. Brandon has simply already learned what Willoughby learns by the end of the novel: that to become a trusted and responsible figure in the modern national community, men of sensation must discipline their sensitivity.

Pride and Prejudice offers us an important glimpse of the cultural reconceptualization of masculinity that accompanies England's modernization. I treat Darcy as an exemplar of a vanishing type of man; he is a resplendent figure who is at once chivalric, rational, and romantic, and I argue that his status as an ostensibly impeccable man highlights his uniqueness. The aristocratic tradition that Darcy embodies and Pemberley institutionalizes is waning, and while it is still greatly admired in the novel, its representatives are dwindling. The novel indicates that as the esteemed nobleman and his accompanying mythology become less common in the modern nation, England must now establish new models of male social identity and begin training non-aristocratic men to assume greater civic responsibilities. I focus on the development and improvement of Mr. Bingley and Mr. Gardiner. Both of these men have benefited from the successes of the trade class in the early nineteenth century, and each receives important guidance in proper masculinity from Darcy; moreover, the special attention that Darcy devotes to Bingley, whose family has risen from the trade industry, suggests that landed men are concerned enough about the future of the nation's masculinity to mentor men of new money.

While *Pride and Prejudice* shows us a society preparing for the transition to a new nation and a new kind of man, *Mansfield Park* dramatizes a society in denial of this transition. The various crises of the Bertram household anticipate the impending collapse of the aristocratic tradition that we see in *Persuasion*. Edmund's sincere effort to re-solidify his family serves as Austen's final fictional attempt to preserve this decaying lifestyle and its model of masculinity. I present Edmund as the last bastion of the declining aristocratic community; the hero's social/sexual subjectivity specifically tries to merge the qualities of manliness—the gentleman and the clergyman—that Burke outlines in his *Reflections on the Revolution in France* (1790). Edmund invests great importance in both identities, and he virulently defends the importance of the ecclesiastical profession against the charges of the sensually stimulating Mary Crawford. The hero's infatuation with Mary tempts him to abandon the discipline of Burke's archaic mode of socially responsible maleness in favor of the pleasures of modernity, but Edmund ultimately anesthetizes his sensitivity to amorous desires. The hero's marriage to his cousin slows the deterioration of his aristocratic family, preserves the integrity of the Bertram line, and perpetuates endangered models of masculinity, but the atavistic quality of this union also reveals the desperation of the aristocracy to reproduce itself.

In *Emma*, the atrophying aristocracy and its model of masculinity become comic. Mr. Woodhouse is a ridiculous male figure who maintains only ceremonial responsibilities in his community. The tradition that Edmund Bertram endeavors to save now appears to have dissipated with little regret. I treat Knightley as an embodiment of what Foucault theorizes as the modern subject whose social/sexual identity is marked by finitude. I agree with Johnson that Knightley is an important figure in the history of masculinity because of his adaptability; he values the agricultural heritage of Donwell Abbey and serves as a pastoral caretaker for the downtrodden of Highbury, but he also rebukes Frank Churchill's excessive gallantry and willingly pursues the company of the rising trade class. Knightley is truly an impressive man who has loaded his finite social/sexual subjectivity with all the masculine characteristics desired by the post-Revolutionary discursive community. He is an extremely well-ordered individual like Henry Tilney, but unlike the hero of *Northanger Abbey*, Knightley is not committed to one model of male sexuality; his is a flexible masculinity, and he has learned to adjust his social/sexual identity to a modern nation. Knightley, moreover, shows how modern men can preserve social/sexual identity, maintain a vital civic role, and keep the company of women by carefully regulating any amorous desire or sexual passion.

In *Persuasion*, Austen finally presents us Wentworth—a man who embraces amorous emotions. Wentworth is a lover who experiences firsthand the personal and cultural consequences of such a social/sexual identity. The pain of his truncated early romance with the heroine lingers throughout the tale, but the naval hero ultimately regains a willingness to experience desire and passion. Wentworth and his naval colleagues are distinct from the previous men of Austen's corpus and Sir Walter Elliot, who embodies the utter demise of the aristocracy and its model of English masculinity.[18] The Elliots must relinquish their landed estate, and while the narrator highlights the decadence of Sir Walter and his circle, she likewise accentuates the sincerity and compassion of the naval community. Wentworth is a sensitive man whose very body bears the marks of seafaring life, but unlike Willoughby or Brandon, the naval hero does not allow his prior experiences of sensation to curb or anesthetize his sensitivity. He remains open to desire

and its social, emotional, and romantic ramifications; his social/sexual identity is essentially insecure, and his maritime marriage to Anne prevents his
sexuality from becoming stultified or disciplined.

My conclusion briefly considers what I theorize as the cultural response
to Anne and Wentworth's dynamic nautical relationship. I discuss the proliferation of small communities that *Sanditon* suggests are quickly appearing
along the English coast. While Mr. Heywood insists that the vast growth of
such oceanside settlements is economically and socially dangerous for the
nation, Austen presents Sanditon as a successful capitalistic venture; it is
a modernized village whose satirized inhabitants have no interest in experiencing the mobility and volatility of the sea that Anne and Wentworth
embrace. Sanditon may be near the water, but the naval community of *Persuasion* will not be spending much time in this well-regulated coastal locale.
Sanditon's modernity prevents individuals from expressing and experiencing potentially destructuring emotions and desires that might disturb the
stability desperately sought by post-Revolutionary England. Sanditon can
tolerate only conventional figures whose desires and passions are disciplined,
predictable, and easily categorized.

This disciplined model of social/sexual subjectivity has become a crucial component of the modern nation and its men. Austen's corpus portrays a nation in the process of becoming modern that is nervous about
its men. These men of Austen's tales respond to this anxiety by developing
stable social/sexual identities capable of enduring such transformation; they
become functional men who help to stabilize the post-Revolutionary nation
and its social structures. In Terry Castle's controversial review of Austen's letters to her sister, she claims "it is a curious yet arresting phenomenon in the
novels that so many of the final happy marriages seem designed not so much
to bring about a union between hero and heroine as between the heroine
and the hero's sister" ("Sister-Sister" 3). Castle's comment frightened many
Austen fans and critics because of its suggestion of lesbianism, but Castle
actually points to the sibling-like quality of Austen's marriages. Indeed,
she presents several of her marital relationships as close friendships that
resemble familial bonds rather than sexual unions. Austen's popularity as a
default-relationship advisor may even stem from the absence of sexual desire
in her novels' concluding marriages. Modern society desperately wants
marriage to be cleansed of the messiness of sex and desire, and Austen's
corpus offers us a valuable example of this burgeoning cultural ambition in
the years following the French Revolution. As England becomes a modern
nation throughout the nineteenth century, passionate male lovers become
liabilities who cannot consistently assume civic responsibilities; such lovers
might be able to exist on the seas, but the post-Revolutionary English nation

needs stable men who will not permit love to interrupt their involvement in hegemonic social structures. Austen's novels may offer us instructions, but they are rarely instructions for lovers; her texts do, however, teach us how heterosexual men can solidify their involvement in the modern national community by dismissing the role of the lover in favor of a disciplined social/sexual subjectivity.

CHAPTER 1

The Emergence of the Modern Nation and the Development of the Modern Man

◄○►

Nationalisms are not simply phantasmagoria of the mind; as systems of cultural representation whereby people come to imagine a shared experience of identification with an extended community, they are historical practices through which social difference is both invented and performed. . . . Nationalism becomes in this way radically constitutive of people's identities, through social contests that are frequently violent and always gendered. (McClintock 260)

Historians have traditionally pointed to the post-Revolutionary period as the era in which the modern European nation emerged.[1] The appearance of the nation-state, moreover, promoted both the modernization of various social structures, like the family, the citizenry, and the military, and the alteration of cultural conceptions of gender and class. Indeed, as Anne McClintock suggests, the very process of nation-building is necessarily gendered and requires a population ordered by social markers. As the modern English nation developed in the years following the French Revolution, political, philosophical, and literary writers actively engaged in public debates about the appropriate social/sexual identities for men and women; moreover, these discussions occurred during a time of economic and social transformation. Foucault concisely explains these shifts when he notes that "at the end of the eighteenth century, the bourgeoisie set its own body and its precious sexuality against the valorous blood of the nobles" (*History of Sexuality, Vol. 1: An Introduction* 127–28). England's industrious middle classes challenged the hereditary authority of the nobility and established new opportunities for non-aristocratic citizens amid the instability of the early nineteenth century. Austen's novels document the effects of both this socioeconomic transition and the late-eighteenth-century debates on the future of the nation; her male characters confront the social anxieties associated with the civic and class instability and respond to gender prescriptions produced by the public discourses of the 1790s.[2]

The reform culture that permeated England in the 1790s created a discursive community that continually addressed this anxiety. Lisa Plummer Crafton points out that the French Revolution initiated "the largest, most far-reaching and broadest 'debate' in [English] literary and cultural history, a war of ideas that encompasses philosophy, theories of history, the study of language, the history of art, gender stereotypes, [and] religion" (x). This decade witnessed sundry textual responses to the radical events in France that outlined proposals to ensure England's future stability as a nation, and these proposals inevitably emphasized the importance of citizens' social/sexual subjectivities. The writers of the 1790s were certainly concerned with more than the classification of gender, but as Doris Y. Kadish indicates, for participants in the post-Revolutionary debates, "the strategy of politicizing gender . . . served many functions." She explains that gender offered the ostensible security of a fixed marker of identity during a period in which "class and other distinctions were uncertain"; Kadish concludes that "gender provided a convenient and universally understandable analogy to be used, even if pure examples of masculinity and femininity were becoming increasingly difficult to find" (3–4).[3] Contributors to the discursive field of the 1790s thus relied upon the social gender structure to provide stable markers of subjectivity integral to their larger reform projects.[4] And since, as McClintock reminds us, the modernizing European nation conceived of the male citizen as "the progressive agent of national modernity (forward-thrusting, potent and historic)," political and literary writers alike in the 1790s offered distinct portraits of an ideal man as integral components of their plans for the future of the English nation (263).

Life, Progress, and Male Hegemony

Such models of masculinity were envisioned within an era of English cultural transformation that corresponded with what Foucault theorizes as "the entry of life into history." He explains that during the final years of the eighteenth century, "Western man was gradually learning what it meant to be a living species in a living world, to have a body, conditions of existence, probabilities of life, an individual and collective welfare, forces that could be modified, and a space in which they could be distributed in an optimal manner" (*History of Sexuality, Vol. 1* 141–42). The opportunities to enhance, alter, or adjust one's physical and material conditions of existence invited men and women to imagine and pursue improvement, and the English nation promoted this culture of progress. Linda Colley explains that post-Revolutionary England created a new patriotism that "served . . . as a bandwagon on which different groups and interests leaped so as to steer it in a direction that would benefit them." Colley adds that "being a patriot was a way of claiming the right to participate in British political life, and ultimately a means of demanding a much broader access to citizenship" (5). Throughout the late eighteenth and early nineteenth centuries, men of the middle classes demonstrated their patriotism in order to enhance their civic identities and social functions; and the modernizing nation welcomed such patriotism because of its growing need for the bodies and sexualities of bourgeois men.

England's newfound appreciation for the potential of bourgeois men derived from the nation's demand for soldiers in the Revolutionary and Napoleonic Wars, laborers in an industrializing economy, and new social leaders in the wake of the declining aristocratic power structure. The nation became conscious of the necessity to maximize the potential of its people, and in 1798, Great Britain conducted its first census and issued the first of two Defence of the Realm Acts. The Act of April 1798 "demanded from each county: details of the number of able-bodied men in each parish, details of what service, if any, each man was prepared to offer to the state, details of what weapons he possessed, details of the amount of live-stock, carts, mills, boats, barges and grain available, details of how many elderly people there were, how many alien and infirm" (Colley 289). England's overt attempt to organize its human and material resources in response to various threats and instabilities exposed the nation's heightened need for the contributions of all its citizens, especially the previously neglected middle classes. The slow atrophy of the aristocracy created civic openings that patriotic bourgeois men attempted to fill in order to improve their social standings and ensure their roles in the English nation and its hegemonic structures.[5] Fulford claims that post-Revolutionary England "wanted a hero to prove its power and manliness against the French," but as he notes, the nation instead became "a society in which traditional models of authority and gender had been discredited without being successfully replaced" (*Romanticism and Masculinity* 6, 9). Connell likewise argues that the downfall of the traditional aristocratic man simultaneously resulted in the ascension of a gentry masculinity that "was closely integrated with the state" and its local and national administration (190). Connell concludes that this civic-based mode of gentry masculinity prospered because of its bifurcation into a new hegemonic form of masculinity and "an array of subordinated and marginalized masculinities" (191). This hegemonic masculinity became the prevailing model of modern Western masculinity that directed aspiring men to maintain power in both the domestic and public spheres.[6]

Leonore Davidoff and Catherine Hall explain that "manhood was to become a central part of claims to legitimate middle-class leadership" (199).

If the patriotic bourgeois man of modern England were to become an active participant and useful component of the civic community, he must not relinquish hegemonic control of his home and wife. The modern man's failure to maintain authority in the domestic realm impeded his ability to act politically, as he could not be a social man without the sexual subjectivity generated by his hegemonic maintenance of home. English bourgeois men thus attempted to make themselves vital members of the English nation by demonstrating both economic and sexual stability; indeed, they pursued sexual stability as a means to justify their public and private social roles. This process inevitably involved what Harriet Guest discusses as a "permeable" relationship between the public and private spheres (15). The man's relationships with his wife and family provided him with the stable sexuality required to function as an efficacious member of the civic community, and his emergent role in the civic community made his body and sexuality increasingly important to the nation.[7] As Joane Nagel argues, "the culture and ideology of hegemonic masculinity go hand in hand with the culture and ideology of hegemonic nationalism" (401). Post-Revolutionary England recognized its need to deploy the potential of middle class men in order to establish a stable and hegemonically ordered nation; England, in turn, offered these men the opportunity to establish their own social/sexual stability by maintaining hegemony at home.

Designing Sexuality in the Modern Nation

The volatility of English culture in the post-Revolutionary years accentuated the social desire for the stabilizing effects of a hegemonic nationalism and masculinity. As we have seen, England recognized its need for the bodies and sexualities of more men, and hence, it likewise realized that these men must be properly taught to train and use their bodies and sexualities. Foucault explains that at the close of the eighteenth century, sex and its regulation became "a concern of the state . . . sex became a matter that required the social body as a whole, and virtually all of its individuals, to place themselves under surveillance" (*History of Sexuality, Vol. I* 116). Men who would become valued members of the public community must first learn how to administer their social/sexual subjectivities to maintain hegemony and promote the nation, and the social discourses that responded to the radical events in France accordingly designed various models of appropriate maleness. These discourses dialogued with an ongoing tradition of male courtesy books that instructed England's men how best to live as sexualized subjects, but unlike the earlier instruction manuals for proper masculinity such as *The Prince*

and *The Book of the Courtier,* the eighteenth and nineteenth centuries witnessed a democratization of this educational process. Since modern England
required the cooperation of its national citizenry, it attempted to regulate the
sexuality of a larger male population. The writers of the 1790s created a discursive field in which they engaged and revised the courtesy book tradition
to present divergent visions of proper masculine sexuality—visions of the
proper male subject as well as his attributes, associations, and civic duties.[8]
The men of Austen's corpus negotiate these models of masculinity in order
to stabilize their social/sexual subjectivities and gain access to the national
community.

Two well-known schools of thought emerged in these politically charged
debates: one associated with the publication of Edmund Burke's widely read
Reflections on the Revolution in France (1790) and the anti-Jacobin writers
of the period, and the other closely linked to the radical thinkers of the dis-
senting tradition, including such Jacobin figures as William Godwin, Mary
Wollstonecraft, and Mary Hays. Seamus Deane maintains that the French
Revolution "polarized British politics to an unprecedented extent."[9] He
explains that "the publication of Edmund Burke's *Reflections on the Revolution in France* in 1790 compelled those who took part in the subsequent
political debate to declare, in however elementary a fashion, the principles
of their political beliefs" (4).[10] Burke's rhetorical response to the French
Revolution clarified his ideas for a future English nation, but his *Reflections*
also forced his discursive opponents to enunciate—via juxtaposition—their
plans for England.[11] Burke and the anti-Jacobins were appalled by the Revolution; they advocated a return to a traditional model of civilization rooted
in firm class and gender distinctions and claimed that every individual must
accept his/her fixed position in society. Burke and his followers also presented a chivalric conception of the noble man strongly influenced by the
popular sentimental male figure of the late-eighteenth-century novel. While
Godwin, Wollstonecraft, and other Jacobin writers briefly supported the
French Revolution, they focused on developing their own ideas for a culture
of progress and reform. They critiqued Burke's ancestral vision of society as
irrational and ridiculed his nostalgic chivalric conception of masculinity as
antiquated and impotent. The Jacobins upheld reason and industriousness
as the guiding principles for any nation and maintained that modern men
must become rational creatures rather than antiquated effeminate figures.

I will trace three threads of this dialogue concerning the proper mode of
English masculinity that consistently appear within the post-Revolutionary
political, philosophical, and literary texts: (1) the utility of chivalric manhood in modern society, (2) the correct balance of rationality and masculine
sentiment, and (3) the manner and quality of relationships between men

and women. Both literary and political works repeatedly addressed these issues to debate different features of the proper English man who could guide and manage the nation; moreover, as England sought to regulate the bodies and sexualities of non-aristocratic men, it attempted to demonstrate both the vital potential of such men *and* the necessity of properly deploying this potency. The Earl of Chesterfield's *Letters to His Son on the Fine Art of Becoming a Man of the World and a Gentleman* (1746–47) may have significantly increased the cultural exigency to illustrate to non-aristocratic men the importance of their bodies and sexualities. Chesterfield's attempt to teach his illegitimate child the life and manners of the aristocracy emphasized dissimulation; he highlighted the value of appearance and impression rather than the more orthodox virtues of knowledge and ethics. At one point in his letters, Chesterfield writes that "to be heard with success, you must be heard with pleasure: words are the dress of thoughts" (288). His praise for well-dressed words rather than appropriate language drew the ire of Dr. Johnson and others, but his larger project threatened to undermine presumably stable markers of *proper* masculinity. The post-Revolutionary English nation could not allow men to learn how to feign proper maleness; England needed an influx of men who knew how to use their sexualities to materially improve themselves and the nation. The various modes of masculinity considered throughout the post-Revolutionary period inevitably returned to the sexuality of the proposed English male, i.e., his sexual style, his sexual behavior, and his sexual desire.[12]

The Merits of Chivalry

The most wide-ranging component of the late-eighteenth-century debates about the appropriate English male was the relevance of chivalric notions of society and masculinity. Edmund Burke, the most influential supporter of chivalric manliness, wrote his *Reflections on the Revolution in France* as a direct response to Richard Price's call for vast democratic "reform." Burke felt Price's vision would annihilate chivalric structures, and he instead offered a politics of nostalgia.[13] While he suggested more progressive political ideas in his other writings, Burke maintained a conservative attitude toward social reform in his *Reflections;*[14] he believed England must retain its monarchical system of government and carefully categorize the privileges and responsibilities of its citizens. He reconsidered the Enlightenment concepts of progress, rationality, and the social contract, and concluded "in this partnership all men have equal rights; but not to equal things. He that has but five shillings in the partnership, has as good a right to it, as he that has five hundred pound has to his larger proportion" (110). Burke's rhetoric echoed Richard Allestree's influential Christian courtesy books, *The Whole Duty of Man* (1661) and *The Gentleman's Calling* (1676), in which Allestree highlighted individuals' "Callings." Allestree explained that "[men's] *Callings* and employments become so various . . . because one man is furnished with an ability, which qualifies him for one sort of calling, another is by his distinct propriety markt out for another" (*Gentleman's Calling* 8). Like Allestree, Burke wanted—and even required—the social participation of all individuals, but he stipulated that people must recognize and respect their fixed positions in society. He discouraged men from pursuing strategies for social improvement and specifically directed them to submit to the authority of organizing civic structures. He demanded that men practice what Gillian Skinner describes as "obligation and dependence" in order to secure a "conservative, Burkean [political] ideal" (155).[15] Burke wanted English citizens to remain loyal to a romanticized notion of a stable nation rather than experience the instability of modernity. He explained that "when antient opinions and rules of life are taken away, the loss cannot possibly be estimated. From that moment we have no compass to govern us; nor can we know distinctly to what port we steer" (129). Burke's rhetoric of fear deemphasized the culture of progress that invited middle-class men to assume larger civic functions and encouraged readers to yearn for an ordered world of time past, as well as the political, economic, and gender systems associated with this mythical period.

Burke again iterated Allestree's influential courtesy books when he argued that manners were an indispensable feature of an ordered society; Burke, however, heightened the nation's current need for such propriety because of the damaging effects of the French Revolution. He described the French Revolution as "the most astonishing [circumstance] that has hitherto happened in the world," and he specifically pointed to its influence on England's system of manners. He acknowledged that "France has always more or less influenced manners in England" (131), but he insisted that "among the revolutions in France, must be reckoned a considerable revolution in their ideas of politeness" (120). He argued that England must return to what he presented as its native ancestral system of economics, politics, and gender, and he asserted that manners were vital to such a national project. He announced that "there ought to be a system of manners in every nation which a well-formed mind would be disposed to relish. To make us love our country, our country ought to be lovely" (129). He repeated Price's patriotic manifesto that men should love their nation, but Burke maintained that this love must revolve around manners rather than radical liberty. Gregory Claeys indicates that for Burke, "manners and civilisation distinguished modern from barbaric societies, and depended crucially upon the spirit of the gentleman and of nobility" (314). Burke invested gentlemanly behavior—and its associative social structures—with the ability to re-stabilize English culture in the wake of the French Revolution, and, thus, Burke's vision of masculinity became vital to his plan for the future of the English nation.

Perhaps Burke's most effective rhetorical device for convincing his readers of the value of the chivalric masculinity he idealized was to announce its death. In one of the most widely discussed passages in his *Reflections*, he mourned the loss of what he believed to be the traditional men and manners of England:

> But the age of chivalry is gone.—That of sophisters, oeconomists, and calculators, has succeeded; and the glory of Europe is extinguished for ever. Never, never more, shall we behold that generous loyalty to rank and sex, that proud submission, that dignified obedience, that subordination of the heart, which kept alive, even in servitude itself, the spirit of an exalted freedom. The unbought grace of life, the cheap defence of nations, the nurse of manly sentiment and heroic enterprize is gone! It is gone, that sensibility of principle, that chastity of honour, which felt a stain like a wound, which inspired courage whilst it mitigated ferocity, which ennobled whatever it touched, and under which vice itself lost half its evil, by losing all its grossness. (127)

Burke bemoaned the apparent demise of men who sustained chastity, honor, and heroic sensitivity, as he believed such male figures were essential to preventing the revolutionaries' ideas about social status and sexual behavior from migrating to England. Tom Furniss explains that "in Burke's analysis . . . the danger of the Revolution is that . . . it promises to *substitute* a bourgeois order *in the place of* traditional structures" (187). Furniss indicates that Burke offered his version of chivalry "as a 'noble' egalitarian code which nevertheless maintains distinctions of rank" (176). Burke's imagined chivalric community ostensibly provided the equality and democratic opportunity sought by the non-aristocratic citizens of a modernizing nation, but it simultaneously preserved hereditary privileges and upheld gallant male behavior. He wanted the nation to rely upon an entrenched political system, whose power structure was maintained by chivalric men.[16] Frans De Bruyn argues that Burke's model man was "a representative and guardian of the nation's history and cultural tradition . . . the very embodiment of customs and manners, and is thus a figure for the entire society to emulate" (49). This ideal male figure was a key component to Burke's overall vision of a future England because he served as both the administrator of a chivalric social system and an exemplar of proper English male sexuality.[17]

Burke's various discursive opponents responded to his *Reflections* by attacking him, the chivalric structures he adulated, and his vision of English masculinity. Joseph Priestley censored Burke for his advocacy of an antiquated system of organizing culture that "nothing but an age of extreme barbarism recommended" (29). Catherine Macaulay likewise challenged Burke's assumption of the naturalness of chivalry to English cultural history; she repositioned chivalry as a social invention that reacted to "the evils arising from ferocity, slavery, barbarism, and ignorance." Macaulay concluded that "now, when the causes no longer exist which rendered them useful, we should rather think of freeing society of all the evils inherent in those false notions of honour which they gave rise to" (*On Burke's Reflections* 54). Macaulay and Priestley denied the relevance of chivalry to the dynamic post-Revolutionary period in which English culture needed to maximize rather than restrict the potential of its populace. They disputed Burke's claims about the benevolent organizing powers of chivalry and suggested England's need for modernized social structures.

Wollstonecraft joined Priestley and Macaulay in decrying Burke as an anachronistic thinker; Wollstonecraft specifically crafted an alternative model of masculinity in opposition to the gallant masculinity idealized by Burke. In *A Vindication of the Rights of Woman* (1792), Wollstonecraft openly derided the chivalric culture and its gentlemanly manners that Burke valued. She divested such behavior of any vital social import and charged, "So ludicrous, in fact, do these ceremonies appear to me, that I scarcely am able to govern my muscles, when I see a man start with eager, and serious solicitude, to lift a handkerchief, or shut a door, when the *lady* could have done it herself" (126). Wollstonecraft ridiculed Burke's model of masculinity as both foolish and revolting. In addition, she argued that such chivalric performances debilitated men by making them irrational, effeminate, and consequently less useful to the national community. She consistently emphasized the responsibility of men to accept the physical preeminence of their bodies; for example, she announced that "in the government of the physical world it is observable that the female in point of strength is, in general, inferior to the male. This is the law of nature; and it does not appear to be suspended or abrogated in favour of woman. A degree of physical superiority cannot, therefore, be denied—and it is a noble prerogative!" (*Vindication of the Rights of Woman* 74).[18] Wollstonecraft urged men to embrace their physical virility as a distinctive mark of their sex, and she requested that they demonstrate this bodily potential through action. As she explained in *A Vindication of the Rights of Men* (1790), "talents are only to be unfolded by industry" (42). Sir Brooke Boothby seconded this argument a year later by insisting that "men are encouraged to every useful exertion by the certainty of enjoying fruits of their industry" (110–11). Unlike Burke, who favored ancestral social structures, Wollstonecraft and Boothby supported a culture of merit and progress based upon a vigor they saw as rational. Wollstonecraft mocked the gallant masculinity that Burke mourned and instead lamented that "the days of true heroism are over, when a citizen fought for his country like a Fabricius or a Washington" (*Vindication of the Rights of Woman* 214). As with Burke, we may learn the most about what Wollstonecraft valued by considering what she eulogized: the virile and accountable man of industry.

Wollstonecraft was particularly harsh on the men who might presumably fit Burke's model of masculinity—soldiers. She claimed that "standing armies can never consist of resolute, robust men; they may be well disciplined machines, but they will seldom contain men under the influence of strong passions, or with very vigorous faculties." Wollstonecraft viewed the men of the military as mechanized figures who could not act or lead with vitality. She explained that such men were "particularly attentive to their persons, fond of dancing, crowded rooms, adventures, and ridicule. Like the *fair* sex, the business of their lives is gallantry.—They were taught to please, and they only live to please" (92–93). She chastised them as physically and psychologically weak men who shunned issues of true national consequence in favor of decoration and ceremony. Wollstonecraft endorsed what G. J. Barker-Benfield terms "standards of healthy citizenship . . . in order to produce virtue [which] looks back to the 'manly' political, moral tradition" (106). Wollstonecraft wanted men to be virile, active, and "other" than women, and she, like Burke, conceived of her proper English man as a central feature of her larger vision of a modern nation. Thomas Gisborne, in his tremendously popular *Enquiry into the Duties of Men* (1794), offered a useful summation of the Jacobin discursive retort to Burke. Gisborne concluded that "the main concern of every Englishman is not with the conduct of his ancestors, but with his own" (I: 101). Like Wollstonecraft, Gisborne emphasized the need for men to accept their own bodily and social responsibilities rather than rehearse the duties of the past. These various criticisms of Burke's desire for gallant and noble men produced a distinct vision of a rational and industrious masculinity that influenced Austen's depiction of men.

The Proper Ratio

The dialogue on the relevance of chivalry to post-Revolutionary English culture was far-reaching and prompted writers of the 1790s to consider additional characteristics for English men, including the appropriate balance such male figures should maintain between rational and sentimental behavior. As we have seen, Jacobin writers of the 1790s criticized chivalry as an arcane social system with an irrational code of propriety. They also charged that chivalry encouraged men to act with uncontrollable sentimentality and unrestrained passion. While such thinkers turned to the Enlightenment tradition to outline a model of masculinity based upon reason and industry, anti-Jacobins relied heavily upon the legacy of the Earl of Shaftesbury's *Characteristics of Men, Manners, Opinions, Times* (1711) and the literary icon of the sentimental male hero to define their proper man. Prominent works such as Samuel Richardson's *Sir Charles Grandison* (1753–54), Laurence Sterne's *A Sentimental Journey* (1768), and Henry Mackenzie's *The Man of Feeling* (1771) offered popular and influential examples of this figure. These and other novels dramatized the wisdom of men who shared Shaftesbury's belief in the primacy and benevolence of emotions. Shaftesbury proposed that "in general all the affections or passions are suited to the public good, or good of the species" and concluded that men are "accordingly good or vicious as the sensible affections stand with them" (250, 255–56). Shaftesbury's work legitimated and indeed elevated the man of feeling as a courteous, trusted, and prudent leader who was fondly memorialized by popular sentimental novels. But by the late eighteenth century, physical sensations and sentimental emotions became an issue of great concern, as English radicals and conservatives alike criticized the excessive overflow of passions associated with the French Revolution.[19] Many Jacobins initially supported the Revolution as the culmination of the rational pursuit of the rights of men, but they eventually became disgruntled with the irrational activity and excessive emotion of the rebels. Conservative anti-Jacobin writers denounced the brutality of the revolt and announced that the French had forgotten how to "feel" properly. Both camps responded to the radical events in France by attempting to delineate equilibriums between reason and emotion that "proper" English men ought to develop.[20]

Burke's *Reflections* was a very good example of this difficult struggle to codify the proper display of male sentiment. His treatise was extremely passionate, as he filled his work with rhetorical flourishes aimed at garnering emotional support for the departed French monarch.[21] Burke, however, was also extremely concerned with the dangerous potential of men's undisciplined feelings. He indicated that "society requires . . . that even in the mass and body as well as in the individuals, the inclinations of men should frequently be thwarted, their will controlled, and their passions brought into subjection" (111). Burke demanded the social subservience and tempered sentiment of men, and he imagined such regulation as reasonable. He criticized the revolutionaries for their uncontrolled emotion and lack of respect for ancestral authority, and proclaimed that "[r]age and phrenzy will pull down more in half an hour, than prudence, deliberation, and foresight can build up in an hundred years" (216).[22] Burke could not endorse what he understood as excessively sensational masculinity that he blamed for the overthrow of a secure hereditary system of politics, economics, and gender relations; nonetheless, he did share Shaftesbury's concern with proper feeling. In his discussion of the horrors of the Revolution, he claimed that "we are so made as to be affected at such spectacles with melancholy sentiments" (131). He compared the violent distress experienced by the French royals to a theatrical performance, and admitted, "I should be truly ashamed of finding in myself that superficial theatric sense of painted distress, whilst I could exult over it in real life" (132). Burke believed that we must express proper emotion within the appropriate context, and he was convinced that English men have a natural ability to feel properly. He concluded by declaring that "[w]e have not (as I conceive) lost the generosity and dignity of thinking of the fourteenth century. . . . We preserve the whole of our feelings still native and entire, unsophisticated by pedantry and infidelity. We have real hearts of flesh and blood beating in our bosoms" (137). Burke wanted England to recapture the sensitivity that he associated with a chivalric system of society. He claimed that men were passionate creatures, and while he believed this passion must be disciplined, he also insisted that modern England could not allow strict rationality to strangle such sentimentality. Burke's *Reflections* produced a complicated social desire that directed the men of Austen's novels to retain emotions while simultaneously submitting to the regulations of entrenched structures.

This powerful desire for a proper man of feeling who upholds the authority of traditional systems of power received challenges from the usual Jacobin discursive opponents. While the literary texts that challenged the ideas of Burke and others about sentiment presented complex male figures who incorporated emotion alongside their commitment to reason, political writers ridiculed Burke and his rhetoric as overly sentimental. Boothby, for instance, referred to the "dangerous tenets" of Burke's work and argued that "all enthusiasm is certainly excess, it begins where reason ends" (6, 13). Macaulay similarly compared Burke's idealization of the fourteenth century to "*methodized sentimental barbarism*" (*On Burke's Reflections* 54). Even Hannah More reported that "some of the blackest crimes which stain the annals of mankind, profligacy, murder, and especially suicide" could be traced "back to this original principle, an ungoverned Sensibility" (II: 100). These writers warned of the risks of emotionalism they associated with Burke's *Reflections,* and Jacobin thinkers grew increasingly concerned about the impact of this sensibility upon English men. Mary Anne Radcliffe specifically addressed the vulnerability of men of sentiment to financially desperate women. She mused, "How many unhappy young men have fallen a sacrifice, both in mind and body, to the diabolical artifices which these poor, miserable, abandoned women are driven to practice for bread!" (419). Radcliffe demonstrated a specific liability of sensibility that threatened to endanger the civic potential of aspiring young English men. She re-worked Burke's genteel rhetoric and charged these men to "act like men, and, as men of honour, support the dignity of their character" (428). Radcliffe's larger goal was, of course, to improve the social opportunities for women, but she also pointed to the damaging effects of hypersentimentality upon men and women alike.

Wollstonecraft was likewise extremely critical of the sentimental masculinity that she identified with Burke's writing and person. She addressed Burke directly: "all your pretty flights arise from your pampered sensibility . . . you foster every emotion till the fumes, mounting to your brain, dispel the sober suggestions of reason" (*Vindication of the Rights of Men* 9). Wollstonecraft decried that Burke, like his man of feeling, was ruled by uncontrollable and irrational passion. She even redefined his advocacy of a noble and genteel sentiment as "sensibility," which she described as "the manie of the day" (8). Wollstonecraft highlighted the dangers of this "manie" to men. She explained that "men who possess uncommon sensibility, whose quick emotions shew how closely the eye and heart are connected, soon forget the most forcible sensations" and are "not spurred on to any virtuous act" (53). Wollstonecraft, like Boothby and Macaulay, was concerned that Burke's text would encourage men to become physically weak and socially feeble. She believed that England must "cultivate [its] reason" rather than adhere to an antiquated chivalric theory of rank and manners, which she claimed had "emasculated [men] by hereditary effeminacy" (*Vindication of the Rights of Men* 60; 40).[23]

Wollstonecraft accordingly espoused rationality as the basis of her plan for a future England and its populace. She felt that men and women could progress by rational and industrious behavior that was limited by Burke's theory of natural rank, gender, and sentiment. She aggressively questioned, "What do you mean by inbred sentiments? From whence do they come? How were they bred? Are they the brood of folly, which swarm like the insects on the banks of the Nile, when mud and putrefaction have enriched the languid soil?" (*Vindication of the Rights of Men* 32). Wollstonecraft's powerful and putrid image implied that Burke's plan for the nation and its man would indeed spoil the promise of the land and its citizens. She refused to accept Burke's proposition of inherent manly sentiments and claimed that "[t]he mind must be strong that resolutely forms its own principles; for a kind of intellectual cowardice prevails which makes many men shrink from the task, or only do it by halves" (*Vindication of the Rights of Woman* 81). Rather than suggesting, as Burke did, that men possessed a priori emotions, Wollstonecraft remained a true empiricist and insisted that men must experience the world and its sensations prior to determining how they "feel."[24] She wanted the modern male of England to renounce Burke's belief in inborn feelings and discern his own passions through rational processes. She understood the importance of emotion and revealed her desire for a man who could "[blend] happily reason and sensibility into one character," but she was adamant that "sensibility is not reason" (132–33).[25] Austen continually presents men who experience difficulties resolving this dialectic between reason and emotion as they attempt to enhance their social/sexual subjectivities and pursue relations with women.

Men and the Rights of Women

The emergence of modern Enlightenment feminism was part of this culture of progress that encouraged the improvement of the nation and its citizens. Prominent works published by Wollstonecraft, Mary Hays, Mary Robinson, and others confronted both traditional gender systems and England's patriotic call for men to exercise hegemonic control over the domestic sphere. While the modern English nation encouraged men to maintain such hegemony as a means to improving their social/sexual identities, these early feminist critics reevaluated longstanding expectations of masculinity as a means to reconstructing femininity. Burke, however, was not interested in modernizing sexual identity; his call for a return to a chivalric system of politics, economics, and gender relations derived from what Johnson describes as Burke's belief that "the continuance of civil order resulted not from our conviction of the rational or metaphysical rightness of certain obligations or arrangements, but rather from our attachment to customary practices" (*Equivocal Beings* 3).[26] Burke implicitly endorsed the distribution of the sexes into the "natural" hegemonic structure delineated by conduct and courtesy books. Such manuals repeatedly emphasized entrenched gender roles and specifically highlighted the need for a woman to care for a man and his public standing. Allestree instructed the wife to "be extremely tender" of her husband "by making all that is good in him as conspicuous, as public as they can; setting his worth in the clearest light, but putting his infirmities in the shade" (*The Ladies Calling* II: 34). The feminist critics who responded to Burke's desire for an ancestral model of gender relations challenged this longstanding perception of the woman as the caretaker of the man. They employed the Enlightenment doctrine of reason to demand a modern conception of the formation and maintenance of gender that did not require aspiring men to retain a hegemonic relationship with women.

Indeed, many of these feminist writers reversed Allestree's influential advice by organizing their claims around the Enlightenment theory that rational men should want to improve the social status of equally rational women. Hays, for example, began her *Appeal to the Men of Great Britain on Behalf of Women* (1798) by describing the nation's male citizens as traditionally "remarkable for an ardent love of liberty"; she then extrapolated that the extant oppression of women and its potential amelioration should be "equally interesting" to men (i–iii). Mary Anne Radcliffe was much more direct in her discussion of the need for men to participate in the social emancipation of women. She indicated that "it was never intended that women should be left destitute in the world, without the common necessaries of life" and concluded by asking, "Then is it not highly worthy the attention of men, men who profess moral virtue and the strictest sense of *honour*, to consider in what mode to redress these grievances!" (409). Radcliffe borrowed from Burke's rhetoric of honorable chivalric masculinity to insist that a proper English man must concern himself with women's social subjection. Even More, in her conservative *Strictures on the Modern System of Female Education* (1799), declared that "men of sense . . . need be the less inimical to the improvement of the other sex, as they themselves will be sure to be gainers by it." More disagreed with many of the leading feminist thinkers of the 1790s, but she felt that if men supported the education of women, such women would be less enamored of gaining equality and more interested in becoming learned and useful (II: 13). These writers produced a cultural desire for men to involve themselves in the social conditions of women, and Macaulay, in her *Letters on Education* (1790), succinctly enunciated the need for such men. She explained that the "happiness and perfection of the two sexes are so reciprocally dependent on one another that, till both are reformed, there is no expecting excellence in either" (216). This notion of a symbiotic relationship between the sexes permeated many of the discussions of gender throughout the decade and ultimately encouraged English men to develop a knowledge and concern for the progress of women.

The Regulation of Love and Desire

English men were specifically asked to reconfigure their amorous relationships with women as part of the social effort to improve the rights and status of women. Courtesy and conduct books had long addressed the issue of love between a husband and wife, and we can trace a growing concern about love throughout the eighteenth century. In 1622, William Gouge claimed that "no dutie on the husbands part can be rightly performed except it be seasoned with loue" (350). Allestree similarly argued that "'Tis Love only that cements the hearts, and where that union is wanting, 'tis but a shadow, a carcass of marriage" (*The Ladies Calling* II: 24). These influential early manuals portrayed love as the fundamental component of marriage, but by the 1700s writers began to warn of the volatility of love. John Essex, for example, advised women to manage the love of marriage. He cautioned young women of "Men who behave themselves with the greatest Decorum and good Manners"; according to Essex, such actions engendered "the Passion of Love . . . [that] at last arrives to be the Cause of so many Extravagances in the world" (124). The anonymous author of *The Lady's Preceptor* (1743), likewise, admonished that "Love is a whimsical Passion" that "gives a visionary Pleasure, but at the same time there is infinite Danger in being led by it" (27). By the end of the eighteenth century, love has ceased to be salutary and has instead become potentially destructive. As John Gregory concluded, "[t]he effects of love among men are diversified by their different tempers. An artful man may counterfeit every one of them so as easily to impose on a young girl of an open, generous, and feeling heart, if she is not extremely on her guard" (84). That which once solidified the marital relationships between men and women now constituted a threat to both naïve young women and the very institution of marriage. Critics of Burke's nostalgic vision for the English nation repeated these warnings about the effects of love upon men, and they consistently pointed to the dangers of wedding a lover.

Wollstonecraft, for example, bemoaned that "husbands . . . are often only overgrown children; nay, thanks to early debauchery, scarcely men in their outward form" (*Vindication of the Rights of Woman* 91). Like Gregory, she instructed that "in the choice of a husband, [women] should not be led astray by the qualities of a lover—for a lover the husband, even supposing him to be wise and virtuous, cannot long remain." She warned of the ephemeral nature of the male lover who began as a "sprightly lover" only to be transmogrified "into a surly suspicious tyrant" (189–90). The male lover, according to Wollstonecraft, was an unstable creature who oppressed the female sex by becoming an irrational despot and weakened the nation by becoming an indolent man. She wanted men to dismiss the dynamic emotions and turbulent malleability of love in favor of a physically strong and focused sexual status. And she was certainly not alone in this discursive endeavor to banish the male lover. Hays insisted that "no reasonable woman, no woman with a spark of common sense, dreams that a husband is to continue a lover, in the romantic sense of the word" (*Appeal* 85). She later addressed the appropriate conduct of men toward women and concluded that "men should be guided by, and act upon, the same principles, in governing the female sex, as in the other transactions of life" (158). While Hays instructed men to treat women as business partners capable of rational exchanges, Hannah More offered more subtle recommendations for the restructuring of amorous relations. She acknowledged that "the sexes will naturally desire to appear to each other, such as each believes the other will best like . . . and each sex will appear more or less rational as they perceive it will more or less recommend them to the other." More granted a certain sensual attraction between men and women, as well as an inclination to adjust the amount of reason employed in such encounters, but she noted that "it is . . . to be regretted, that many men, even of distinguished sense and learning, are too apt to consider the society of ladies, rather as a scene in which to rest their understandings, than to exercise them" (II: 42). More, Hays, and Wollstonecraft echoed eighteenth-century conduct and courtesy books with their cautionary treatments of love, and they established a cultural desire for men to pursue romantic relations with reason rather than passion.

Austen's fiction consistently explores the cultural dangers associated with male lovers, including the risks incurred by young women who become romantically involved with such men; moreover, Austen's corpus demonstrates that men who abandon erotic desire in favor of social/sexual security inevitably enjoy functional marriages, improve their social/sexual identities, and become useful to the modern English nation. The many qualifications for the proper English man produced in the discursive field of the 1790s created a dynamic zone of nation and masculinity. These various literary and political discourses delineated social expectations for English maleness that the male characters of Austen's corpus attempt to satisfy in order to become active participants in the post-Revolutionary nation. Her narratives continually portray men who willingly embrace a lack of love in order to secure their social/sexual subjectivity. Her male characters craft secure aesthetics of existence in response to the many desires produced by post-Revolutionary literary and political discourses; they can never meet all the standards developed for the model national male figure, but by relinquishing their roles as lovers they ensure their immunity from the destabilizing powers of amorous desire. Post-Revolutionary England was desperate to reestablish order and structure; it could not allow men to experience the diversity and dynamic flexibility involved in passionate love. Austen was aware of the delicate state of the nation, and she demonstrated how various men responded to this crisis by managing their emotions, regulating their sexual behavior, and renouncing love.

CHAPTER 2

Rationalizing the Anxieties of
Austen's Juvenilia

Henry Tilney's Composite Masculinity

◄○►

You will meet with a thousand publications tending to impress your mind with the idea, that you are a free independent being. . . . But believe your mother, when she assures you, that high ideas of independence are dangerous . . . retain a strong sense of your dependence upon your master, your parents, and your Creator; you will then act uprightly and consistently. (Jane West, in Letters Addressed to a Young Man on His First Entrance into Life I: 39–40)

Young Men are often hasty in their resolutions—and not more sudden in forming, than unsteady in keeping them. (Mrs. Vernon, in Lady Susan 245)

Her greatest deficiency was in the pencil—she had no notion of drawing—not enough even to attempt a sketch of her lover's profile, that she might be detected in the design. There she fell miserably short of the true heroic height. At present she did not know her own poverty, for she had no lover to pourtray. She had reached the age of seventeen, without having seen one amiable youth who could call forth her sensibility; without having inspired one real passion, and without having excited even any admiration but what was very moderate and very transient. (Austen, Northanger Abbey 4)

Mrs. Vernon's comment reveals a prominent cultural concern of the post-Revolutionary years: the unstable young man of England who is rashly pursuing too many resolutions and consistently failing to fulfill them. As Jane West's instructions to her fictional son suggest, the philosophical and political discourses of the 1790s that publicly discussed the proper means of reforming and improving English masculinity established distinct yet specific models for appropriate maleness that the nation's men were urged to imitate. Austen's juvenile writings, written throughout the latter years of the eighteenth century, provide humorous and often ridiculous portraits of men who respond to these textually produced expectations for masculinity by attempting to change, improve, and even perfect their sexualized aesthetics of existence. The men of Austen's juvenilia attempt to achieve hegemonic social/sexual stability through their relationships with women, but they are inevitably frustrated as lovers; they are duped, compromised, and even abandoned.[1] Although we do not note in the juvenilia a clear negotiation of the specific prerequisites for proper masculinity created by the discourses of the late eighteenth century, Austen's early texts offer examples of insecure young men and portray a nation nervous about its future male social/sexual subjects. I will examine three early tales that illustrate the challenges experienced by youthful English men as they attempt to craft culturally approved aesthetics of existence; "Jack and Alice," "Catharine," and *Lady Susan* dramatize England's extant uneasiness about its young masculinity and provide examples of adolescent male figures whose struggles with love exacerbate this national anxiety.[2]

Austen's humorous explanation of Catherine Morland's failure to draw her lover bespeaks an additional problem concerning England's men: the heroine cannot even imagine her hero, whom both she and readers anticipate, because of an apparent absence of valiant young males in her society. Austen's remarks, moreover, foreground Catherine's romantic expectations for her future lover, Henry Tilney. Tilney, like the anxious men of the juvenilia, is presented as a self-conscious figure, but he successfully organizes his social/sexual subjectivity. Henry is able to rehearse various modes of masculinity prescribed by the discourses of the 1790s because he maintains a strict adherence to the Enlightenment principle of the rational individual—the exact model about which West warns the young recipient of her *Letters*. While Henry demonstrates both his chivalric and sentimental training, as well as his interest in the social status of women, his various "male" performances are always regulated by reason. His intellectual control enables him to maintain a well-managed aesthetic that the men of Austen's juvenile writings could not, but Austen ultimately shows how Tilney's commitment to logic leads to a similar end: Henry, like his fictional male predecessors in Austen's juvenile texts, is revealed to be an inept lover who is unwilling to accept the radical multiplicities of Deleuzian love. Henry, as opposed to the male subjects of the juvenilia, is a socially functional modern man; he has heard and responded to specific socially produced desires by crafting a comprehensive aesthetic of existence that enables him to monitor his social/sexual behavior and consciousness.[3] His is a masculinity of restraint, and his restricted sexuality is marked by the excessive regulation that the anti-Jacobins parody. Henry is a hegemonic man whose social/sexual security helps to secure the future of the English nation, but Austen illustrates how his rationalized masculinity inhibits his ability to explore the volatility of passionate love.

The men of her juvenilia are quite clearly not complete men capable of fulfilling sundry requirements for proper English maleness, yet their fictional representations reveal Austen's early concern with the instability of the nation's young men. Her juvenile works offer compelling portraits of absurd men who expose their insecurities as they try to solidify their social/sexual identities. Charles Adams, the primary male figure of "Jack and Alice," may be Austen's most hilarious representation of the English male's attempt to fix his sexuality; Adams actually imagines himself to be perfect—or at least perfectible. Austen informs us that "Charles Adams was an amiable, accomplished and bewitching young Man; of so dazzling a Beauty that none but Eagles could look him in the Face" (*Catharine* 11). The narrator portrays him as an angelic man who is both graceful and attractive, and he appropriately attends a masquerade party wearing "a Mask representing the Sun." She continues to explain that "The Beams that darted from his Eyes were like those of that glorious Luminary tho' infinitely superior. So strong were they that no one dared venture within half a mile of them" (12).[4] This comic portrait emphasizes Adams's supposed excellence, but it also subtly suggests his precarious insecurity. He is not content existing as a normal man; he seeks perfection, and this ambition requires him to perpetually explore new ways of enhancing himself.

Adams's infatuation with this goal of solipsistic male perfection recalls Godwin's assertion that men are perfectible; Godwin urged men to "express the faculty of being continually made better and [receive] perpetual improvement," but Austen details the absurd nature of her mock-hero's arrogant efforts to achieve impeccability (*Enquiry* I: 93). Austen notes that "the singularity of his appearance, the beams which darted from his eyes, the brightness of his Wit, and the whole *tout ensemble* of his person had subdued the hearts of so many of the young Ladies, that of the six present at the Masquerade but five had returned uncaptivated" (13). Austen's comments deride Adams's lofty perception of himself, and his excessive confidence neither enables him to pursue effectively romantic passions nor garners for him the amorous attentions of women. Indeed, we learn that "the cold and indifferent heart of Charles Adams . . . preserved its native freedom; polite to all but partial to none," and following his stern dismissal of his sole female suitor, "he still remained the lovely, the lively, but insensible Charles Adams" (14). He knows how to be courteous, and Alice is enthralled by his person, but he appears uninterested in and perhaps incapable of experiencing or exchanging passionate sensations.

While he is not able to pursue romantic possibilities, Adams still knows he must marry, and he is clearly concerned with his future wife. He announces, "whoever she might be, [she] must possess Youth, Beauty, Birth, Merit, and Money" (19). He demands perfection for himself, and he requires a similar level of excellence in the woman who may be his wife. After he refuses the proposal of marriage offered by the heroine's father, Adams explains:

> I look upon myself to be . . . a perfect Beauty—where would you see a finer figure or a more charming face. Then, sir I imagine my Manners and Address to be of the most polished kind; there is a certain elegance, a peculiar sweetness in them that I never saw equaled and cannot describe. . . . I am certainly more accomplished in every Language, every Science, every Art and every thing than any other person in Europe. My temper is even, my virtues innumerable, my self unparalleled. Since such, Sir, is my character, what do you mean by wishing me to marry your Daughter? . . . I expect nothing more in my wife than my wife will find in me—Perfection. (23)

Adams's lofty marital expectations and grandiose conception of himself effectively preclude his involvement in a love relationship as he could never locate an equally magnificent specimen. The comic and violent resolution of the brief tale demonstrates the severe dangers precipitated by Adams's pursuit of individual and spousal perfection: Austen announces his marriage to the conniving Lady Williams in the narrative's final sentence.[5] Adams's relentless pursuit of excellence has led to ridiculous and harsh consequences, as he must now tolerate the treacherous activity of this older female advisor. The narrator illustrates how Adams, the seemingly flawless male, is incapable of discerning her deceptive powers; for all his greatness, Adams falls victim to the lures of the manipulative Lady Williams and is shown to be both fallible as a man and inept as a lover.[6]

"Catharine, or the Bower" offers another important example from the juvenilia of England's unease with the attitudes and behavior of its youthful masculine citizens. Catharine's domineering and disciplining aunt, Mrs. Percival, is especially frightened by the potential threat adolescent men pose to young women; she forbids her niece from attending social balls, fearing "that it would not be possible to prevent [Kitty] Dancing with a *Man* if she went" (201). Later, Mrs. Percival explains that "there is certainly nothing like Virtue for making us what we ought to be, and as to a young Man's, being young and handsome and having an agreable person, it is nothing at all to the purpose for he had much better be respectable" (218). Mrs. Percival's comments reveal both a strong anxiety about the appropriate education and activity of contemporary English men and a powerful nostalgia for men of old. She openly criticizes "the shocking behaviour of modern young Men, and the wonderful Alteration that had taken place in them, since her time, which she illustrated with many instructive anecdotes of the Decorum and Modesty which had marked the Characters of those whom she had known, when she had been young" (220). Mrs. Percival, like Burke, is convinced that English masculinity is no longer what it once was, and she is quite frightened by what she sees as its devolving condition. This apprehension becomes a central issue in the narrative, most prominently through Austen's depiction of Edward Stanley.

Stanley descends from a family of "Large Fortune and high Fashion," and we learn that this fortunate son has recently "returned from France" (191, 207).[7] He enters the narrative boldly, arriving at the Percival residence while Kitty's relations have departed for the ball. He has little difficulty introducing himself to the heroine, as he confidently proposes: "Miss Percival, what do you say to my accompanying you [to the ball]? And suppose you were to dance with me too?" (209). He has none of the caution and reserve that Mrs. Percival demands in young men. He is excited about the opportunity to attend the social event with the heroine, but he regrets that he "shall cut a sad figure among all your Devonshire Beaux in [his] dusty, travelling apparel." He requests time and supplies to improve his appearance, instructing Kitty, "You can procure me some powder perhaps, and I must get a pair of Shoes from one of the Men" (209). He takes great care in making-up his face and person, recalling the stereotypical behavior of the French effete, and Kitty learns that his desire to improve his appearance "had not been merely a boast of vanity . . . as he kept her waiting for him above half an hour" (209).[8] Austen presents Stanley as an extremely self-conscious man who adheres to arcane expectations about the physical appearance of a socially proper male. He may be a "modern" man, according to the definition of Mrs. Percival, but he follows antiquated models of English and French masculinity—although these may be perverted modern models.

Kitty becomes quite enamored of Stanley despite, or perhaps because of, his modernized chivalric behavior.[9] Austen explains that while her heroine "had not yet seen enough of him to be actually in love with him. . . . There was a Novelty in his character which to *her* was extremely pleasing; his person was uncommonly fine, his Spirits and Vivacity suited to her own, and his Manners at once so animated and insinuating, that she thought it must be impossible for him to be otherwise than amiable. . . . He knew the powers of them himself" (224). Edward is clearly not the kind of man whom Kitty is accustomed to meeting. He is elegant and gallant, appears conscious of his own artifice, and employs this facade effectively. Kitty later notes "the power of his Address, and the Brilliancy of his Eyes," adding that "the more she had seen of him, the more inclined was she to like him, and the more desirous that he should like *her*" (225). Stanley definitely has an opportunity

to behave as a lover, but the heroine's anticipation of potentially reciprocated amorous emotions is thwarted when she learns the following morning
that "Mr. Edward Stanley was already gone" (225). Upon hearing this news,
Kitty initially chides herself as a "silly" and "unreasonable" woman, but she
soon decides that "it is just like a Young Man, governed by the whim of the
moment, or actuated merely by the love of doing anything oddly! Unac-
countable Beings indeed!" (225–26).[10] Although Kitty is definitely intrigued
by the novelty of Stanley's masculinity, she seems completely willing to
dismiss his unpredictable actions as simply what young men do. And yet,
Austen demonstrates how his quick departure actually reflects the powerful
social pressures that prompt young English men to avoid the dangers associated with potential amorous behavior.

Camilla, Kitty's confidant and Stanley's sister, eventually explains the
young man's abrupt exit. Camilla tells Kitty that her brother extended "his
Love to you, for you was a nice Girl he said, and he only wished it were in
his power to be more with You. You were just the Girl to suit him, because
you were so lively and good-natured, and he wished with all his heart that
you might not be married before he came back."[11] Camilla openly assures
the heroine that Edward "certainly is in love with you," and she portrays
her brother as a young man captivated by Kitty—a young man who must
abandon her company because of the dictates of his father. Camilla informs
Kitty, "Oh! you can have no idea how wretched it made him. He would not
have gone this Month, if my Father had not insisted on it" (227). Unlike
romantic lovers, Edward Stanley, and his apparent strong love for the heroine, succumbs to a patriarchal system of power and discipline.[12] He follows
Jane West's advice, avoiding the dangers she associates with enlightened
young men's "high ideas of independence" and maintaining his "strong
sense of dependence" upon his father (Letters Addressed to a Young Man I:
39–40). Kitty envisions her lost lover as an extremely melancholic man who
is "Obliged to tear himself from what he most loves, [whose] happiness is
sacrificed to the vanity of his Father!"; but Austen presents Edward as an
inept lover; he is a man who seems interested in romance and is definitely
effective in garnering the amorous emotions of a woman, but he is incapable
of developing or reciprocating such passions (228). Austen depicts him as a
young man compelled to respect the desires of patriarchy rather than pursue
a desubjectifying love relationship.

In Lady Susan, Austen provides a third early example of a stultified
male lover who is continually controlled and manipulated by his society's
desires. Reginald De Courcy is initially quite fascinated by the opportunity
to meet Lady Susan, the radically independent heroine who is perhaps the
most rebellious female of Austen's corpus.[13] We are told that "Reginald

[had] long wished . . . to see this captivating Lady Susan," even though he is quite critical of the titular character prior to their first meeting (211).[14] Lady Susan describes him as "a handsome young Man, who promises me some amusement," and concludes that "there is something about him that rather interests me, a sort of sauciness, of familiarity which I shall teach him to correct (217).[15] Lady Susan plans to retrain Reginald, suggesting both the malleability and the vulnerability of the youthful English male. And Lady Susan's efforts are rather successful. Mrs. Vernon, Reginald's sister, instructs their mother that her son's "admiration was at first very strong, but no more than was natural . . . but when he has mentioned [Lady Susan] of late, it has been in terms of more extraordinary praise, and yesterday he actually said, that he could not be surprised at any effect produced on the heart of Man by such Loveliness and such Abilities" (218). Reginald, according to Mrs. Vernon, has fallen victim to the seductive powers of Lady Susan, who claims that she has simply "subdued [Reginald] entirely by sentiment and serious conversation, and made him . . . at least *half* in Love with me" (220). Lady Susan emphasizes Reginald's utility rather than his emotional commitment, describing him as a suitable substitute for other men no longer in her service, and admitting that "he is quite agreable enough . . . to afford me amusement, and to make many of those hours pass very pleasantly" (221). Reginald can be made to serve a purpose, and Lady Susan is convinced that she can mold and direct his affections to her ends.

Reginald's father also attempts to influence the behavior of his tractable son. Sir De Courcy writes to Reginald, "I know that young Men in general do not admit of any enquiry even from their nearest relations, into affairs of the heart; but I hope . . . that you will be superior to such as allow nothing for a Father's anxiety." He is aware of the uncomfortable circumstances of a father's investigation into a son's love interests, but Sir De Courcy is deeply concerned about Reginald's potentially overwhelming romantic passions. Sir De Courcy tells Reginald that he "must be sensible that as an only son and the representative of an ancient Family, your conduct in Life is most interesting to your connections. In the very important concern of Marriage especially, there is everything at stake" (222). Reginald's father, echoing the sentiments of Burke's *Reflections,* emphasizes the familial and social responsibilities that his son must uphold; the De Courcy patriarch insists that it is his "Duty to oppose a Match, which deep Art only could render probable, and must in the end make wretched" (223). Like the father of Edward Stanley, Sir De Courcy exercises his paternal authority in an attempt to discipline the behavior and emotions of his son. Reginald's father is part of an older generation of English men and seems to share Mrs. Percival's doubts about the worthiness and stability of modern males. He urges his son to curb destabilizing amorous emotions, and his regulatory efforts imply a societal apprehension about young English masculinity.[16]

Mrs. Vernon claims that Sir De Courcy is correct to be cautious about his son's behavior as a lover. She reports that Lady Susan continues to "[call] forth all [Reginald's] tender feelings," leading him to express strange new emotions (229). Lady Susan also notes the newfound sensitivity of Reginald; she informs her confidant, Mrs. Johnson, that her newest project is "sometimes impertinent and troublesome. There is a sort of ridiculous delicacy about him" (230). She concludes, "This is *one* sort of Love—but I confess it does not particularly recommend itself to me" (231). She has supposedly enjoyed her recent encounters with Reginald, including her attempts to reform his character, but she now regrets his overflow of sentiments and proclaims that "Artlessness will never do in Love matters" (236). She will not tolerate Reginald's apparently "honest" feelings, and even though she retrained him, she no longer appreciates her trainee once he has become a lover.[17] Lady Susan seems frightened that Reginald might become overwrought with uncontrollable passion, like Sir Peter Osborne, the Lovelace-esque figure of Mary Hays's *The Victim of Prejudice* (1799). Osborne is an emotional male who employs "adulation and offensive gallantry" to court Mary, the novel's heroine; she reports that Osborne "renewed his persecutions with a disgusting audacity, insulted me with licentious proposals, contrived various methods of conveying to me offers of a splendid settlement, and reduced me to the necessity of confining myself wholly to the house" (51, 96). At the close of the tale, Hays references the example of Osborne and cautions the English male: ". . . let him learn, that, while the slave of sensuality, inconsistent as assuming, he pours, by *his conduct,* contempt upon chastity" (174). Austen presents Reginald as a young man in danger of becoming such a slave to his emotions, and Lady Susan is appalled at the possibility. Like Wollstonecraft, she wants nothing to do with young male lovers who are at best volatile and potentially destructive.

Reginald's obsession with Lady Susan prevents him from renouncing his interest in the powerful older woman until the close of the narrative. He finally writes to Lady Susan and announces, "The spell is removed. I see you as you are" (263). He cites various reports of the woman's scandalous behavior and bids her good riddance, charging that she mistreated him, especially as he "was an encouraged, an accepted Lover!" (264). Reginald is angry and frustrated; he acted the role of a lover but was treated as surrogate entertainment. Austen's text documents the dangers young male lovers experience, but it also highlights the ongoing social regulation of English men's romantic interests. Once the news of Reginald's break from Lady Susan reaches his mother, Lady De Courcy quickly promotes a new strategy to "try to rob him of his heart once more" (268). She plans to foster a love relationship between Reginald and Frederica, Lady Susan's troubled daughter. In the brief conclusion to the novel, Austen informs us that "Frederica was therefore fixed in the family of her Uncle and Aunt, till such time as Reginald De Courcy could be talked, flattered, and finessed into an affection for her—which, allowing leisure for the conquest of his attachment to her Mother . . . might be reasonably looked for in the course of a Twelvemonth" (272). Although Reginald has successfully dismissed the lure of Lady Susan, he must now negotiate new expectations for his affections and new marital schemes orchestrated by his family. He has admittedly failed as a lover; he is not allowed to pursue his own amorous emotions, and this discipline of the masculine subject reveals both a cultural anxiety about the uncontrollable quality of male lovers and a social desire to manage their sexualities.

While Austen's juvenile tales do not maintain the consistent engagement with the political and literary discourses of the 1790s that we see in her full-length works, these texts document her early interest in the nation's anxiety about its young male citizens. The juvenilia provide us with images of nervous English men who realize that they must modify and improve their aesthetics of existence, but these male figures remain uncertain of the necessary alterations. They are merely aware of the "dangers to which young men are, in this age *particularly exposed*," about which Jane West warns her fictional son in *Letters Addressed to a Young Man on His First Entrance into Life* (1803). West explains that these hazards "are multiplied in a considerable and tremendous degree by the remarkable change which has taken place in manners" (I: xxii). The men of Austen's juvenilia face a great challenge; as they struggle to become proper male figures, the very standards for appropriate masculinity are shifting. They specifically experience insecurity and frustration as lovers because they pursue romantic and/or marital possibilities that threaten to destabilize their social/sexual subjectivities. Austen depicts Henry Tilney, the hero of *Northanger Abbey,* as a similarly self-conscious male figure who manages to control his anxieties through his ardent devotion to rationality. While Austen exposes the instabilities of the men of her juvenile texts, she shows how Henry relies upon the dictates of reason to inform his language, guide his actions, and regulate his performances as a modern man of England. She presents Henry as an impressively complete masculine figure who successfully performs numerous versions of proper English masculinity by rationalizing the features of these sexual models.

Austen's characterization of Henry Tilney as a rational man recalls an important literary archetype of the late-eighteenth-century novel: the philosophical advisor. Jacobin and anti-Jacobin novelists debate the value of an empiricist epistemology by personifying such men and dramatizing both the benefits of reasonable thought and the dangers of stern logic. Jacobin writers such as Mary Hays and Gilbert Imlay attempt to document England's need for men of reason in their fictional accounts. Mr. Francis, the benevolent distant consultant of Hays's *Memoirs of Emma Courtney* (1796), informs the heroine that a man "who tamely resigns his understanding to the guidance of another, sinks at once, from the dignity of a rational being, to a mechanical puppet, moved at pleasure on the wires of the artful operator" (49). According to Mr. Francis, men must exercise their own intellectual capacities or run the risk of becoming controlled by the machinations and desires of another. He prophesizes that "reason will fall softly, and almost imperceptibly, like a gentle shower of dews, fructifying the soil, and preparing it for future harvests" (50). Mr. Francis imagines rationality as a fortifying and regenerative force that promises to foster the spirit of reform in the nation. Austen often presents Tilney as a fictional descendant of Mr. Francis; Tilney similarly employs reason to evaluate the behavior of others, administer his own actions, and theorize future possibilities. The hero of *Northanger Abbey* is also reminiscent of P.P.—Esq., the wise counselor of Gilbert Imlay's utopian novel *The Emigrants* (1793), who also emphasizes the tyranny of social control and the essential importance of reason. P.P. explains that "Men will no longer continue to be attached to forms, and therefore it becomes a folly to reverence a system, that has not for its basis, reason and truth" (199). He later adds that "all men who are conscious of having acted in every respect like gentlemen, *always court enquiry and investigation*" (239).[18] P.P. redefines a proper gentleman as an empirical scientist who resists inherited modes of thought and determines his ideas through sensory experience. Austen's portrayal of Henry suggests the strong influence of such earlier fictional figures like Mr. Francis and P.P.; Henry is committed to rationality, and he depends upon reason to order his social/sexual subjectivity.

While Jacobin writers' advocacy of Enlightenment models of masculinity clearly influences Austen's characterization of Henry Tilney, his aesthetic of existence is also informed by anti-Jacobin novelists such as Sophia King and Elizabeth Hamilton, whose texts strongly ridicule such a rational man. King's *Waldorf: Or, the Dangers of Philosophy* (1798) recounts the adventures of Lok, a dangerous philosophical male who "offered a new system of philosophy, which at once leveled sacred and political ties." Lok has no respect for the ancestral cultural policies that Burke valued, and King's anti-hero instead affirms that "[m]atrimonial opinions, and a belief of God, were . . . absurdities" (I: 33). King also notes how Lok believes that "*[v]irtue* and *vice* are equally analogous; the *excess* of virtue is virtue no longer, but, degenerating into superstition, prejudice, and austerity, becomes *vice*" (I: 76).[19] King's tale highlights the hazards of men who excessively employ reason to guide

their opinions and actions; Austen's novel likewise details Henry's susceptibility to the dangers of obsessive reason and his efforts to avoid such peril.
Hamilton's *Memoirs of Modern Philosophers* (1800) narrates another story
of an obnoxiously deluded philosopher, Vallaton, whose loyalty to reason
perverts his ethical principles. Vallaton boldly insists that "duty is an expression merely implying the mode in which any being may be best employed
for the general good," and concludes that "in the eye of a philosopher no
promise is, or ought to be, binding" (I: 38–39; II: 275). Like Lok, Vallaton
critiques Burke's conception of individual duty and instead promotes a
proto-Benthamite model of social economics.[20] His love of logic leads him
to favor the primacy of utility and prevents him from honoring social contracts such as marriage and citizenry. Henry Tilney's rational attitudes and
actions are not as extreme as those modeled by Lok and Vallaton, but Austen
creates her hero within the discursive context of these earlier fictional men.
Henry's rationalized composite social/sexual subjectivity empowers him to
perform various modes of masculinity, but Austen's text also illustrates the
social/sexual consequences of his adherence to reason.

Henry is indeed a stern Enlightenment thinker who relies upon the laws
of logic. When Catherine announces to Miss Tilney "that something very
shocking indeed, will soon come out in London," a famous dialogue follows in which the two young women misconstrue the actual subject of their
conversation. Henry's role in this dialogue serves as a template for the hero's
use of rationality to acquire knowledge and mold his aesthetic of existence.
Catherine explains that *it* "is to be more horrible than any thing we have
met with yet. . . . It is to be uncommonly dreadful. I shall expect murder and
every thing of the kind" (87–88). The heroine bills the upcoming event as
both real and sublime, but Henry will not allow his sister to conceptualize
reality as wonderful or confusing. The hero's empiricist mindset demands
that he designate anything fantastic as irrational and ultimately insignificant;
his commitment to reason also forces him to establish limits and categories
for acceptable "true" experience.[21] Henry rebukes his female companions:
"Come, shall I make you understand each other, or leave you to puzzle out
an explanation as you can? No—I will be noble. I will prove myself a man,
no less by the generosity of my soul than the clearness of my head" (87).[22]
Henry feels compelled to perform an ostensibly chivalric duty, and while he
accentuates the artifice of his gallant behavior, he also presents his "noble"
task as an intellectual accomplishment. He chides his sister by explaining
that "[Catherine] talked of expected horrors in London—and instead of
instantly conceiving, as any rational creature would have done, that such
words could relate only to a circulating library, [Eleanor] immediately pic-
tured to herself a mob of three thousand men assembling in St. George's

Fields" (88). Henry's adherence to Enlightenment thought compels him to employ reason as a universal epistemological panacea; he is convinced that *any* rational person would arrive at such a "logical" conclusion and distinguish reality from imagination.[23]

Henry's stern rationality may remind us of earlier fictional figures like Mr. Francis and P.P., but Austen's hero has also been exposed to the chivalric archetype upheld by Burke and modeled by General Tilney. Austen notes that Henry's father, "like every military man, had a very large acquaintance," and her remark recalls Wollstonecraft's harsh diatribe on the proficient sociability of soldiers; indeed, the General maintains other features of such an affected gallantry, including his fondness for decorating and his interest in planning potential marital relationships (73).[24] He is also a careful practitioner of chivalric propriety, and when Catherine visits the Tilneys at Bath, Austen indicates that "to such anxious attention was the General's civility carried, that not aware of her extraordinary swiftness in entering the house, he was quite angry with the servant whose neglect had reduced her to open to door of the apartment herself." Following their meeting, "the general attended [Catherine] himself to the street-door, saying every thing gallant as they went down stairs, admiring the elasticity of her walk, which corresponded exactly with the spirit of her dancing and making her one of the most graceful bows she had ever beheld, when they parted" (79). On Catherine's exit, the General will not risk the indelicacy of his servant, yet Austen portrays his gallant speech and bow as both ridiculously artificial and carefully planned to promote a mutual affection between the young heroine and his son.[25] Henry's father demonstrates for the hero some of the utility of chivalric masculinity, but the narrator ultimately reveals the strategizing quality of the General's "noble" actions, specifically his sudden decision to send Catherine home unattended.

While Henry employs features of the chivalric system exemplified by his father, he is keenly aware of the artifice involved in the etiquette of this ancestral mode of behavior.[26] Henry's knowledge of such decorum is clear in an early exchange with the heroine. Austen relates: "After chatting some time on such matters as naturally arose from the objects around them, he suddenly addressed her with—'I have hitherto been very remiss, madam, in the proper attentions of a partner here; I have not yet asked you how long you have been in Bath; whether you were ever here before; whether you have been at the Upper Rooms, the theatre, and the concert, and how you like the place altogether'" (11–12). Austen juxtaposes "naturally" occurring subjects to the chivalric niceties in which Henry is quite skilled. He has learned that a proper English man must make these inquiries of a new female acquaintance, and while he is able to perform this task, Austen highlights the comedic quality of his language. She notes how Henry "affectedly [softens] his voice" and responds "with affected astonishment" (12). Henry is not sincerely invested in the chivalric model of masculinity like his father or gallant literary figures such as Vivaldi, the romantic hero of Ann Radcliffe's *The Italian* (1797). Radcliffe describes Vivaldi as "a knight of chivalry, who would go about the earth fighting with everybody by way of proving [his] right to do good"; he truly believes in the value of noble masculinity, but Henry recognizes the artifice involved in the genteel code of manners that accompanies this archaic ideal of male sexuality (122). He even explains to Catherine, "Now I must give one smirk, and then we may be rational again" (12).[27] Henry's initial appearance in the novel reveals his proficiency in chivalric conduct, but he is quick to return to the rationality upon which he depends to administer his aesthetic of existence.

Henry again demonstrates his exposure to the chivalric paradigm of gender and society in his well-known explanation of marriage as a country dance. He denounces the impropriety of John Thorpe for attempting to interrupt his dance with the heroine, insisting that "he has no business to withdraw the attention of my partner from me." Henry explains to Catherine, "We have entered into a contract of mutual agreeableness for the space of an evening, and all our agreeableness belongs solely to each other for that time. . . . I consider a country-dance as an emblem of marriage. Fidelity and complaisance are the principal duties of both" (56). Henry's language recalls the conservative rhetoric of Burke's *Reflections;* as Burke insists that men and women must honor the "contracts" of a time past, including such policies as gender subordination, ancestral descent, and monarchical authority, Henry claims that men and women must honor a dance as a social agreement.[28] Henry continues to analyze his metaphor of marriage for the bewildered heroine: "You will allow, that in both, man has the advantage of choice, woman only the power of refusal; that in both, it is an engagement between man and woman, formed for the advantage of each; and that when once entered into, they belong exclusively to each other till the moment of its dissolution" (57). He acknowledges the subordination of the woman in this arcane gender structure, and he emphasizes the intent of both the dance and the marital union to facilitate the individual and social security of the participants. Henry may be aware of the artifice involved in such a gender system; he occasionally accepts elements of a chivalric culture as conventional and even useful.[29]

And yet Henry remains committed to the primacy of rationality, and he infuses his chivalric training with reason to provide security and social harmony at two key moments in the narrative: (1) while driving Catherine to Northanger, and (2) following his discovery of the heroine in his mother's chamber. On the drive to Northanger, Catherine observes that "Henry drove so well,—so quietly—without making any disturbance, without parading to her, or swearing at them. . . . And then his hat sat so well, and the innumerable capes of his great coat looked so becomingly important!" (123). Catherine's thoughts reflect her romantic sentiments, but they also serve to distinguish the impressive horsemanship skills of Henry from the obnoxious boasts and insecure actions of John Thorpe, who cannot control his horses from "[dancing] about a little at first setting off" (44).[30] Unlike Thorpe, Tilney is not concerned with impressing the heroine by the accomplishments of his horse or the price of his gig; the hero, rather, plays the role of a well-disciplined gentleman-coachman, regulating the power of the horse and providing Catherine with safe and comfortable travel. He again rationally deploys chivalric behavior when he unexpectedly finds Catherine in his deceased mother's chamber. After he learns of the heroine's imaginings about his father's role in the death of his mother, Henry invokes reason and declares, "Dear Miss Morland, consider the dreadful nature of the suspicions you have entertained. . . . Remember the country and the age in which we live. Remember that we are English, that we are Christians. Consult your understanding, your own sense of the probable, your own observation of what is passing around you" (159).[31] Henry presents his view of England as a land of tranquility, beneficence, and communal participation as rational, and his Enlightenment epistemology likewise encourages him to dismiss the heroine's speculations. Austen notes "Henry's astonishing generosity and nobleness of conduct, in never alluding in the slightest way to what had passed" (161). He avoids embarrassing Catherine by discussing her secret trip to his mother's chamber, and while Henry's adherence to reason enables him to resolve this difficult situation calmly, it also leads him to uphold a chivalric conception of the nation as a pastoral and secure land, effectively preventing him from considering the heroine's suspicions about the General.

Henry depends upon reason to order his perception of the world and his composite aesthetic of existence, but his devotion to intellectual powers does not prevent him from rehearsing the sentimental mode of masculinity—even if such performances are artificial. Austen exposes Henry's conventional sentimentality following Catherine's attempt to express her regret for rudely passing the Tilneys in John Thorpe's gig. The heroine explains that she "begged Mr. Thorpe so earnestly to stop; I called out to him as soon as ever I saw you . . . and, if Mr. Thorpe would only have stopped, I would have jumped out and run after you." The narrator then asks, "Is there a Henry in the world who could be insensible to such a declaration? Henry Tilney at least was not" (71). This language highlights the constructed quality of Henry's sensitivity to emotional language; he is aware of a social desire for men of sentiment, and he is able to play this part when needed, but Henry inevitably evaluates emotions rationally. When discussing the legitimacy of sensational gothic novels, Henry insists that "the person, be it gentleman or lady, who has not pleasure in a good novel, must be intolerably stupid. I have read all Mrs. Radcliffe's works, and most of them with great pleasure. The Mysteries of Udolpho, when I had once begun it, I could not lay down again.—I remember finishing it in two days—my hair standing on end the whole time" (82). Henry's comments indicate both his intellectual appreciation of the gothic novel as a valid genre of literature and his sensitivity to the feelings aroused by the sublime art. Unlike John Thorpe, who arrogantly asserts that "novels are all so full of nonsense and stuff," Henry has learned to value the sensations produced by these texts (31).[32]

While Austen's hero demonstrates his capacity to feel sensibly, he will not allow his feelings to overpower his disciplined rationality; he carefully elucidates that his admiration of Radcliffe's novels is primarily because they offer pleasurable experiences. Henry's practiced approach to sensation is also apparent in his "lecture" on the picturesque. Austen informs us that Henry's explanations of the picturesque "were so clear that [Catherine] soon began to see beauty in every thing admired by him. . . . He talked of fore-grounds, distances, and second distances—side-screens and perspectives—lights and shades" (87). This narration reminds us of the excessively romantic attitude of her heroine, but Austen's comment also emphasizes Henry's rational understanding and control of the picturesque. He is affected by the beauty of pictorial sensations, and he can explain such sublime artistic experiences clearly, cataloguing and describing various components and qualities of natural splendor. He appears to act much like Mr. Subtile, the satirized philosophical figure of Isaac D'Israeli's Vaurien (1797), who endeavors to "arrange the vast diversities of nature . . . to methodize what is spontaneous and to attempt to enumerate all its endless varieties" (62). Like Mr. Subtile, Henry offers rational explanations for seemingly irrational phenomena such as the picturesque and the sublime. He is convinced that he can order the world in a clear and logical fashion, and while he can mimic the traditional behavior and discourse of a man of feeling, his sensitive performances are always regulated by reason.

Henry's adherence to reason likewise informs his interest in the cultural status of women. Wollstonecraft, Hays, and other Enlightenment feminist thinkers of the late eighteenth century criticized the inherited social perceptions of women as illogical creatures and emphasized their intellectual capacity. Henry seems conscious of both lines of argumentation, and despite the often presumptuous quality of his language, he attempts to uphold women as essentially rational beings.[33] Following his arrogant explanation of the misunderstanding between his sister and the heroine concerning the riotous events in London, Eleanor chides her brother: "And now, Henry . . . that you have made us understand each other, you may as well make Miss Morland understand yourself—unless you mean to have her think you intolerably rude to your sister, and a great brute in your opinion of women in general" (88). Henry responds to this charge by insisting that "no one can think more highly of the understanding of women than I do. In my opinion, nature has given them so much, that they never find it necessary to use more than half" (89). Henry's comment is obnoxious, but it also reveals his belief in women's intellectual abilities.[34] Tilney reminds us of an earlier fictional Henry, the virtuous hero of Elizabeth Inchbald's *Nature and Art* (1796), who also treated women as enlightened creatures. Inchbald recounts that the "first cause of Amazement to Rebecca," Henry's future wife, "was that he talked with *her* as well as with her sisters" (47). Austen's Henry, like Inchbald's hero, advocates the rational capacity of the female sex, and he engages in intelligent conversations with men and women alike. Terry Castle suggests that Tilney "*is* an admirer of female understanding; what he regrets (though he never says so directly) is that women do not take their own intelligence seriously enough"; Henry seems to have responded to Hays's request that men express concern with the social subordination of women, and as Castle concludes, "Austen's hero, one suspects, has read his Wollstonecraft too" (Introduction xxiii). Per Wollstonecraft's dictates, Henry upholds the potential of women's minds, remains devoted to reason, and becomes neither a gallant military man like his father nor a male lover.[35]

Unlike the other young men of the novel, Henry will not play the part of the foolish male lover; Austen presents James Morland, John Thorpe, and Captain Tilney as unmanaged males whose impulsive actions help to accentuate the disciplined rationality of Tilney. Austen describes James, who becomes engaged to the ridiculous Isabella Thorpe, as "the anxious young lover . . . who [comes] to breathe his parting sigh before" he leaves to request the consent of his father (95). He is adept at playing the role of the romantic suitor, demonstrates his advanced sighing skills, and eventually experiences great frustration reminiscent of the men of Austen's juvenilia. John Thorpe also displays the stereotypical traits of an emotionally enamored male throughout the first volume, as he continually attempts to impress the heroine with his horse, his gig, and his acquaintances. Isabella finally warns Catherine that John is "over head and ears in love with you," and at the end of the first volume he appears foolish, as he attempts to subtly court Catherine (112). Thorpe addresses Catherine: "A famous good thing this marrying scheme, upon my soul! A clever fancy of Morland's and Belle's. What do you think of it, Miss Morland? *I* say it is no bad notion" (97). Austen presents

Thorpe as an arrogant lover whose stratagems garner no effect from the heroine. Neither John nor James is a committed man of reason like Henry, and they are thus vulnerable to the irrational power of amorous emotions.

Henry, however, carefully regulates his susceptibility to romantic passions, and this approach encourages him to reconceptualize love as a rational phenomenon. When Catherine becomes concerned for her brother because of the extensive attention Isabella offers Captain Tilney, Henry reminds the heroine, "You have no doubt of the mutual attachment of your brother and your friend; depend upon it therefore, that real jealousy never can exist between them; depend upon it that no disagreement between them can be of any duration. Their hearts are open to each other, as neither heart can be to you; they know exactly what is required and what can be borne" (119–20). Henry speaks of love as a stable force, and he disregards Catherine's hypothesis of mutable love as he earlier dismissed her belief in the mimetic quality of gothic novels. He cannot fathom emotions based upon uncontrollable forces, and later in the story he presents love as a skill one develops. When Henry engages the heroine in a humorous conversation about her fondness for flowers, he informs her, "now you love a hyacinth. So much the better. You have gained a new source of enjoyment. . . . And though the love of a hyacinth may be rather domestic, who can tell, the sentiment once raised, but you may in time come to love a rose" (138). Henry treats amorous passions as learned abilities that one can study and master. He explains to Catherine, "I am pleased that you have learnt to love a hyacinth. The mere habit of learning to love is the thing" (139). Henry's comments are witty, but they also illustrate his understanding of love as an acquired talent—not unlike his proficiency as a gentleman-horseman—that can be rationally improved and deployed.

Henry is forced to reconsider his disciplined conception of love when he learns of the rumored engagement between his brother and Isabella. Our hero is initially quite confused and exclaims that "Frederick will not be the first man who has chosen a wife with less sense than his family expected"; he adds, "When I think of his past declarations, I give him up. . . . It is all over with Frederick indeed! He is a deceased man—defunct in understanding" (165–66). Although the news of a planned union between Captain Tilney and Isabella poses a significant challenge to Henry's theory of love, he behaves as a true Enlightenment thinker and dismisses his improper brother as unreasonable. He cannot tolerate an irrational sibling for the same reasons he cannot accept emotions that are illogical; he thus denounces his brother. Critics have not paid enough attention to the disillusionment and frustration Henry experiences after he learns of Frederick's folly.[36] This scene forces the hero to reevaluate not only his understanding of amorous passions but also his strategy for organizing his social/sexual subjectivity. The dictates of reason, on which he has depended to guide his judgments and direct his behavior, can explain neither the volatility of male lovers nor the instability of illogical emotions that he has recently witnessed. Austen now conveniently allows Henry to return to his pastoral parsonage at Woodston, as he can no longer endure the irrational events that he experiences at the gothic abbey.[37] Henry's removal to Woodston, followed by the planned visit of his father, Eleanor, and Catherine, also provides Austen with an important opportunity to distinguish the highly disciplined and rational son from his gallant father.

Henry shares none of the General's concerns with interior decorating or gardening; he maintains a rustic domestic sphere that leads his father to inform Catherine, "We are not calling it a good house. . . . We are not comparing it with Fullerton and Northanger—We are considering it as a mere Parsonage, small and confined, we allow, but decent perhaps, and habitable" (172). The minimalism of the hero's residence reflects the simplicity of his activities at Woodston. He joins the heroine and his other visitors on "a saunter into other meadows, and through part of the village, with a visit to the stables to examine some improvements, and a charming game of play with a litter of puppies just able to roll about" (173). While Henry's Woodston living is not a bona fide farm, he enjoys an agrarian existence reminiscent of the agricultural lifestyles modeled by numerous fictional men of late-eighteenth-century Jacobin novels. Like Delmont, the wise male figure of Charlotte Smith's *The Young Philosopher* (1798), who explains, "Farming . . . never attracted me by the lucrative prospects it offered, but because I hoped to keep myself independent by it," Henry maintains a basic dwelling at Woodston that enables him to remain free from the authoritative control of his father (III: 12). Delmont eventually questions how "any man ever *can* so submit" to the authority or ideas of another "who has the power of earning his bread by the sweat of his brow" (I: 226–27). Delmont's comments may anticipate Henry's commitment to his own rationally acquired ideas, yet they also remind us of the financial independence that Austen's hero has secured. Woodston, as opposed to the Abbey, is a rational and simple domain where Henry can regain his disciplined aesthetic of existence and observe Catherine away from his family's gothic estate.

Henry's time at Woodston may remind him of the Enlightenment epistemology on which he relies to craft his aesthetic of existence, but the next time we see the hero he appears on the brink of performing the role of a romantic lover. And yet, his arrival at Fullerton, following his father's rude dismissal of Catherine, is both predictable and dramatically disappointing. Henry "proposes" to Catherine on their walk to the Allens' residence, but

Austen only informs us that her heroine "was assured of his affection; and that heart in return was solicited, which, perhaps, they pretty equally knew was already entirely his own." The narrator explains that "though Henry was now sincerely attached to [Catherine], though he felt and delighted in all the excellencies of her character and truly loved her society, I must confess that his affection originated in nothing better than gratitude, or, in other words, that a persuasion of her partiality for him had been the only cause of giving her a serious thought. It is a new circumstance in romance, I acknowledge, and dreadfully derogatory of an heroine's dignity" (198). Austen draws attention to the artificial quality of her romantic ending and the rationalized affections of her hero. We do not witness Henry's supposedly romantic behavior, but we are told that he loves the heroine's company and appreciates her character. The narrator even "confesses" that Henry's feelings for Catherine are the logical result of a sense of gratitude he experiences because of the heroine's great esteem for him. Like Inchbald's Henry, for whom "love, however rated by many, as the chief passion of the human heart, [was] but a poor dependent, a retainer upon other passions; admiration, gratitude, respect, esteem, pride in the object," Tilney maintains stable and ostensibly rational preferences for the heroine rather than uncontrollable amorous passions (49). Deleuze explains that "the pluralism of love does not concern only the multiplicity of loved beings, but the multiplicity of souls or worlds in each of them" (*Proust and Signs* 7). Henry will not allow such multiplicity to become exposed in either himself or the object of his "affection." He retains the solidity of his well-crafted composite masculinity and avoids the destabilizing dangers of love. Although Henry has played the part of the archetypal romantic hero in defying his father's orders and proposing to Catherine, Austen highlights Henry's adherence to a rational conception of sexual relations and love.[38]

Austen remains self-conscious about her concluding marriage throughout the final chapters of the novel. She notes the General's attempt to forbid his son from pursuing the heroine, "but, in such a cause, [the General's] anger, though it must shock, could not intimidate Henry, who was sustained in his purpose by a conviction of its justice."[39] Austen adds that her hero "felt himself bound as much in honour as in affection to Miss Morland, and believing that heart to be his own which he had been directed to gain, no unworthy retraction of a tacit consent, no reversing decree of unjustifiable anger, could shake his fidelity, or influence the resolutions it prompted" (202). Henry appears determined to marry Catherine not because of his strong affection for her, but because he was urged to gain a "heart" for her by his father—and Henry will not allow himself to renounce an emotion he has rationally attained. His bold actions incur the risk of disownment, but he

considers such an abjuration of learned sentiments as unjust and unreasonable. Tilney's stance is again reminiscent of the position taken by Delmont,
who announces that "a man would have in every thing else not only a *very*
ordinary, but a very sordid mind, who would give up the freedom of that
mind to the miserable hope of a legacy" (I: 226). Like Delmont, Austen's hero
clings to his Enlightenment epistemology and advocates the preeminence
of a man's reason over his familial connections. He momentarily rehearses
the part of a male lover, but unlike the men of Austen's juvenilia, his performance is rationally managed.

Henry will not forfeit his logically developed interest in the heroine, but
the "lovers" will also not proceed in their plans without the General's assent;
Austen's hero, unlike the many satirized philosophers of late-eighteenth-
century anti-Jacobin texts, will not abuse or recklessly employ the dictates
of reason. The narrator indicates that Henry's and Catherine's "tempers
were mild, but their principles were steady, and while his parent so expressly
forbad the connexion, they could not allow themselves to encourage it. . . .
His *consent* was all that they wished for." They are not romantically inclined
enough to marry without parental sanction; they proceed cautiously, and
even though Henry's "present income was an income of independence and
comfort," the hero and heroine choose not to marry until they receive the
General's approval (203). Unlike most lovers in Austen's corpus, Catherine
and Henry are not in need of financial support, yet their stability does not
impel them to act impetuously or irrationally. Henry's father eventually
does support their marriage, but not because he suddenly realizes the benefits of such a union; Austen attributes the patriarch's change of heart to
the overwhelming emotions created by his daughter's marriage to "a man
of fortune and consequence." Austen notes that this event strongly affected
the General, producing "an accession of dignity that threw him into a fit of
good-humour, from which he did not recover till after Eleanor had obtained
his forgiveness of Henry, and his permission for him 'to be a fool if he liked
it'" (204).[40] The hero's father, who is susceptible to the power of gallantry
and nobility, is unable to control himself and simply permits Henry's "foolishness." The General's volatility ironically precipitates the rational love of
Henry and Catherine. Henry's steadiness prevails; he acquires a marital
status and retains the capacity to rationally perform various roles prescribed
for the English man.

Henry's successful endeavor to satisfy the distinct desires produced for
socially proper English maleness is attributable to his consistent devotion
to reason. He crafts and maintains a composite aesthetic of existence that
enables him to rehearse assorted manly duties without relinquishing his
rational masculinity. The men of Austen's juvenilia, like Henry, are self-

conscious figures who experience great anxiety about their social/sexual subjectivities, but they lack the ordering force of Henry's strict Enlightenment epistemology and are thus exposed as incompetent and foolish men. Austen's presentation of her hero in *Northanger Abbey* emphasizes how his perpetual reliance upon the dictates of reason ensures his hegemonic stability—even as he rehearses diverse and contradictory modes of appropriate English masculinity. Henry's rationalized sexuality allows him to demonstrate his chivalric training, his learned sentimentality, and his interest in the condition of women, but Austen dramatizes how his dedication to reason ultimately inhibits his ability to participate in desubjectifying love relations. Henry, like the ridiculous male figures of the juvenilia, must establish an approved sexuality in order to participate fully in the early-nineteenth-century reformed national community; he crafts a well-disciplined masculine identity, and Austen demonstrates how his rational marriage to Catherine precludes him from experiencing the multiplicity and instability of Deleuzian love. He will not permit himself to accept the illogical, overwhelming, and destructuring powers of amorous passions. Henry's rationalized aesthetic of existence regulates the explosive potential of his relationship with Catherine and maintains the security of his composite masculinity.

CHAPTER 3

Austen's Sensitive Men

Willoughby, Brandon, and the Regulation of Sensation

I could not be happy with a man whose taste did not in every point coincide with my own. He must enter into all my feelings; the same books, the same music must charm us both. . . . Mama, the more I know of the world, the more am I convinced that I shall never see a man whom I can really love. I require so much! (Marianne Dashwood in Austen, Sense and Sensibility 14–15)

That is what I like; that is what a young man ought to be. Whatever be his pursuits, his eagerness in them should know no moderation, and leave him no sense of fatigue. (Marianne Dashwood in Austen, Sense and Sensibility 38)

The relation to self that constitutes the end of the conversion and the final goal of all the practices of the self still belongs to an ethics of control. (Foucault, The History of Sexuality, Vol. 3: The Care of the Self 65)

Marianne Dashwood critiques the rational mode of masculinity adhered to by men like Henry Tilney and the disciplined model of masculinity followed by men of restraint like Edward Ferrars, and she instead announces her expectations of a male lover who remains inexhaustibly passionate. Marianne wants men to dismiss the restrictive structures of modern society and feel power(fully). Marianne encourages men to embrace and vocalize their emotions and energies, and for the young heroine such explicit passion is an essential character trait of her idealized lover. Her reflections strongly influence our readings of her two suitors: the mature Colonel Brandon and the youthful Willoughby. Both Brandon and Willoughby are well-schooled in the tradition of male sensibility, and they demonstrate their susceptibility to feeling throughout the narrative. Austen's *Sense and Sensibility* (1811) relates the story of each man's romantic pursuit of Marianne, but it also dramatizes the dangers that confront sensitive men; moreover, the novel documents the efforts of these men to regulate their emotions and order their aesthetics of existence by adhering to models of male behavior prescribed by post-Revolutionary discursive forces. Brandon has learned to temper his sentimentality by reverting to Burke's conception of a modern chivalric man; Willoughby painfully discovers that he, too, must limit his volatile passions, but he instead relies upon Enlightenment principles of rationality to mitigate the risks of his impulsive behavior. Most importantly, Austen dramatizes how both sensible male characters must abandon the role of the male lover to secure their hegemonic social/sexual subjectivities. Brandon and Willoughby craft socially functional aesthetics of existence, yet Austen's text illustrates how their accomplishments depend upon their control of emotions.

Austen's presentation of these men's struggles to regulate their sensibilities resembles the Hellenic process of self-formation that Foucault introduces in *The History of Sexuality, Vol. 2: The Use of Pleasure*.[1] Foucault indicates that the success of the ancient Greek world depended upon the individual's understanding of "the relationship with the self that enabled a person to keep from being carried away by the appetites and pleasures, to maintain a mastery and superiority over them . . . to remain free from interior bondage to the passions, and to achieve a mode of being that could be defined by . . . the perfect supremacy of oneself over oneself" (31). This efficient Greek system of self-discipline promoted a citizenry based upon individual self-surveillance, including the supervision of irrational passions. Brandon and Willoughby participate in a modern version of this method of self-formation; and yet, there is an important distinction between Brandon and Willoughby's self-regulation and the ancient Greek practice. Foucault points out that for the proper Greek man, the control of sensation actually becomes a source of great pleasure "in which the relation to self takes the form not only of a domination but also of an enjoyment without desire and without disturbance" (*The History of Sexuality, Vol. 3* 68).[2] Brandon and Willoughby, however, discover that they must manage what Deleuze and Guattari theorize as the diversity and unpredictability of love to ensure their abilities to meet other standards for proper English masculinity; for Austen's modern English men, the discipline of their feelings promotes their social/sexual regulation rather than their sensual pleasure.

Austen introduces both sensitive men following the Dashwoods' move to Barton Cottage, and we quickly discover that Colonel Brandon has already regulated his susceptibility to sentiment. Sir John Middleton initially describes the Colonel as the "only . . . gentleman there besides himself . . . a particular friend who was staying at the park, but who was neither very young nor very gay" (28). Austen echoes Sir John's sketch of Brandon as a stoic yet genteel man; she depicts her elder hero as "silent and grave," adding that "his appearance . . . was not unpleasing, in spite of his being in the opinion of Marianne and Margaret an absolute old bachelor, for he was on the wrong side of five and thirty." The narrator concludes that "though his face was not handsome his countenance was sensible, and his address was particularly gentlemanlike" (29). Austen's narration highlights the maturity and reserve of Brandon, but it also suggests his extant sensibility; he is an older gentleman who has felt and experienced a diversity of sensations. And while he currently seems neither interested in nor capable of exposing such sensitivity, he has the knowledge and tact to listen attentively to Marianne's music; he "heard her without being in raptures . . . and she felt a respect for him on the occasion, which the others had reasonably forfeited by their shameless want of taste" (30). Marianne appreciates Brandon's refined sophistication, especially his sensitivity to musical pleasure, but she criticizes him for not appearing "animated enough to be in love" and adds that he "complain[s] of rheumatism. . . . the commonest infirmity of declining life" (31–32). She recognizes Brandon as a man of sensibility who has disciplined his emotions to such an extent that he can no longer experience erotic love. Indeed, the Colonel refrains from the destabilizing behavior of a male lover, and he is too old and rheumatic to perform the virile masculine behavior requested by Wollstonecraft and her followers; he instead reverts to the safety of Burke's model of chivalric masculinity to order his aesthetic of existence.

Austen presents Willoughby, unlike Brandon, as both a virile man and a lover. The youthful suitor originally appears as a "gentleman carrying a gun, with two pointers playing round him." When he observes Marianne's fall, he "put down his gun and ran to her assistance." He "offered his services, and perceiving that [Marianne's] modesty declined what her situation rendered necessary, took her up in his arms without farther delay, and carried her down the hill" (35). Willoughby's actions may resemble those of a romanticized chivalric hero coming to the rescue of the ailing maiden, but he also demonstrates his virility by exerting great physical strength and endurance. Austen notes his "manly beauty and more than common gracefulness," and Marianne constructs him as an "equal to what her fancy had ever drawn for the hero of a favourite story."[3] He is an impressive male specimen who makes a heroic entrance, "and he then departed, to make himself still more interesting, in the midst of a heavy rain" (36). Austen initially constructs Willoughby as a storybook hero: mysterious, handsome, and virile. The excitable heroine concludes, "Every circumstance belonging to him was interesting. His name was good, his residence was in their favourite village, and she soon found out that of all manly dresses a shooting-jacket was the most becoming" (37). She immediately identifies Willoughby as the manifestation of her ideal man who remains physically powerful and emotionally unrestrained.

Sir John confirms many of Marianne's quickly formed impressions of Willoughby. He dubs the young man "as good a kind of fellow as ever lived. . . . A very decent shot," and declares "there is not a bolder rider in England" (37). Sir John's remarks remind us of Willoughby's superior physical skills: he knows how to ride and hunt, and he performs such activities in a bold manner. Sir John also informs us of Willoughby's fondness for sensual and social activities by noting his ability to dance "from eight o'clock till four, without once sitting down" (38). He is a tireless dancer whom Marianne praises for his "perfect good-breeding," his ability to unite "frankness and vivacity," and his declaration that "of music and dancing he was passionately fond" (39–40). He pays her great attention while she recovers from her injuries, and the heroine learns that he is a great and passionate reader, leading her to conclude that "Willoughby was all that her fancy had delineated" in her earlier attempts to outline the ideal male companion. Willoughby amazingly appears to fulfill all of Marianne's standards for an acceptable man, but Austen foreshadows the perilous social consequences of his impressive feat when Elinor notes that he "[slighted] too easily the forms of worldly propriety, he displayed a want of caution" (41–42). Willoughby may be an imposing man trained in the traditions of sensibility, but he has not curtailed his passions, and this lack of discipline encourages his involvement in desubjectifying amorous activities that engender dangerous sexual and social consequences. Austen establishes and ultimately traces an important distinction between Marianne's admirers; while Brandon relies upon traditional chivalric behavior to organize his aesthetic of existence, Willoughby will eventually turn to rational principles to order his unstable social/sexual subjectivity.

And yet, Willoughby shows few rational tendencies early in the story. His love of sensation and his fervent disregard for customary behavior remind us of Montague, the maligned rake of Mary Hays's feminist reform novel, *Memoirs of Emma Courtney* (1796). Montague is "blown about by every gust of passion" and "had never given himself time to reason, to compare, to acquire principles"; Hays adds that Montague was "accustomed to feel, and not to reason" (37). Willoughby shares Montague's faith in the infallible accuracy of sensory perceptions, and Austen's male figure also too often neglects rational thought in favor of emotional urges. Willoughby acts impulsively, maintains no profession, and like many of the vilified male figures of Jacobin novels, shows little inclination toward assiduous behavior. Sir John informs the Dashwoods that "Mr. Willoughby had no property of his own in the country . . . he resided there only while he was visiting the old lady at Allenham Court, to whom he was related, and whose possessions he was to inherit" (37–38). Willoughby demonstrates no ambition to enhance his standing in the modernizing nation through his own labor and instead prefers to trust in the beneficence of his aged aunt. He may be a striking young man, but he enjoys neither the direction of aspiring middle-class men nor the independence of rational male characters. Austen differentiates Willoughby from fictional men such as Henry Tilney and the many farmers of Jacobin novels who pursue industrious agricultural work rather than depending upon a familial inheritance. Willoughby is completely opposed to Enlightenment principles of progress, many of which were adopted by late-eighteenth-century feminist thinkers such as Wollstonecraft and Hays. Willoughby does not appear interested in achieving hegemonic security through his relations with women; rather, he experiences pleasures and sensations during his time with Marianne. Austen's novel, however, ultimately illustrates how Willoughby must reconfigure his method of relating to/with women. He must embrace the advice of Wollstonecraft and Hays—specifically their insistences that men respect the rational capacity of women and dismiss the role of the lover within marriage—to ensure his participation in the emerging national community.

While Willoughby eventually sacrifices amorous activity for conjugal stability, Brandon has already relinquished the behavior of a lover. Elinor displays great concern for Brandon's delicate constitution, especially in comparison to his youthful counterpart. She seriously questions "what could a silent man of five and thirty hope, when opposed by a very lively one of five and twenty" (42). Brandon appears too mild, with a reserve that "appeared rather the result of some oppression of spirits, than of any natural gloominess of temper," to compete with the aggressive hunter for the young heroine's attention. The Colonel has previously felt emotions, and although he is not "naturally" melancholic, he has learned to regulate his passions by adhering to the chivalric model of masculinity advocated by Burke. Willoughby claims that Brandon "is just the kind of man . . . whom every body speaks well of, and nobody cares about; whom all are delighted to see, and nobody remembers to talk to" (43). Willoughby's comment suggests the social acceptability of a male like Brandon. He is a culturally approved man who causes no disturbance and garners no notice because he has constructed his aesthetic of existence in accordance with the specific requests of the post-Revolutionary discursive field. He appears to have all the essential characteristics of a proper English man—save a wife—with no prominent insufficiencies.

Despite Brandon's hesitancy to pursue romantic love, he is nonetheless highly skilled at feeling and appreciating sensation. Willoughby may be more dramatic in his display of emotion, but Austen informs us that Brandon remains "on every occasion mindful of the feelings of others" (53).

He is reminiscent of the benevolent paternal figure of Ann Radcliffe's *The Romance of the Forest* (1791), Arnand La Luc, who is similarly described as "ever sensible to the sufferings of others" (258). Radcliffe claims that La Luc's "mind was penetrating; his views extensive; and his systems . . . were simple, rational, and sublime" (245). Like La Luc, Brandon expresses empathy and compassion throughout the story; in addition, both men have panoramic minds and display a remarkable ability to accept both the laws of reason and sublime happenings. Elinor instructs Willoughby and her sister that the Colonel "has seen a great deal of the world; has been abroad; has read, and has a thinking mind." She declares that she has "found him capable of giving me much information on various subjects" and notes that "he has always answered my inquiries with the readiness of good-breeding and good nature" (43). Elinor reconfigures the Colonel as an experienced and oft-consulted reference manual, and she concludes that he is "a sensible man, well-bred, well-informed, of gentle address . . . possessing an amiable heart" (44). Elinor correctly identifies the Colonel's education and experience, as well as his training in both sensibility and chivalry; this background informs both his sensitivity and his sense of duty to others.

Brandon is especially concerned about his abandoned niece, Eliza, and when he receives news of her whereabouts, his interest in her welfare becomes paramount. Austen notes that he "changed colour, and immediately left the room" (54). The Colonel is sensually affected by the report of Eliza's abandonment, but he quickly suppresses these passions and acts as a dutiful man. He cancels the party to Whitwell and departs for London, informing Willoughby and his other guests, "I cannot afford to lose *one* hour" (55). Brandon sincerely regrets both the abrupt nature of the day's canceled event and his sudden exit, but he immediately begins his journey on horseback, after bowing silently to Marianne (56). The narrator emphasizes the Colonel's chivalric behavior whenever he becomes emotionally overwrought; rather than allowing himself to become flushed with sentiment, he mounts his horse, heroically departs to save an endangered woman, and offers a humble bow to his would-be lady. Austen carefully distinguishes Brandon's heroic performance from the actions of many obnoxiously chivalric men showcased in the fiction of the 1790s. For example, the Colonel is clearly distinct from Coke Clifton, the villain of Thomas Holcroft's radical novel, *Anna St. Ives* (1792), who is devoted to "a high sense of fashionable honour" and "well acquainted with foreign manners" (5; 117). Unlike Clifton, Brandon is not a foolish practitioner of arcane French customs; the Colonel is a responsible man who maintains great compassion for Eliza and relies upon chivalric traditions to keep his masculinity structured. His journey to London is crucial to the development of the narrative because it precipitates Willoughby's mysterious departure from Barton, but it also illustrates how Marianne's suitors revert to alternative models of male social/sexual subjectivity whenever their sensations become overwhelming. While Brandon relies upon ideals of duty to guide his actions, Willoughby is initially obsessed with pleasurable sensations promised by social activities such as the outing to Whitwell. The novel demonstrates how Brandon's strategy promotes a model of masculinity better suited to stabilize English men, domestic settings, and the post-Revolutionary nation.

Following Brandon's departure, Austen stresses the instability promoted by Willoughby's libertine behavior; the young suitor provides Marianne with a horse and later captures a lock of her hair. Both incidents suggest Willoughby's physical intimacy with the heroine: the gift of the horse recalls the unrestrained passion often associated with artistic renderings of the animal, and the shearing of Marianne's hair certainly reminds us of a similarly aggressive man's activity in Pope's "Rape of the Lock" (49; 51). Austen's young lover may be named after the rakish figure of Francis Burney's *Evelina* (1778), but his courtship strategies resemble the undisciplined sentiments exhibited by William from Inchbald's *Nature and Art* (1796). Inchbald claims that "William indeed was gallant, was amorous, and indulged his inclination to the libertine society of women"; she adds that William was "well versed in all the licentious theory" and "thought himself in love, because he perceived a tumultuous impulse cause his heart to beat, while his fancy fixed on a certain object, whose presence agitated yet more his breast" (41; 45). Like William, Willoughby is schooled in excessively romantic conduct, and he, too, quickly convinces himself of the sincerity of strong feelings derived from his experiences of physical sensations. Willoughby becomes even more forward in the absence of Mrs. Smith. He escorts Marianne, without an attendant, around what they presume to be his future home at Allenham.[4] He acts as a confident lover, and while Marianne is undoubtedly exhilarated by Willoughby's amorous performances, even the young heroine becomes concerned about his resources. As she reflects on the possibility of sharing Mrs. Smith's house with her passionate lover, she "could easily conceive that marriage might not be immediately in their power; for though Willoughby was independent, there was no reason to believe him rich." She knows that he "lived at an expense to which" his present income "could hardly be equal, and he had himself often complained of his poverty" (61). Marianne is aware of her lover's financial limitations and the impossibility of their sudden marriage, but she remains convinced that Willoughby will be her lover, her husband, and a landed gentleman. And yet, Austen reveals that Willoughby is primarily a pleasure seeker who has little interest in the responsibilities of an English gentleman modeled by men such as Mr. Darcy and Mr. Knightley.

Willoughby may unwisely assume a level of future financial security, but he never announces an inheritance; and unlike Brandon, he shows no inclination to perform the social duties of the aristocratic gentleman, such as administering an estate and caring for dependents. Rather, Willoughby is enamored of the simplicity and charm of Barton Cottage. He insists that "not a stone must be added to its walls, not an inch to its size, if my feelings are regarded" (62). Willoughby appears much like Pierre de la Motte, the indebted fugitive of *The Romance of the Forest,* whom Radcliffe describes as "a man whose passions often overcame his reason, and, for a time, silenced his conscience" (2). Willoughby experiences a similar emotional engulfment, as he is incapable of accepting either the rationality of time or the mutability of human existence. He neither wants his friends nor their house to alter; he is attached sentimentally to Barton and implores, "Tell me that not only your house will remain the same, but that I shall ever find you and yours as unchanged as your dwelling; and that you will always consider me with the kindness which has made every thing belonging to you so dear to me" (63–64). He echoes Wordsworth's desire to remember always "spots of time." Willoughby wants to capture and continuously return to moments and people of great sensation. He appears to have little ambition for either the aristocratic life proposed by the discourses of Burke and his followers or the culture of merit and progress theorized by the Jacobins. While he has a strong admiration for the past, his nostalgia is not for a lost chivalric system and its noble man. Austen presents Willoughby as a passionate male who is fond of a simple lifestyle and frustrated by the conflicting desires of the modern English nation.

Austen's narrative shatters Willoughby's attempt to experience continuously the simple sensations aroused by his time at Barton. He is able to remain near this "spot" only a day longer; distraught with emotion, he informs the Dashwood family (after attempting to reveal the matter to Marianne) that "Mrs. Smith has this morning exercised the privilege of riches upon a poor dependent cousin, by sending me on business to London" (65). Willoughby's explanation accentuates both his unstable social/sexual standing and the authoritative function of his female relation, whose influential power reminds us of the efforts of Wollstonecraft and other Enlightenment feminist thinkers to expand the social conception of women.[5] Mrs. Smith employs her financial standing to affect Willoughby's behavior, and as Phoebe Smith notes, she is specifically concerned with preventing "Willoughby from following the dictates of his heart to marry Marianne" (11). Mrs. Smith prompts her nephew to discipline his overwhelming passions for the heroine and concern himself with the "business" of developing a hegemonic social/sexual subjectivity through marriage. In leaving he declares, "I will not torment myself any longer by remaining among friends whose society it is impossible for me now to enjoy." Willoughby does not make a heroic exit like Brandon; instead, the young virile suitor exits pining of his suffering and indicting his aged female relation. Elinor notes this severe alteration in his manner and claims that his present actions are "so unlike a lover, so unlike himself" (66). Elinor's remarks suggest both the common perception of Willoughby as a lover and the nascence of a significant alteration in his aesthetic of existence. Mrs. Smith compels him to leave Barton after she learns of his scandalous affair with the second Eliza; he no longer maintains strong passions for Miss Williams, and his abandonment of her and their newborn child exposes Willoughby's improper training as a man of feeling. Austen illustrates how Willoughby must now dismiss his romantic passions for Marianne to acquire a socially sanctioned masculine subjectivity; modern England cannot allow its young men to act impulsively with fervent passion. Austen specifically demonstrates that he must address the dictates of Enlightenment feminist thought: Willoughby must establish a new appreciation for the social potential of women, relinquish his identity as a lover, and adopt rational principles to craft a nationally proper masculinity.

Austen foreshadows such a change in Willoughby's emotional demeanor, but when Marianne travels to London she eagerly expects to encounter the same passionately exuberant man. The narrator notes that the heroine "was internally dwelling on the perfections of a man, of whose whole heart she felt thoroughly possessed, and whom she expected to see in every carriage which drove near their house" (121). While Austen's narration reveals the excessively romantic attitude of Marianne, it also reminds us of the contradictory expectations for proper English masculinity that Willoughby must negotiate; he has traveled to London in accordance with the directives of Enlightenment and feminist writers for a man of reason, yet he is still idealized as a lover by the heroine. His actions in London reflect this tension as well as an impending change in his aesthetic of existence. He no longer behaves as a passionate and virile figure unconcerned with custom and propriety;[6] the influence of Mrs. Smith and his own financial need have clearly forced him to reorder his sexuality in accordance with the desires of modern English society. While Brandon maintains regular contact with the Dashwood sisters, Willoughby's endeavor to restructure his sexual subjectivity forces him to hide from the heroines. When he eventually encounters Marianne, after Elinor notices him in a crowded room of a London party, Austen indicates that "he immediately bowed, but without attempting to speak to her, or to approach Marianne, though he could not but see her" (152). He now tries to behave in a manner for which he had earlier rebuked Brandon: Willoughby would like to be noticed by all and approached by none.

Willoughby adopts the socially approved behavior of a reserved man who rehearses the customary chivalric niceties modeled by Henry Tilney, but Marianne, unlike Catherine Morland, refuses to allow such hackneyed propriety. She demands, "Good God! Willoughby, what is the meaning of this? Have you not received my letters? Will you not shake hands with me?" (152). She rebukes his disciplined emotions, but Willoughby, who now seeks social/sexual security, can no longer dismiss the stable models of hegemonic masculinity provided by codifying structures such as chivalry and reason. The narrator claims that Willoughby could not avoid confronting Marianne, "but her touch seemed painful to him, and he held her hand only for a moment. . . . all this time he was evidently struggling for composure." Willoughby is still a man of feeling, but he will not permit himself the opportunity to enjoy or reciprocate physical sensations, especially previously felt sensations.[7] He can only speak briefly to his former lover before he "turned hastily away with a slight bow and joined his friend" (153). Austen highlights Willoughby's determination to regulate his powerful emotions with the order promised by the cold logic of an extreme rationalist; his decision to solidify his social/sexual subjectivity through marriage is a rational choice informed by business. Like Brandon, Willoughby will not be able to banish completely his propensity to feel, but the narrator records his attempts to strategically manage his sensations.

The London scenes also document a different but equally difficult struggle for Brandon, who has already successfully disciplined his susceptibility to emotion. The narrator notes that the Colonel continually visited the heroines at Mrs. Jennings's home; "he came to look at Marianne and talk to Elinor" (145). Despite his extant desires for Marianne, Brandon restrains from actively pursuing their pleasurable potential; he instead performs as a chivalric gentleman who remains concerned about his ward and passively admires his beloved. He arrives at Berkeley-street one afternoon looking "more than usually grave" and "sat for some time without saying a word." He informs Elinor that her "sister's engagement to Mr. Willoughby is very generally known" and then questions, "Is every thing finally settled? Is it impossible to—? But I have no right, and I could have no chance of succeeding." He is nonplused and effectively silenced by his own thoughts and abridged words. He can only tell Elinor that for Marianne he "wish[es] all imaginable happiness; to Willoughby that he may endeavour to deserve her" (149–50). Brandon momentarily adopts the mindset of a lover, only to leave his performance incomplete. He may appear to imitate the ancient Greek model of self-formation, garnering ostensible satisfaction from his well-ordered masculinity, but he has actually constructed a carefully regulated aesthetic of existence that does not permit the volatile emotions engendered by love.

Austen presents Brandon much as Mr. Dudley, the virtuous paternal figure of Jane West's *A Gossip's Story* (1797), who "possessed in eminent degree the virtues of the head and the heart . . . [and] knew how to reduce his desires to that moderate standard, which is most likely to produce content" (I: 13–14). The Colonel, like Mr. Dudley, is a man learned in both knowledge and sensibility, but he most importantly knows he must contain his feelings to ensure the safety of his sexuality and the comfort of his social existence.

After Willoughby's formal break with Marianne, Brandon successfully explains—at least to Elinor—the primary reasons for his regulated sensations. He struggles to relate the story of the Elizas, including Willoughby's scandalous activity with his young ward. He compares his love for the first Eliza to Willoughby's relationship with Marianne and informs Elinor that he and the first Eliza "were within a few hours of eloping together for Scotland" (179). He discusses the plight of his romantic childhood love, her divorce from his brother, and her death; his account again reveals his strong commitment to a sense of duty inspired by his adherence to a chivalric form of masculinity. We learn that after he finally located the abandoned first Eliza, Brandon nursed her during her final moments of life and accepted the dying mother's child as his responsibility (181). The Colonel's account of earlier events invites us to revise our conception of his character. He again appears very similar to Mr. Dudley, whose mind was "awakened to all the impressions of duty both to his Maker and his fellow-creatures" and "[possessed] sufficient strength to overcome the extreme indulgence of hopeless grief." West indicates that "though [Mr. Dudley] found it impossible to forget that he once was most happy, he acquiesced with patient resignation in the limited enjoyments which his situation allowed" and preserved "the anxious tenderness of the paternal character" (I: 15). Like Mr. Dudley, Brandon reveals his youthful romantic happiness, but he is now a responsible and resigned patriarchal man who can neither forget the pain of his troubled past nor actively pursue new experiences of pleasure. While his discussion with Elinor provides scandalous information concerning Willoughby, Brandon's story also demonstrates his commitment to emotional discipline and his allegiance to Burke's conception of a noble and dutiful masculinity.[8]

The Colonel's history, likewise, reemphasizes his training in the traditions of sensibility. Like Mr. Dudley and Willoughby, Brandon, too, was once a passionate lover. He has stabilized his subjectivity, but he is not yet a complete modern English man, as he still lacks the social/sexual security engendered by a hegemonic marital relationship. Unlike Willoughby, however, the Colonel benefits from a solid financial standing because, as Johnson reminds us, the "days of [his] subjugation to a corrupt father and older brother are happily behind him" (*Jane Austen* 70). England has updated its economy, and Brandon is no longer subjected to archaic traditions that dictated familial roles; the Colonel's economic and social stability enables him to perform two prominent actions in the final stages of the novel that confirm his commitment to the traditions of sentimentality and chivalry: his offer of the Delaford living to Edward Ferrars and his service as Elinor's attendant and Mrs. Dashwood's escort during Marianne's illness. When he learns of Mrs. Ferrars's strategy to impede the planned marriage between Edward and Lucy Steele by withholding her son's inheritance, the Colonel is astonished at the "impolitic cruelty . . . of dividing, or attempting to divide, two young people long attached to each other" (246). He is sensible of the feelings of young lovers—even if he will no longer behave as a lover himself—and critical of the coarse heartlessness exhibited by Mrs. Ferrars. In addition, his gift of the Delaford parsonage to Edward recalls a chivalric economic structure in which land was administered by a feudal lord. His genteel beneficence circumvents the authority of Mrs. Ferrars and provides Edward with a domestic sphere, a safe opportunity to marry without the risks of love, and a chance to solidify his involvement in the modern national community.

Yet Brandon sees his action as neither heroic nor noble. He remains a disciplined man who reveals little interest in gallant ceremonies. He does not even want to make the offer himself; he requests, rather, that Elinor present the living to Edward. Miss Dashwood lauds the Colonel's generosity toward a man he does not know and insists that there "are not many men who would act as he has done . . . few people who have so compassionate an heart!" (249). Even the timid Edward realizes that Brandon "is undoubtedly a sensible man, and in his manners perfectly the gentleman" (253). The comments of Elinor and Edward remind us of Brandon's sensibility as well as his adherence to a chivalric model of maleness. He is a sentimental man schooled in genteel behavior, but he prefers the role of a dutiful protector and provider to the gallant activity of a glorified hero. The Colonel's behavior is reminiscent of another of Jane West's kind-hearted paternal figures, Mr. Herbert, who presides over *The Advantages of Education: Or, the History of Maria Williams* (1793). West announces that "integrity seems [to be] the predominant feature of [Herbert's] soul. He has the greater share of independence, of sentiment, than I ever knew a man possess. Nothing can persuade him to alter a conduct which he considers to be conscientious; and he fears no person's resentment, when engaged in the cause of virtue" (II: 225). Like Mr. Herbert, Brandon believes in the sincerity of his own emotions, and he is determined to act upon them regardless of the social consequences. As a man of sensibility, the Colonel trusts his feelings, but he has also trained his sensations to prevent the possibility of an uncontrollable overflow of passions, and this careful discipline allows him to remain perpetually useful to his modernizing society without relinquishing his sensitivity.

When the Dashwood sisters remove to Cleveland, the Colonel quickly follows and continues his service to Marianne and Elinor. Brandon remains a dutiful companion of the heroines, but Miss Dashwood also notes the "needless alarm of a lover" in "[Brandon's] looks of anxious solicitude on Marianne's feeling, in her head and throat, the beginning of a heavy cold" (267).[9] Austen documents how Brandon remains sensibly affected by Marianne's sickness; it frightened him, and the narrator notes that he "tried to reason himself out of fears" (270). When Elinor later approaches him about her sister's worsening condition, the Colonel listens "in silent despondence;—but her difficulties were instantly obviated, for with a readiness that seemed to speak the occasion . . . [he] offered himself as the messenger who should fetch Mrs. Dashwood." Brandon is still sensitive to sensations, but he will once again perform as a responsible chivalric figure, offering to transport the mother of Marianne to her bedside. Austen informs us that "whatever he might feel, [Brandon] acted with all the firmness of a collected mind, made every necessary arrangement with the utmost dispatch, and calculated with exactness the time in which [Elinor] might look for his return" (272). While he appears to perform as a romantic hero, he still acts in a controlled and ordered manner, outlining his travel plans and determining his timeframe. Despite his well-trained susceptibility to feeling, Brandon is organized and regulated.

Following Brandon's departure, Willoughby arrives at Cleveland and attempts to acquire from Elinor news of Marianne's health. He stammers, "Your sister . . . is out of danger. I heard it from the servant. God be praised!—But is it true?—is it really true?" Elinor attempts to remain silent, but Willoughby proclaims, "For God's sake tell me, is she out of danger, or is she not?" (278). He is emotionally overtaken with his concern for the heroine's health, and paralleling Brandon's inability to inquire coherently of Marianne's marital arrangements, Willoughby can only stutter his words. When Miss Dashwood inquires the reason for his surprising visit, he provides an ambiguous response: "I mean . . . to make you hate me one degree less than you do *now*." He continues, "I mean to offer some kind of explanation, some kind of apology, for the past" (279). Willoughby knows that his recently related history has transformed his social reputation, and he asks Elinor for the opportunity to account for his behavior. He begins his story by defending his innocent initial attractions to Marianne and the Dashwood family at Barton. He informs Elinor that at that time he "had no other intention, no other view in the acquaintance than to pass my time pleasantly while I was obliged to remain." He claims that Marianne's person and charms "could not but please me" and acknowledges that originally his "vanity only was elevated" by her affection (280). He suggests that his time with Marianne at Barton was sensibly pleasurable and claims that while he was susceptible to such sensations he was also ignorant of the dangers associated with amorous emotions. Willoughby presents his incipient romantic desires for the young heroine as accidental, but as Austen's novel suggests, even men who unintentionally adopt the pose of a lover endanger the social/sexual security of themselves, others, and the nation.

As Willoughby's compromised masculinity is in part due to his economic instability, he also attempts to explain his precarious financial status. He declares that his "fortune was never large" and indicates that he "had always been expensive, always in the habit of associating with people of better income than [himself]" (280). He is a connoisseur of pleasure, and although he had always maintained hope in the possibility of a significant inheritance after the death of his aunt, Willoughby indicates that "it had been for some time [his] intention to re-establish [his] circumstances by marrying a woman of fortune" (280). Unlike Delmont and other industrious men of Jacobin novels who plan to earn their sustenance through agricultural labor, Willoughby's monetary hopes rest upon a familial inheritance and a marriage to a wealthy woman. He is honest about his desires for an ample income, and he freely admits that marrying Marianne "was not a thing to be thought of." He concludes that he "was acting in this manner, trying to engage her regard, without a thought of returning it" (280). Willoughby announces both his coarse desire for affluence and his careless, but eventually powerful, interest in Marianne. He grants, "I did not know the extent of the injury I meditated, because I did not *then* know what it was to love" (280).[10] He expresses his own surprise at developing sincere amorous emotions for Marianne. His comments recall the irrational and uncontrollable quality of love; they also remind us that even a man who performs briefly as a romantic lover risks significant consequences. Willoughby once developed powerful amorous passions for Marianne, but he has now learned that aspiring modern men must view love as a rational activity based upon pecuniary and utilitarian concerns rather than desire. West describes *The Advantages of Education* as a fictional attempt "to counteract the evils incident to the romantic conclusions which youths are apt to form" (I: iv). Austen's novel, likewise, illustrates how modern English men must treat romantic passions like a dangerous narcotic; the only sure way to prevent possible peril is to practice total abstinence.

Willoughby, of course, did not keep such a vow, but he learned that he must regulate his susceptibility to emotions and sensations because "a circumstance occurred—an unlucky circumstance, to ruin all [his] resolution, and with it all [his] comfort" (281). According to Willoughby, when Mrs. Smith discovered his scandalous activity with Eliza, she threatened to relinquish her future financial support, although she did offer to "forgive the past, if [he] would marry Eliza" (283). Willoughby acknowledges that he once maintained romantic feelings for Miss Williams, but their affair now seems childish and immature. He briefly appears to behave as a man of sensibility who will not accept a passionless marriage complemented by a large inheritance from his aged aunt, but he is also not willing to pursue his ostensibly sincere love for Marianne without some degree of economic stability. He now reverts to the safety of rational behavior displayed by men like Henry Tilney. Willoughby acts in a "reasonable" manner, as he departs for London, "[believing himself] secure of [his] present wife, if [he] chose to address her" (283). He opts to dismiss his passions and the sentiments of the male lover to pursue the social standing facilitated by an economically promising marriage. His rational decision also implies a consciousness of his previous irresponsible performances as a lover; he must now turn to stern Enlightenment codes to repair the damage amorous feelings inflicted upon his masculinity.[11] He has also come to appreciate the mandates of late-eighteenth-century feminist thinkers. He respects the new social presence of women like his aunt, and as Wollstonecraft instructs, he does not confuse his responsibilities as a husband with the identity of a lover. Indeed, he concludes that his own "domestic happiness is out of the question" (291). Willoughby will not enjoy marital bliss, and it is precisely his willingness to forgo the felicity of amorous experiences that allows him to stabilize his social/sexual subjectivity.

Following Willoughby's confession and explanation, Austen allows Brandon a similar opportunity to reconfigure himself through his unheard conversation with Mrs. Dashwood. The emotional mother effectively recreates Brandon, describing him as a desperate sentimental man who will also be a useful addition to her family. She tells Elinor that he "opened his whole heart to me yesterday as we travelled," and according to Mrs. Dashwood, the Colonel has loved Marianne "ever since the first moment of seeing her." Mrs. Dashwood concludes that Brandon's regard was "infinitely surpassing anything that Willoughby ever felt or feigned, as much more warm, as more sincere or constant. . . . Such a noble mind!—such openness, such sincerity!—no one can be deceived in *him*" (295). She depicts Brandon as a passionate lover who is well trained in sentimental behavior, but she also highlights his social stability. Mrs. Dashwood admires "His fortune too" and explains that "at my time of life . . . everybody cares about *that;*—and although I neither know, nor desire to know, what it really is, I am sure it must be a good one" (297). Mrs. Dashwood's characterization of the Colonel establishes him as a man suitable to serve as Marianne's protector and ostensible lover. He is a disciplined man of sensibility who relies upon his "noble mind" to manage his aesthetic of existence. Brandon's control of his passions prevents him from enduring the volatile consequences of love, and his financial standing enables him to revert continually to chivalric male activities to participate in the national community.

Austen concludes her novel by reporting both Marianne's eventual marriage to the regulated Colonel and Willoughby's frustrated marital status. Austen suggests that Brandon "still sought the constitutional safeguard of a flannel waistcoat" and concludes that he "was now as happy, as all those who best loved him, believed he deserved to be" (333). Her ambiguous narration reminds us of the Colonel's melancholic past and sentimental training, but it also suggests the limits—and the publicly anticipated limits—of his conjugal bliss. Brandon's experience of pleasure derives from his control rather than his overflow of sensations, and the narrator implies that even his friends do not expect him to experience exuberant joy. Austen adds that Marianne "restored his mind to animation, and his spirits to cheerfulness," and "her whole heart became, in time, as much devoted to her husband, as it had once been to Willoughby" (334).[12] Marianne can recharge the Colonel's sensibility and facilitate his social life, but she can only love him as much as she did Willoughby—and even that will take time. Marianne briefly appears like the far more timid Catherine Morland, whom Tilney hopes will learn to love different flowers. The restricted nature of her commitment to the Colonel may be crass, but is also essential, as he could not successfully manage an immoderate amorous experience. Brandon is more financially stable than Willoughby, but it is his emotional discipline that distinguishes him as a socially functional mate for Marianne. He will not allow passions to overwhelm himself or his wife, and his control also allows him to perform various social roles prescribed for the proper English man.

The narrator shows how Willoughby can also successfully fulfill numerous expectations for the appropriate national man once he relinquishes his amorous inclinations.[13] Willoughby, like Brandon, does not enjoy unbridled domestic pleasure, but he eventually discerns how to accept the compromises involved in his socially sanctioned conjugal relationship. He was not forever heartbroken, nor did he abandon the world; rather, "he lived to exert, and frequently to enjoy himself" (334). He remains a virile man of sensibility, as he continues to relish the possibility of physical sensations. Austen notes, "His wife was not always out of humour, nor his home always uncomfortable; and in his breed of horses and dogs, and in sporting of every kind, he found no inconsiderable degree of domestic felicity" (334). Like Brandon's ambiguous future "happiness," Willoughby's joy in life appears limited and somewhat perverted. His "domestic felicity" involves almost everything but his wife, and while he is certainly not a miserable hermit, like Gulliver, he seems more interested in his horses than his supposed lover. Austen illustrates how Willoughby's decision to discipline his susceptibility to emotions helps him to meet other post-Revolutionary expectations for English masculinity. He can still hunt, ride, and appreciate sensations, but he must no longer allow his emotions to overtake his reason. He has established a secure aesthetic of existence by acting rationally, and while he is now able to participate in the burgeoning modern nation, he must perpetually abstain from the multiplicities and volatilities of love to maintain his status.

Neither Willoughby nor Brandon is able to exist as an unchecked man of sensibility, and Austen demonstrates how each suitor must avoid amorous emotions to ensure his secure domestic life. Willoughby restrains his susceptibility to romantic love by relying upon rationality to direct his behavior, while Brandon consistently relies upon the socially accepted chivalric model of behavior to order his sexuality. Willoughby may become more disciplined, but he is clearly still a man in training who is learning to respond to the dictates of reason and the requests of Enlightenment thinkers such as Wollstonecraft. Brandon is already disciplined, and while he may not be an extremely exciting male figure, Austen suggests that he is the kind of man who is of great use to the nation during the cultural unrest of the early nineteenth century. The Colonel still must solidify his social/sexual subjectivity, and his need for amelioration prefigures Austen's later depictions of aspiring tradesmen who strive to develop and broaden their identities as English men in order to assume more significant social responsibilities; moreover, Brandon's guarded masculinity also anticipates the stable sexualities of social administrators like Mr. Darcy and Mr. Knightley, who perform vital leadership roles in their communities. Marianne may idealize a passionate man, but Austen's story illustrates that post-Revolutionary English society desires carefully disciplined masculine subjects who will assume the responsibility of guiding England through its post-Revolutionary transformation. These men, of course, must still marry to establish hegemonic identities and reproduce a national citizenry, but as Wollstonecraft argues and Austen's text dramatizes, functional and secure marriages must not involve Deleuzian love.

CHAPTER 4

Austen's Tradesmen

Improving Masculinity in Pride and Prejudice

While the novels of Austen's contemporaries, with very few exceptions, are given over to crises of social and marital disintegration, Pride and Prejudice *is a categorically happy novel, and its felicity is not merely incidental, something that happens at the end of a novel, but is rather at once its premise and its prize. In its readiness to ratify and to grant our happiness,* Pride and Prejudice *is almost shamelessly wish fulfilling. The fantasies it satisfies, however, are not merely private—a poor but deserving girl catches a rich husband. They are pervasively political as well.* (Johnson, Jane Austen 73)

[A] relationship with the self . . . is not simply "self awareness" but self-formation as an "ethical subject," a process in which the individual delimits that part of himself that will form the object of his moral practice, defines his position relative to the precept he will follow, and decides on a certain mode of being that will serve as his moral goal. And this requires him to act upon himself, to monitor, test, improve, and transform himself. (Foucault, The History of Sexuality, Vol. 2: The Use of Pleasure 28)

Much of *Pride and Prejudice*'s enduring appeal is no doubt due to the reputation of the novel as a "shamelessly" happy story in which, as Johnson notes, the characters realize their dreams (*Jane Austen* 73).[1] This perception, of course, is primarily based upon the romantic account of Elizabeth and Darcy's love relationship. Elizabeth is one of the more alluring female figures in the history of English letters, and Darcy is admired as both an ancestral man of England and a lover.[2] He is a phenomenal male figure, and the heroine sarcastically announces early in the tale that she is "perfectly convinced . . . that Mr. Darcy has no defect" (50). Mrs. Gardiner, however, later explains to Elizabeth that the benevolent patriarch of Pemberley "wants nothing but a little more liveliness, and *that*, if he marry *prudently*, his wife may teach him" (288). According to the heroine's aunt, Darcy must "learn" to overcome his cautious reserve and appreciate the energy of other individuals; and though Austen reveals throughout her corpus how love can destabilize lesser men, the hero of *Pride and Prejudice* is the exceptional man who benefits from his amorous experiences. Indeed, he eventually relates to the heroine: "[Y]ou taught me a lesson, hard indeed at first, but most advantageous. By you, I was properly humbled. I came to you without a doubt of my reception. You shewed me how insufficient were all my pretensions to please a woman worthy of being pleased" (328).[3] Darcy's love for Elizabeth—a love that is not Deleuzian but ostensibly edifying—helps him to accept his proper social function, and as Johnson concludes, Austen ultimately depicts him as "singularly free from the faults that underline comparable figures elsewhere" (*Jane Austen* 73). Darcy presides over this shamelessly happy story as an exemplar of English masculinity, and his extraordinary social/sexual subjectivity suggests the lack of any remotely equivalent men.

Darcy's preeminent class position as the current head of an ancient, landed, yet untitled family immediately distinguishes him from the other men of the novel. In addition, he is an outstanding man because of his ability to satisfy the various and distinct socially produced desires for proper English masculinity generated by the discursive field of the 1790s. He is a physically imposing man who is eager to fish with Mr. Gardiner at Pemberley (235); he can be a coldly rational man, as he demonstrates by his unwillingness to allow Bingley to risk his recent rise in society by embracing an irrational love; and he also exposes great sensibility, as in his second proposal when he "expressed himself . . . as sensibly and as warmly as a man violently in love can be supposed to do" (325). Although he is a versatile man, Austen most clearly portrays Darcy as an adherent to Burke's model of chivalric masculinity, and as Alistair Duckworth explains, "he has a Burkean regard for the wisdom of his ancestors" (129). Darcy carefully follows Burke's outline for a man of ancestral heritage; he is noble, well mannered, and upholds the majesty and tradition of his Pemberley estate that symbolizes his aristocratic lineage and grounds his cultural authority.[4] His outstanding social/sexual standing, buttressed by the grandeur of Pemberley, allows him to serve as an administrator of social morality who effectively orchestrates and evaluates the activity of the novel. Darcy's exceptional status as a disciplined man who is virile yet genteel, romantic yet responsible, anticipates both the impending collapse of idealized Burkean masculinity and an important cultural shift in England's expectations for its male leaders.

Austen's mature novels suggest that the post-Revolutionary English nation can no longer rely solely upon Burkean aristocratic men like Darcy to provide civic and moral guidance; as *Mansfield Park, Emma,* and *Persuasion* illustrate, country gentlemen are aging, and the noble ideals they once embodied are quickly atrophying. While this decline of the aristocratic man and his Burkean principles is not apparent in *Pride and Prejudice,* Austen's novel does accentuate Darcy's singular status, and his marriage to Elizabeth effectively ensures that the next generation's Mr. Darcy will lack true aristocratic lineage. There are simply no other men of Darcy's standing or grandeur in the narrative, and in her later tales Austen portrays the decay of Burkean masculinity quite clearly. In the latter half of the novelist's corpus, she demonstrates that the modernizing nation will not be guided solely by men of the aristocracy, and as we begin to see in *Pride and Prejudice*, England must prepare for and expect important civic activity from its rising trade class that Mary Evans and other Austen scholars have observed in her novels. Evans notes that Austen's texts dramatize how in the early 1800s "a largely rural world of agricultural production gave way . . . to an urban world of mechanized industrial production" (3–4).[5] *Pride and Prejudice* specifically portrays two men, affiliated with the trade class that emerges from this urban industrial growth, who attempt to improve themselves and enhance their responsibilities in the modern English state: Mr. Bingley and Mr. Gardiner.

Gardiner is a successful and respected man of trade, and while Bingley is not himself a member of the trade class, his descent from a prosperous family of trade continues to mark him throughout the novel; he may no longer work, but he is still defined as a man *from* trade. Neither Bingley nor Gardiner enjoys the status and power of Darcy, but Bingley has substantial financial means, and Gardiner displays a genteel Burkean demeanor usually reserved for a nobleman. They cannot become complete men like Darcy, but they are able to ameliorate their sexualized aesthetics of existence. Foucault explains that the ancient Greek practice of molding an aesthetic of existence did not entail "the individual . . . [making] himself into an ethical subject by universalizing the principles that informed his action; on the contrary, he did so by means of an attitude and a quest that individualized his action [and] modulated it" (*History of Sexuality, Vol. 2* 62). Bingley and Gardiner must create individualized rather than idealized social/sexual subjectivities by focusing on specific anxieties and needs that will enable them to enlarge their roles and responsibilities in their social communities: Bingley orders his aesthetic of existence around the pursuit of pleasure, while Gardiner organizes his around a sense of duty. These men of/from trade do not threaten to usurp Darcy's role as a civic and moral administrator, but as successful members of England's emerging middle classes, Gardiner and Bingley embody what Ernest Gellner dubs the "idea of progress" that "European thought since the eighteenth century has come to assume" (3). Gellner explains that following the French Revolution, "Life has come to be lived *on an upward slope*. The nature of things has a bias towards improvement. Improvement is both anticipated and required" (4).[6] Bingley and Gardiner's social advancements help them to become more involved in early-nineteenth-century English society, but their class positions ultimately prevent them from joining or intimately participating in the nation's ancient history.

While *Emma* and *Persuasion* offer more poignant portraits of a newly emerging class structure and the decaying aristocracy, *Pride and Prejudice* dramatizes how England and its ancestral leaders are beginning to recognize the social potential of new classes of men, represented by Bingley and Gardiner, who have either wealth or a sense of duty—but not both. Indeed, Darcy's close relationship with Bingley suggests that the gap between new and old money is shrinking, and the hero's kindness and collaboration with Gardiner demonstrate an astonishing degree of cooperation between the aristocracy and the tradesmen of London. Darcy, like his arrogant aunt, is certainly not interested in abandoning his ancestral privilege. Austen's novel makes explicit his extant preeminence as an English male, but the hero's relationships with these men of/from trade illustrate an important transition in the nation's conceptions of class and masculinity. To ensure that the increasing involvement of this new-money class is properly regulated, even men of/from trade must be taught traditional modes of English maleness and trained to make appropriate contributions to the state. Men like Bingley and Gardiner are not expected (or allowed) to become established cultural leaders, but Austen's narrative documents their increasingly prominent role in the civic community.[7] They improve themselves and expand their social roles, but their historical class status permits them to become only apprentices and assistants of Darcy—not his partners in guiding the moral and social development of the national community. Ernest Renan, in his canonical "What Is a Nation?," points out that "a nation is a soul, a spiritual principle. Two things, which in truth are but one, constitute this soul or spiritual principle. One lies in the past, one in the present. One is the possession in common of a rich legacy of memories; the other is present-day consent, the desire to live together, the will to perpetuate the value of [this] heritage" (52). Austen's tradesmen actively engage the events of the present national community, and their prosperity facilitates their personal enrichment, but they do not and cannot share the aristocratic historical tradition of England that is romanticized by Burke and personified by Darcy. Their status as men of trade, whose money was recently earned rather than ancestrally inherited, prevents them from fully joining the mythologized English national heritage. They are improving, and as they improve they become more valuable to the present and future of the state, yet they always already exist as historically inferior men because of their class.

Bingley is introduced long before the appearance of Gardiner, and we soon learn that the former has both ample financial resources and a definite plan for social improvement. As a poster child for the successes of the trade class, he embodies the great economic potential of this segment of society. And Austen's text reveals a strong cultural anxiety about him—especially his penchant for destabilizing love relationships. Even a landed aristocratic man like Darcy is concerned with the development of this newly wealthy man; Austen's hero both tutors Bingley in Burke's model of traditional male behavior and encourages him to discipline his amorous desires. The novel documents the pressures and difficulties Bingley experiences as he attempts to meet the desires produced by Burke and other post-Revolutionary writers for proper English masculinity. Austen's portrayal of Bingley thus also instructs other prosperous men, who have recently emerged from the trade class, of the lessons they must learn to become integral participants in the national community. Bingley is "a young man of large fortune from the north of England"; he is "gentlemanlike" and has "a pleasant countenance, and easy, and unaffected manners," but his money is both earned and new (1; 7). Like many ascendants from the rising trade class, he has significant monetary holdings, but Austen exposes early in the novel that he is still quite inferior to the administrator of the Pemberley estate. She relates that Darcy "was much handsomer than Mr. Bingley" and that "in understanding Darcy was the superior" (8; 13). Bingley is a compelling figure because he approaches the masculine excellence upheld by Darcy. He occupies a new position in the social hierarchy somewhere above the trade class and below the gentry, and this precarious space severely complicates his social/sexual subjectivity. John McAleer explains that Bingley's family is "passing from the middle class into the gentry," and "they exhibit the uneasiness such a transition involves" (73).[8] Bingley is expected to continue his family's social rise, and Austen's text details his struggles to accomplish this task while performing as a lover.

Bingley, like Gardiner, must specifically learn to act as a Burkean man of England to gain acceptance as an appropriate male figure and potential future leader. As an exemplar of Burke's ideal of English masculinity, Darcy remains an especially important influence on Bingley, and this man of new money knows that his efforts for self-improvement largely depend upon his ability to follow the model of maleness offered by the administer of Pemberley. Bingley playfully asserts that "if Darcy were not such a great tall fellow, in comparison with myself, I should not pay him half so much deference" but then quickly admits that he does "not know a more aweful object than Darcy" (44). Bingley's remarks on the awe-inspiring quality of his friend foreground the influence of the hero on the "inferior" men of the story; but while Bingley knows he must learn from the example set by Darcy, he is also conscious of his shortcomings as a man from trade. Austen notes that "Mr. Bingley inherited property to the amount of nearly an hundred thousand pounds from his father, who had intended to purchase an estate, but did not live to do it" (12). It is now Bingley's responsibility to enshrine the family's new cultural position, yet he knows he cannot simply copy the architectural drawings for the Darcys' residence. When Bingley's sister encourages him to model his future estate after Pemberley, he answers that he "will buy Pemberley itself if Darcy will sell it" and explains to his sibling that it would be "more possible to get Pemberley by purchase than by imitation" (33). Bingley recognizes his own limitations *and* his own potential; he realizes that he could never fully pattern his future home after the ancestral Pemberley because he lacks the heritage of the Darcys. Bingley's comments also remind us of his significant cash holdings; if Darcy's grand estate were somehow for sale, Bingley theoretically could buy it. Unlike Darcy who maintains proud connections to the history of a specific domestic realm, Bingley is a man of the present, who acknowledges that "whatever I do is done in a hurry . . . and therefore if I should resolve to quit Netherfield, I should probably be off in five minutes" (36). He informs Mrs. Bennet that "when I am in the country . . . I never wish to leave it; and when I am in town it is pretty much the same. They have each their advantages, and I can be equally happy in either" (37).[9] Bingley is neither personally nor financially tied to a specific domestic domain; he and his income are mobile. While he understands that his continued advancement will require him to acquire an estate, he knows that such a purchase could only simulate a home like Pemberley.

Bingley certainly respects Pemberley and the ancestral legacy that Darcy's family estate symbolizes, but Bingley's attempts to improve his social/sexual subjectivity inevitably revolve around his primary concern: the pursuit of pleasure. Darcy may be unimpressed by the Meryton ball, but Bingley informs his friend, "I never met with so many pleasant girls in my life, as I have this evening; and there are several of them you see uncommonly pretty" (9). Bingley is a pleasure seeker who enjoys social events, especially interactions with attractive women, and his acquired wealth allows him to fulfill such desires. He becomes particularly interested in Jane, and Austen reports that while he housed her at Netherfield during her illness, "his anxiety for Jane was evident, and his attentions to herself most pleasing" (30). Bingley even experiences pleasure in caring for Miss Bennet, and when she is finally ready to leave her bed at Netherfield, he "was full of joy and attention. The first half hour was spent in piling up the fire, lest she should suffer from the change of room" (47). Bingley also maintains his fondness for dancing and remains committed to his plan to host a ball at Netherfield. When his sister challenges his idea for a ball by announcing that there are "some among us to whom a ball would be rather a punishment than a pleasure," he declares, "If you mean Darcy . . . he may go to bed, if he chuses, before it begins." Bingley momentarily dismisses the example of Darcy's tastes, and after Miss Bingley counters by suggesting that "[i]t would surely be more rational if conversation instead of dancing made the order of the day," her brother explains, "Much more rational, my dear Caroline, I dare say but it would not be near so much like a ball" (48). Early in the novel, Austen emphasizes Bingley's pursuit of pleasures—even irrational pleasures—but she later dramatizes how Darcy instructs his understudy to manage such volatile enjoyment.[10]

Following Bingley's privately sponsored ball, Austen relates that "[he] was all grateful pleasure" to accept an invitation to dine with the Bennets. He is unable to make this proposed meeting because his training in Burkean male behavior begins to take precedence over his preference for pleasure (93). Miss Bingley informs Jane that "the whole party have left Netherfield by this time, and are on their way to town; and without any intention of coming back again" (105). This regrettable news invites us to speculate on Darcy's hegemonic direction of Bingley's activity. Although Elizabeth is certain that Bingley is not acting on his own volition, Jane insists that his removal to London "must be his own doing.—He is his own master" (106). Jane is often dismissed as a simpleton, but she clearly understands Bingley's responsibility to focus his own aesthetic of existence; she upholds the power of the successful bourgeois subject to mold his own position in the modernizing national community. Elizabeth, however, is certain that Bingley "was really fond of Jane . . . and much as she had always been disposed to like him, she could not think without anger, hardly without contempt, on that easiness of temper, that want of proper resolution which now made him the slave of his designing friends, and led him to sacrifice his own happiness to the caprice of their inclinations" (119). Elizabeth identifies what she understands to be Bingley's weakness, that is, his ductility, and the heroine charges him with becoming too susceptible to the dictates of others, especially Darcy. According to the heroine, the same easiness of temper that enables Bingley to excel as an amiable entertainer is also the primary reason for his inability to pursue his own desires. Darcy certainly sways Bingley's plans, but the latter's impressibility should not be read only as an indication of his utter inferiority. Bingley's significant monetary holdings facilitate his social improvement and his pursuit of pleasure, yet he knows his wealth is not ancestral; hence, he must establish a hegemonic social/sexual identity and learn Burkean masculinity to solidify his new class position in the nation—and Darcy is still the best teacher around.

We discover more about the powerful social forces that influence Bingley and his desires from Elizabeth's conversations with Darcy during her visit to Hunsford. Indeed, as befits Bingley's deference, we hear far more about Bingley's actions from others than we do from himself. When the heroine asks Darcy if "Mr. Bingley has not much idea of ever returning to Netherfield again?" the hero responds, "I have never heard him say so; but it is probable that he may spend very little of his time there in future. He has many friends, and he is at a time of life when friends and engagements are continually increasing" (158). Darcy highlights the demanding quality of Bingley's dynamic class position; at this unstable point of his life, as he assumes new cultural identities and responsibilities, he must consider the heightened importance of his business acquaintances, personal relations, and social engagements. Colonel Fitzwilliam Darcy also speaks with Elizabeth about the insecure tradesman. The Colonel informs the heroine, "I really believe Darcy *does* take care of [Bingley] in those points where he most wants care. From something that [Darcy] told me in our journey hither, I have reason to think Bingley very much indebted to him" (164). Darcy is an active sponsor of Bingley who has taken special care to direct the tradesman's efforts to learn "proper" English masculinity, and Fitzwilliam specifically reports that "[Darcy] congratulated himself on having lately saved a friend from the inconveniences of a most imprudent marriage, but without mentioning names or any other particulars, and I only suspected it to be Bingley from believing him the kind of young man to get into a scrape of that sort" (165). As Fitzwilliam's comment indicates, Bingley is known as a man apt to become overly impressed by irrational sensual charms—a man who needs to be reminded of the dangers of love and the powerful social forces that ought to inform an aspiring English man's behavior. Darcy's concern for and tutelage of Bingley again suggest the hero's recognition that wealthy men of trade like Bingley are becoming vital resources in England's future—and these men must be taught to discipline their passions to ensure their maturation as stable men of the nation.

Bingley's misguided pursuit of pleasure is, according to Darcy, specifically dangerous to the tradesman's efforts to improve his masculinity and secure his new social standing. After Elizabeth's rejection of the hero's initial proposal, he admits to offering such advice to the pliable Bingley. Darcy tells Elizabeth he has "no wish of denying that [he] did every thing in [his] power to separate [his] friend from [the heroine's] sister"; Darcy adds that he "had often seen [Bingley] in love before" (170; 175). The hero knows that his aspiring friend is susceptible to the perils of overwhelming amorous passions, and while he acknowledges that he has deceived Bingley by encouraging him to seek alternative ways to safely stylize his sexuality, Darcy firmly believes that what he did "was done for the best" (177). As a wealthy man without a noble family background, Bingley's reckless pursuit of pleasure is liable to engender a fall in society that would negate his family's recent rise. Darcy recognizes that such vulnerable men cannot risk the dangers associated with amorous

emotions, and he is specifically anxious about Bingley, whose wealth qualifies him to become a prominent player in the modern post-agrarian state.
Following Darcy's admission of responsibility, the heroine offers a revised
assessment of Bingley. She notes that "[Bingley's] affection was proved to
have been sincere, and his conduct cleared of all blame, unless any could
attach to the implicitness of his confidence in his friend" (189). Elizabeth
may acquit him, but her comments also point to his continued dependence
on the example and instructions of Darcy. Bingley yields to Darcy's authority
as a man of national heritage who can provide accurate instructions on how
to meet Burke's qualifications for male civic organizers.

Elizabeth's awareness of Bingley's struggle to mold his own sexual subjectivity after Darcy's powerful example of Burkean masculinity allows her
to observe acutely how Bingley's distinct class position alters his behavior.
When she encounters Bingley at Pemberley, she appreciates his "unaffected
cordiality with which he expressed himself, on seeing her again," and Austen
notes that he "looked and spoke with the same good-humored ease that he
had ever done" (230). In spite of his efforts to become a Burkean man, Bingley speaks and acts without ceremony. He even exposes his extant romantic
interest in Miss Bennet when he tells Elizabeth that it "was a very long time
since he had had the pleasure of seeing [Jane] . . . it is above eight months.
We have not met since the 26th of November, when we were all dancing
together at Netherfield" (231). Bingley's precise memory is an impressive
indication of his feelings for Jane, but it is not clear that he is a secure man
capable of pursuing his own desires without first clearing his actions with
Darcy. We must wait for the re-arrival of Bingley and Darcy in Meryton to
identify the integrity and focus of the former's aesthetic of existence. Bingley
is "both pleased and embarrassed" upon his arrival at Longbourn; he once
more illustrates his emotional and physical sensitivity by remaining susceptible to the potency of amorous experiences (297). Elizabeth even records
"how much the beauty of her sister re-kindled the admiration of her former
lover. When first he came in, he had spoken to her but little; but every five
minutes seemed to be giving her more of his attention" (299). Bingley is still
animated by and pleased with Jane, who now declares that "he is blessed
with greater sweetness of address, and a stronger desire of generally pleasing than any other man" (304). Bingley is obsessed with pleasing—pleasing
Jane, pleasing Darcy, and even pleasing the annoying Mrs. Bennet—and he
has likewise become a very skilled seeker of pleasure, but while pursuing
pleasure permits him to improve his social/sexual subjectivity, this focus for
his aesthetic of existence will not enable him to fulfill Burke's desire for a
chivalric male who can provide civic and moral leadership.

Bingley's wealth, nevertheless, does allow him to establish a stable social/

sexual identity based upon the pursuit of pleasure. After the announcement of the engagement between Bingley and Jane, Elizabeth reflects upon their future marriage. Austen narrates, "in spite of his being a lover, Elizabeth really believed all his expectations of felicity, to be rationally founded, because they had for basis the excellent understanding, and super-excellent disposition of Jane, and a general similarity of feeling and taste between her and himself" (308). Elizabeth, like Darcy, is concerned about Bingley's proclivity to love unreasonably, but she logically forecasts a life of contentment for the couple because of their mutual tastes and tempers; they are both unassuming individuals who simply want to enjoy pleasure. Bingley has consistently demonstrated his tendency to comply with the commands of others, and as we soon learn, even his return to Netherfield was authorized by Darcy, who advises Elizabeth that

> Bingley is most unaffectedly modest. His diffidence had prevented his depending on his own judgment in so anxious a case, but his reliance on mine, made every thing easy. I was obliged to confess one thing, which for a time, and not unjustly, offended him. I could not allow myself to conceal that your sister had been in town three months last winter, and that I had known it, and purposely kept it from him. He was angry. But his anger, I am persuaded, lasted no longer than he remained in any doubt of your sister's sentiments. He has heartily forgiven me now. (330)

Darcy's "confession" indicates his continued influence on the diffident Bingley.[11] Darcy finally accepts that while Bingley's money makes him an eligible man to assume a greater role in the leadership of England, he is simply not capable of regulating his pursuit of pleasure, even if such discipline could enhance or even ensure his role in the future nation.

Bingley cannot achieve the masculine excellence of Darcy, but Austen's aspiring man *from* trade has certainly come a long way, and he and Jane will now leave Meryton to seek their pleasure.[12] Austen relates that "Mr. Bingley and Jane remained at Netherfield only a twelvemonth. . . . The darling wish of his sisters was then gratified; he bought an estate in a neighbouring county to Derbyshire, and Jane and Elizabeth, in addition to every other source of happiness, were within thirty miles of each other" (342). Bingley finally attains the all-important estate that grounds him as a landed man of the nation, but this home is purchased and still thirty miles from the splendor of Pemberley. For all Darcy's influence on his friend, Bingley can only approach the sphere of the remarkable romantic hero. While Bingley's acquisition of the estate helps to aggrandize his aesthetic of existence, he remains socially and sexually inferior to Darcy. Bingley has tried to learn from Darcy throughout the narrative, but he is ultimately a man of new money—derived from trade—who is enamored of pleasure rather than cultural prestige. His relationship with Jane is not Deleuzian, but it may anticipate a new telos for romantic male behavior; his love for Jane promotes his pleasure rather than his social/sexual stability. Bingley must depend upon his money instead of his marriage or lineage to form his hegemonic identity, and though his grand residence materially marks him as a nationally prominent man, he uses his financial resources to pursue pleasure rather than the discipline of Burkean masculinity. Bingley exists as an ersatz gentleman without an ancestral heritage; still Austen's novel demonstrates a strong social interest in training such men in the traditional modes of English masculinity. Bingley's is not a complete success story, but it does offer a blueprint for other thriving men of new money to follow.

Mr. Gardiner is such a prosperous man of trade, but since he has not inherited significant wealth he does not have the financial resources that Bingley uses to pursue extensive material pleasures and purchase an estate. Despite his lack of ready cash, he is a responsible man who acts as a dutiful Burkean guardian for the Bennet family. The narrator presents Gardiner as a happily married older tradesman who has trained his amorous desires; he is neither a cherished romantic love figure like Darcy nor an ambitious seeker of sensual pleasure like Bingley. Austen initially mentions Gardiner as Mrs. Bennet's "brother settled in London in a respectable line of trade" (23). As an urbanite, he is a rarity in Austen's fiction, yet the narrator notes that he is also "a sensible, gentlemanlike man, greatly superior to his sister as well by nature as education." Indeed, Austen claims that "the Netherfield ladies would have had difficulty believing that a man who lived by trade, and within view of his own warehouses, could have been so well bred and agreeable" (124–25). Gardiner is an impressive male figure who, despite his class standing, appears to fulfill Burke's expectation for well-mannered masculinity.[13] Gardiner does not receive Darcy's direct tutoring; nevertheless, he still attempts to perform many of the duties prescribed by Burke for proper English men (75). Indeed, Gardiner displays many of the attributes required of a Burkean man, save the requisite ancestral standing and class status. While Gardiner does not become a prominent figure until late in the novel, Austen draws specific attention to his classed identity near the end of the second volume. As Elizabeth awaits a planned tour of the Lake District with her aunt and uncle, the narrator informs us that "Mr. Gardiner would be prevented by business from setting out till a fortnight later in July, and must be in London again within a month; and as that left too short a period for them to go so far . . . they were obliged to give up the Lakes" (211–12). These comments emphasize the restrictions Gardiner experiences because of his business obligations. Like Bingley, Gardiner has commitments that force him to adjust his social activities and modify his aesthetic of existence.

The shorter alternative holiday through Derbyshire, on which the Gardiners are joined by the heroine, highlights the tradesman's social grace and personal versatility. The most important events of this journey are, of course, the travelers' visits to Pemberley. Austen notes Mr. Gardiner's "willingness" to view Darcy's landed estate, and she reports that his "manners were easy and pleasant" in his discussions with the nostalgic housekeeper, Mrs. Reynolds, who perpetually praises the hero (213; 218). Gardiner is polite, well mannered, and amenable to a doting caretaker, remaining "highly amused by the kind of family prejudice, to which he attributed her excessive commendation of her master" (219).[14] He is not offended by Mrs. Reynolds's lavish admiration of Darcy; rather, he adopts Burke's theory of ancestral privilege and accepts that it is natural for servants to admire their masters. While at Pemberley, Gardiner also reveals his skill as an outdoorsman, and we are told that "though seldom able to indulge the taste, [Mr. Gardiner] was very fond of fishing" (223). Mr. Darcy offers Gardiner free license to fish on the grounds of Pemberley, and after originally opting not to accept this invitation, the tradesman soon joins Darcy and others in a fishing party "at Pemberley by noon" (235). Mrs. Gardiner speaks of her husband as a man "who was fond of society," and his behavior at Pemberley illustrates his comfort with different classed domains and distinct modes of culturally approved masculine activity (232). He is a flexible man, but his economic situation eventually disqualifies him from becoming either a true Burkean man or a leader in the modern nation.

Gardiner nonetheless attempts to perform as a heroic Burkean figure following the shocking news of Lydia's elopement by providing familial leadership and attempting to restore order. In the subsequent London scenes, Austen portrays Gardiner's ability to rehearse traditional chivalric duties and reveals his inability to match Darcy's model of Burkean masculinity. Immediately after Elizabeth's explanation of the events surrounding Lydia's affair, "Mr. Gardiner readily promised every assistance in his power" (247). He offers his services like a sacrificial hero, and his relatives understand him as such an altruistic man. Jane even assures herself, "now that my dear uncle is come, I hope every thing will be well" (252). As an urban resident, Gardiner is especially helpful in the mission to locate Lydia, and upon arriving at Longbourn, he provides "general assurances of his affection for [Mrs. Bennet] and all her family, [and] told her that he meant to be in London the very next day" to "assist Mr. Bennet in every endeavour for recovering Lydia." He also tries to calm his relatives by reminding them "not [to] give way to useless alarm . . . though it is right to be prepared for the worst, there is no occasion to look on it as certain" (253). Mr. Gardiner is given and willingly performs the role of family champion who will structure chaos and ensure domestic peace. In addition, he encourages his family to be reasonable. Prior to beginning his quest to save Lydia and comfort his family, Gardiner pledges to "prevail on Mr. Bennet to return to Longbourn, as soon as he could, to the great consolation of his sister, who considered it as the only security for her husband's not being killed in a duel" (259). Austen's comment again reminds us of Mr. Gardiner's graciousness. He has the impressive ability to endure Mrs. Bennet's excessively irrational fears about her husband's activity in London with poise. Although he adopts features of a heroic male, he is still a business man, and this class status encourages him to act pragmatically.[15]

Mr. Gardiner demonstrates his new responsibilities by laboring arduously to locate Lydia in London, but while Austen presents him as a familial guardian she also emphasizes how he continues to think and act as a tradesman. He sends Mr. Bennet home, and Gardiner soon writes his brother-in-law to inform him that "after you left me on Saturday, I was fortunate enough to find out in what part of London they were" (266). He breaks the news that Lydia and Wickham are "not married," but he instructs Mr. Bennet that if he is "willing to perform the engagements which I have ventured to make on your side, I hope it will not be long before they are" (267). Mr. Gardiner appears as a master detective and an effective matchmaker. He has both found the missing lovers and arranged a workable scenario for them to wed. His experience in trade again serves him well; it allows him to negotiate a deal that will benefit all parties and mitigate potential consequences. Gardiner cannot completely mend the damage that the improper actions of Lydia and Wickham have caused, but he does provide a feasible solution that minimizes additional injury. We learn from Mrs. Gardiner and others that Wickham has incurred a large financial debt that must be paid prior to his marrying Lydia, and Mr. Gardiner has apparently made arrangements to settle this financial matter. Gardiner's involvement in Lydia and Wickham's elopement even includes a ceremonial function in his niece's marriage. Lydia, upon her return to Longbourn, tells her sisters that her uncle was to give her away at her wedding, but he "was called away upon business to that horrid Mr. Stone" (282). Lydia's comment recalls Gardiner's ubiquitous professional demands that consistently interrupt his other activities, but the youthful Bennet girl's account also accentuates the tradesman's inability to perform traditional patriarchal duties such as the offering of a young bride. Although Gardiner rehearses many of the skills required for Burkean masculinity, his class status and business obligations continually prevent him from fully assuming such a social/sexual identity.

Lydia continues her story by noting that following Mr. Stone's untimely request for her uncle's assistance, she was momentarily frightened that her nuptials must be delayed, but she soon realized that "the wedding need not be put off, for Mr. Darcy might have done as well" (282). Lydia's remark reminds us of the ever-increasing modern interchangeability of aristocratic men like Darcy and tradesmen like her uncle; Darcy assumes the role of Gardiner, and as Lydia suggests, the administrator of Pemberley is a suitable replacement. Lydia's report also prompts Elizabeth to inquire of her aunt about the presence of Mr. Darcy at Lydia's wedding. Mrs. Gardiner's subsequent letter to Elizabeth provides information regarding the hero's activity in London and further details on Mr. Gardiner's attempts to extend his social duties. Mrs. Gardiner specifically narrates the account of Darcy's arrival at Cheapside and his discussions with Mr. Gardiner. She assures her niece that her "uncle would most readily have settled the whole" of Wickham's debt, but as she explains, Darcy insisted that "nothing was to be done that he did not do himself" (286). Austen's language accentuates Darcy's romantic subjectivity, his great social power, and Gardiner's classed limitations as a tradesman. He apparently has the available cash to pay Wickham's substantial obligations, but as Austen shows, Gardiner must defer to Darcy's authority; while the tradesman is willing to assume the responsibility of the sacrificial heroic figure who can restore order and structure to civilized society, Darcy will not permit a man of trade to play this part. The hero may be interested in promoting the development and improvement of men from the trade class, but he is not yet prepared to relinquish or share the Burkean role of administering civil society and its ethical codes. *Pride and Prejudice* suggests that bourgeois men like Gardiner and newly ascendant men like Bingley are becoming necessary to the maintenance of the English nation, but the novel also illustrates aristocratic men's desire to preserve their extant privileged status as the curators of England's moral order.

Mrs. Gardiner closes her letter by telling the heroine that "at last your uncle was forced to yield, and instead of being allowed to be of use to his niece, was forced to put up with only having the probable credit of it" (286). And indeed, when Elizabeth had initially heard of the planned nuptials between Lydia and Wickham, she confidently pronounced, "Oh! it must be my uncle's doings! Generous, good man, I am afraid he has distressed himself. A small sum could not do all this" (268). The heroine was confident that her uncle had been her family's benefactor, despite the great financial sacrifice such altruistic actions would have required, and she presented him as a noble man who had miraculously resolved the crisis. Later, however, Mr. Gardiner only offers "intreaties that the subject might never be mentioned to him again" (276). Elizabeth may imagine Mr. Gardiner as a heroic Burkean male, but he knows better than to claim this identity for himself. After Elizabeth writes to her uncle to express her appreciation, Mrs. Gardiner indicates to her niece that her "letter . . . gave [Mr. Gardiner] great pleasure, because it required an explanation that would rob him of his borrowed feathers, and give the praise where it was due" (286). He appreciates the heroine's gratitude, but he is happier to acknowledge who truly saved Lydia and her family from shame. Mr. Gardiner is a man of integrity who is eager to renounce credit for Darcy's generous actions. Gardiner has raised himself in society by his endeavors in trade, but he is not interested in continuing this rise under false pretenses. Although he does not possess the financial means to operate as an aristocratic male, he organizes his attempts to improve his aesthetic of existence around many of the values upheld by Burke as essential to the proper man of England. At the novel's close, Austen informs us that "with the Gardiners, [Darcy and Elizabeth] were always on the most intimate terms" (345). The narrator's concluding comment recalls the comparison between Darcy and Bingley, who are only thirty miles removed from each other. Gardiner is also "close" to the masculine excellence embodied by Darcy and perpetually "visits" this zone of romantic splendor. And while his class status as a respectable tradesman allows him to ameliorate his aesthetic of existence, this same class position prevents him from acting as a public guardian of his community.

Although they fall shy of Darcy's romantic masculine preeminence, both Gardiner and Bingley manage to improve their sexualized subjectivities by focusing their aesthetics of existence around specific concerns. Neither Bingley nor Gardiner is an extraordinary romantic lover like Darcy, but they consistently attempt to enhance themselves and serve as important examples of the Enlightenment theory of the human potential for improvement developed by Godwin. Godwin explains that "we are all of us endowed with reason, able to compare, to judge and to infer. The improvement therefore, which is to be desired for one, is to be desired for another" (I: 146). Gardiner and Bingley personify this egalitarian mantra as they strive to secure their participation in the dynamic post-Revolutionary English nation. They are ultimately unable to perform all the roles and responsibilities that Burke outlines for a proper man of England, but they are nonetheless impressive male figures whom the nation needs. And yet, despite the social improvement modeled by *nouveau riche* men like Bingley and tradesmen like Gardiner, Austen's presentation of Darcy remains an archetype of romantic masculinity. A personal ad in the July 29, 1999, issue of *The Stranger,* a Seattle-based entertainment newspaper, announced: "**Single Irish Female:** 27yo blnd/blu 5'10" Irish-Catholic background. Olympia seeks Mr. Darcy. Beach, travel, sports fan, bookstores, autumn, Guinness, leisurely Sunday mornings: all good." The listing illustrates the continued attractiveness and prominent versatility of the hero of *Pride and Prejudice*. Darcy is still "desired," and we continue to uphold his financial and social standing as vital features of an idealized man. Bingley and Gardiner will never measure up to this standard of male perfection, but the prominent emergence of the middle classes throughout the nineteenth century forces the modern English state to concern itself with men who are not necessarily ideal. Austen's novel reflects an important cultural crisis of the post-Revolutionary years: grand men of pure aristocratic ancestry, like the aristocratic tradition itself, are atrophying, and England must now garner important civic contributions from men of/from trade like Bingley and Gardiner—men who have demonstrated great ambition for personal and social improvement. They will never become legendary romantic lovers, and they are not capable of reviving ancestral lines of descent, but they embody a spirit of progress and amelioration that drives the modernization of the English state.

CHAPTER 5

Exposing Burkean Masculinity,
or Edmund Confronts Modernity

—◄○►—

The manners I speak of, might rather be called conduct, *perhaps, the result of good principles; the effect, in short, of those doctrines which it is their duty to teach and recommend; and it will, I believe, be every where found, that as the clergy are, or are not what they ought to be, so are the rest of the nation. (Edmund Bertram in Austen,* Mansfield Park *84)*

Nothing is more certain, than that our manners, our civilization, and all the good things which are connected with manners, and with civilization, have, in this European world of ours, depended for ages upon two principles; and were indeed the result of both combined; I mean the spirit of a gentleman, and the spirit of religion. (Burke, Reflections *129–30)*

[T]he aim of the modern art of government, or state rationality, namely, [is] to develop those elements constitutive of individuals' lives in such a way that their development also fosters the strength of the state. (Foucault, "'Omnes et Singulatim'" 322)

In *Pride and Prejudice,* Austen anticipates the emergence of a new class of men of/from trade and points to the diminishing number of grand Burkean men like Darcy; in *Mansfield Park,* she explores the cause of this decline, as she dramatizes how England's post-Revolutionary culture exposes contradictions in Burke's model of aristocratic masculinity. Edmund Bertram desperately attempts to embody both the principle of religion and the principle of the gentleman that Burke presents as essential to a civilized nation, but as Austen's novel suggests, such a synthesis is becoming more difficult and less functional in the modern world. Burke's ideal of English maleness is closely aligned with a larger call for nostalgic cultural reformation; he insists that "people will not look forward to posterity, who never look backward to their ancestors" (83). He believes that post-Revolutionary England must recapture the spirit of an earlier civilization regulated by an edifying religious presence and directed by valorous gentlemen like Mr. Darcy. And Burke claims that proper men must be heroic and genteel—dutiful and sensitive. In his famous discussion of the French revolutionaries' treatment of Marie Antoinette, he claims that "in a nation of men of honour and of cavaliers," he would have expected "ten thousand swords must have leaped from their scabbards to avenge even a look that threatened her with insult" (127). He admires a chivalric code of male conduct, but he is also moved by this memory and asserts that "we are so made as to be affected at such spectacles with melancholy sentiments" (131). Burke charges such sentimental gentlemen with the responsibility of securing the nation, and while such a task might have prompted males to be both heroic and sensitive in England's past, *Mansfield Park* presents a modern culture that is no longer conducive to this antiquated sexual identity, behavior, or consciousness.

Austen's tale specifically documents Edmund's labors and consistent failures to meet Burke's expectations for a gentleman and a religious leader in post-Revolutionary England. He is eager to perform the clerical duty of serving as a moral exemplar to the nation, and he alternatively displays great sensibility and heroism throughout the novel, but he is unable to reconcile such duties and behaviors with the modern sensations and experiences that Mary Crawford invites him to pursue. Although Edmund initially views his responsibilities as a member of the clergy as heroic, he is repeatedly tempted by a new mode of valor that seeks sensual exhilaration and pleasure. He becomes enamored of the capacity of a modernized masculinity, and Austen tracks his attempts to craft such an exciting aesthetic of existence. While he is certainly tempted by sensuality, he ultimately chooses to limit his opportunities to experience such pulsations; he instead clings to Burke's model of masculinity, resolidifies his aristocratic family, and reclaims his vocation as a heroic clergyman by marrying his cousin. Edmund discovers that he cannot exist as a Burkean man in the modern English nation, so he decides to marry internally and remain stable within the atavistic culture of the past. He eventually heeds Burke's warning that "when ancient opinions and rules of life are taken away, the loss cannot possibly be estimated. From that moment we have no compass to govern us; nor can we know distinctly to what port we steer" (129). The pseudo-incestuous union of Edmund and Fanny symbolically does recuperate a sense of cultural direction by halting the collapse of the Bertram family, ensuring the continuation of its legacy, and reestablishing the disciplinary function of the clerical gentleman. Edmund's love for Fanny is most certainly not Deleuzian; the hero's marriage to his cousin is neither romantic nor passionate, but it is safe, and as the novel suggests, the English aristocracy needs such safeguarding in the early nineteenth century.

The collapse of the Bertram family is symptomatic of the larger post-Revolutionary cultural demise of the English aristocracy, and Austen's is not the only novelistic treatment of the modern difficulties facing the nation's historical elite. Walter Scott's *Waverley* (1814), published in the same year as *Mansfield Park,* addressed the tenuous state of England's aristocracy and specifically documents the hero's attraction to and ultimate rejection of its treasured chivalric code. Like Edmund, Waverley grows up strongly influenced by his father, but Waverley's father, unlike Sir Bertram, is no longer interested in maintaining long-established structures. Waverley's uncle, Sir Everard, however, is still quite invested in atrophying chivalric customs, and he actively attempts to instruct his nephew in the importance of such traditions. Scott notes that Sir Everard spent much time "[examining] the tree of his genealogy, which [was] emblazoned with many an emblematic mark of honour and heroic achievement" (8). Scott emphasizes his hero's ambivalence toward such training early in the narrative; he "yawned at times over the dry deduction of his line of ancestors, with their various intermarriages, and inwardly deprecated the remorseless and protracted accuracy with which the worthy Sir Everard rehearsed the various degrees of propinquity." Still, Scott observes that "if . . . he sometimes cursed in his heart the jargon of heraldry, its griffins, its moldwraps, its wyverns, and its dragons, with all the bitterness of Hotspur himself—there were moments when these communications interested his fancy and rewarded his attention" (16). Both Waverley and Edmund are young aristocratic men who, as they develop their sexualized aesthetics of existence within a shifting English culture, must negotiate the long-standing cultural importance of chivalry and its code of masculinity.

Waverley and Edmund likewise become torn between the lure of ancestral systems and the inconsequence of such antiquated machinery in the modernizing world. Alice Chandler argues that Scott's works "deal with a past that is passing away," and she notes that "Scott knows that historical change is not to be resisted" (31). The Bertrams are not as receptive to a potential cultural transition, and Austen illustrates how familial and national pressures encourage Edmund to view the regulation of his masculinity as essential to the future of the aristocracy and its chivalric mores. Waverley is likewise urged to continue chivalric traditions cherished by his uncle, and when the hero encounters Charles Edward and his fellow rebels attempting to usurp the English throne, he becomes enamored of the finery associated with the Great Pretender. Scott's narrator reports, "Unaccustomed to the address and manners of a polished court, in which Charles was eminently skilful, his words and his kindness penetrated the heart of our hero, and easily outweighed all prudential motives" (193). As Edmund is overwhelmed by the sensations associated with the modern urban lifestyle of Mary Crawford, Waverley is overwhelmed by the splendor associated with the Great Pretender's chivalric performance; but when Waverley "looked closer upon the state of the Chevalier's court . . . [he had] less reason to be satisfied with it" (250).

Scott's hero eventually dismisses the relevance of such chivalric traits and traditions and accepts the realities of modern life, while Edmund ultimately reverts to such an archaic model of masculinity to safeguard his masculinity from the dangers of England's post-Revolutionary culture—including the risks involved with Mary Crawford's sensuality. Although he pursues the potential of various modern temptations throughout the novel, Edmund clings to a hegemonic social/sexual subjectivity rooted in an antiquated version of chivalric heroism and clerical gentility.

Scott's novel portrays the increasing inconsequence of England's ancestral lore as an inevitable result of the modern nation-state, but Austen's *Mansfield Park* dramatizes the desperate attempts of the English aristocracy to retain its status as the nation's civic and moral leaders.[1] The text documents many failures to accomplish this end and specifically dramatizes the embarrassments of the Bertram family; moreover, Austen's work offers Edmund and Fanny as the new (and likely last) hope for the family's, and perhaps the aristocracy's, resurgence; Edmund will act as the sacrificial hero who can restabilize ancestral English ideals cherished by Burke, and the heroine will serve as a pure and fecund woman who has the potential to cleanse the current generation of the aristocracy and reproduce the next. Austen may specifically memorialize England's need for such sacrificial hero(in)ism during the tale's strange stargazing scene. When Edmund and Fanny wander out on the lawn to engage in some casual stellar viewing, the hero notices the constellation Arcturus in the sky, and Fanny observes the bear, but she announces, "I wish I could see Cassiopeia" (102).[2] Her desire to see Cassiopeia invites us to consider the passive heroine as an Andromeda figure longing for an image of her distant mother. And indeed, Fanny does become a virginal offering of sorts; she is sent to her wealthy family, embodies a feminine innocence unmatched by the other young women of the novel, and accepts her role as the next maternal figure of the aristocracy. Such a mythological reading of this scene also anticipates the emergence of a Perseus figure who will valorously save Fanny from her chains. Edmund is, of course, the ideal individual to fulfill such a heroic role. He will serve as Fanny's educator, protector, and counselor; in addition, he will become her husband. He learns to value Fanny's importance to his family and herself, and per Burke's request he treats her with great sensibility. When Edmund finally accepts the severity of his family's demise, he quickly reconfigures his sexualized aesthetic of existence to wed his cousin, safeguard the future of the Bertrams, and symbolically preserve the nation's aristocracy.

Throughout the tale, Edmund, as a future member of the clergy, is invested in the condition of both his family and the nation. It is in and through this ecclesiastical identity that he endorses a strong sense of social morality and represents a proper mode of conduct for others. As a clergyman he advocates individual responsibility and subservience to a higher authority, whether that be nation, God, or family. He continually deploys what Foucault terms pastoral power—"the individualizing of power" or "the development of power techniques oriented towards individuals and intended to rule them in a continuous and permanent way" ("*Omnes et Singulatim*'" 300). Edmund's ecclesiastical duties require him to "assume responsibility for the destiny of the whole flock and of each and every sheep" ("*Omnes et Singulatim*'" 308). He exercises such power to ensure that all members of his community behave properly and assume specific and useful social roles. He is a concerned man who, like Knightley, attempts to make certain that each individual is cared for and instructed to support the nation.[3] Austen particularly details Edmund's consistent anxiety throughout the novel with his family, and specifically with the activities and ideas of young women; he takes steps to protect women, but he also encourages them to sacrifice their bodies and desires for the state. He realizes that the biological and cultural future of the aristocracy depends upon adolescent women's (re)productions—and hence, the morals and training of women like his sisters and Mary Crawford are of national import. These females are the most likely candidates to bear the next generation of the aristocracy, but they fail to maintain moral values and ancestral principles, and thus the task of reproducing the nation's future leaders falls on the heroine.

Fanny's untainted femininity is indeed key to England's emerging conception of a national community, for as Nira Yuval-Davis points out, "it is women—and not (just?) the bureaucracy and the intelligentsia—who reproduce nations, biologically, culturally and symbolically" (2).[4] McClintock adds that the English nationalistic fervor that developed in response to the French Revolution assigned female citizens a specific duty. She explains that "Britain's emerging national narrative gendered time by figuring women (like the colonized and the working class) as inherently atavistic—the conservative repository of the national archaic" (264). Fanny may not enjoy high social standing like the Bertram girls and Mary Crawford, but the heroine can still become a vital member of the national community by assuming this conservative atavistic function. Fanny is not lured by the possibilities of the modern urban world; she prefers the nostalgic pleasures of the country and the quiet of the drawing room sofa. The narrator indicates late in the novel that Edmund's regard for Fanny is "founded on the most endearing claims of innocence and helplessness, and completed by every recommendation of growing worth" (429). Fanny is not a physically impressive specimen, but

Edmund learns to value Fanny for her purity; she has apparently not been adulterated by the complexities and vices of post-Revolutionary culture. Yuval-Davis concludes that women are taught to assume a "'burden of representation,' as they are constructed as the symbolic bearers of the collectivity's identity and honour, both personally and collectively" (45). Fanny embraces such responsibility, as she, rather than the Bertram girls, comes to embody the hope of the aristocracy—physically and metaphorically; still, she is not able to reach her potential without the heroic sacrifices of Edmund, who exercises his pastoral power to direct her development.

Austen's initial depictions of Edmund and Fanny emphasize both his sensitive concern for the heroine and the potentially overwhelming sensitivity of young English aristocratic men. Prior to Fanny's arrival at Mansfield, the narrator foregrounds the Bertram family's anxiety about the latent sensuality of its adolescent boys. Mrs. Norris, in her attempt to dissuade Sir Thomas from bringing Fanny to Mansfield, cautions, "Suppose her a pretty girl, and seen by Tom or Edmund for the first time seven years hence, . . . I dare say there would be mischief" (4). The loquacious aunt's fear of her nephews' vulnerability to "pretty girls" reminds us of the cultural unease about male youth that Austen dramatizes in her juvenilia. England's future aristocratic men, like the Bertram boys, have been preserved in isolated environments, and the introduction of unknown females—especially ones who might be/become physically appealing—is viewed as potentially dangerous. Post-Revolutionary culture was certainly aware of the great peril of undisciplined young men, and Jane West's *Tale of the Times* (1799) detailed the great volatility of intemperate aristocratic men like Monteith, whose "passions were naturally very strong; and, never having been taught the necessity of restraining them, they were increased by continual gratification, till they somewhat resembled the impetuous torrent" (III: 193–94). Mrs. Norris's comment suggests the possibility that the ignorant young Bertram men might follow Monteith's example, and Austen proves the obnoxious aunt wise with her portrayal of Tom Bertram, who "was careless and extravagant" (17). Tom is not a responsible man, and his decadent lifestyle, replete with debauchery and foolishness, mirrors that of the Prince Regent.[5] The elder Bertram son personifies the impending demise of the traditional aristocratic male leader, and his lavish lifestyle even forces Edmund to relinquish the small living initially intended for him; as Austen suggests, "the younger brother must help to pay for the pleasures of the elder" (19). And because the elder son neglects his duties as both a model of ethical behavior and a future family leader, Edmund must assume these roles—responsibilities that are integral to maintaining an ancestral stock and its hegemonic functions.

Indeed, Austen presents Edmund in direct opposition to Tom. She notes how the hero's "strong good sense and uprightness of mind, bid most fairly for utility, honour, and happiness to himself and all his connections" (18). He clings to his genteel upbringing, and his training certainly qualifies him to provide valuable civic service, but his loyalty to an archaic model of masculinity leaves him inexperienced with the sensual possibilities of the modern world. This ignorance is not a significant detriment early in the novel, as he successfully employs his antiquated Burkean sensitivity to attend to Fanny within the safe confines of Mansfield. Edmund first meets his cousin when he finds her "sitting crying on the attic stairs" and "tried to console her" (12). He appears as a counselor and comforter who listens to her and attempts to ease her discomfort; he even offers to assist Fanny in writing a letter to her beloved brother William (13–14). The narrator relates that the heroine "felt that she had a friend, and the kindness of her cousin Edmund gave her better spirits" (14).[6] He continues to care for his cousin, acting as a sentimentalized Burkean male who remains sensitive to the pangs of others—especially women; this early encounter, moreover, anticipates Edmund's activity as Fanny's advisor who can instruct the heroine to direct her body and talents for the good of the nation. Edmund is an emotional Burkean male whose ancestral heroism is viable at his family's residence, but when the boundaries of Mansfield are broached, the antiquated nature of the hero's masculinity is exposed.

And Mansfield's borders are soon crossed and its security threatened when Sir Thomas travels to Antigua. The departure of Edmund's father creates a leadership void in the family that compels the hero to accept an early audition as a replacement patriarch. Austen indicates that "in Edmund's judgment" the departing father "had sufficient confidence to make him go without fears" for the conduct of the remaining children (28). Even Lady Bertram observes "how well Edmund could supply [Sir Thomas's] place in carving, talking to the steward, writing to the attorney, settling with the servants" (29). He can perform the mundane husbandry of a benevolent Burkean man within a controlled domestic sphere, but he quickly encounters new challenges engendered by the improper conduct of young women. Edmund is critical of modern English women, especially those who involve themselves too greatly with physical and social ornaments. He concludes that "[t]he error is plain enough . . . such girls are ill brought up. They are given wrong notions from the beginning. They are always acting upon motives of vanity—and there is no more real modesty in their behaviour *before* they appear in public than afterwards" (44–45). Edmund speaks as a confident man of moral integrity who is sincerely concerned with the education and activities of the nation's youthful female subjects.

While Edmund eventually identifies his sisters as examples of such inappropriate aristocratic women, Mary Crawford initially epitomizes the modern female who both appalls and stimulates the hero. Indeed, Edmund's first conversations with Mary revolve around her overt criticism of Sir Bertram's stern education of his daughters. Austen notes that "Edmund was sorry to hear Miss Crawford, whom he was much disposed to admire, speak so freely of her uncle. It did not suit his sense of propriety and he was silenced" (51). He may be fond of Mary, but he is also nonplussed by her disregard for aristocratic gender training. She seems disinterested in inherited gender identities, and though her attitude clashes with the hero's strong convictions about a woman's national responsibility, he is nonetheless intrigued by this urban woman—especially her charming talent for the harp. He "spoke of the harp as his favourite instrument, and hoped to be soon allowed to hear her"; and even when Mary speaks despairingly of the naval profession, he "reverted to the harp, and was again very happy in the prospect of hearing her play" (53–54). Edmund is unwilling, and perhaps unable, to discuss rationally Mary's attacks on traditional national structures such as the patriarchal aristocracy or the military, but he does employ his Burkean sensibility to appreciate her music. Mary challenges the contemporary feasibility of Edmund's archaic sexuality, and the hero soon turns to his innocent cousin for advice. He informs the heroine that "it is [Mary's] countenance that is so attractive. She has a wonderful play of feature!" (56). He knows that Miss Crawford's careless talk of Sir Thomas "was very wrong—very indecorous," but he nevertheless admires her face, her "warm feelings and [her] lively spirits" (57). And despite her impropriety, Austen informs us that Edmund "was beginning . . . to be a good deal in love" (58). Johnson evaluates the novel's romantic relations and argues that "the men in *Mansfield Park* are nervous about female sexuality"; she concludes that "Edmund, for example, is alternately spellbound and horror stricken by Mary Crawford" (*Jane Austen* 108). Edmund's traditional training as a Burkean man of sensibility endangers him as he pursues a relationship with this sensual modern woman. He becomes overwhelmed by the sensations Mary produces, and his aesthetic of existence is especially threatened by his emerging amorous desires that tempt him to disregard familial and national responsibilities in favor of pleasure.

Edmund is not an established aristocrat like his father or Darcy, and, hence, Austen's hero struggles to uphold antiquated chivalric traditions in a modern culture replete with new pressures and pleasures. For example, after learning that Fanny is unable to participate in the equestrian activities of the household, he creates a complex scenario by deciding that "Fanny must have a horse" (31). He again acts as a sensitive and heroic protector of this passive heroine, but he soon offers to provide Miss Crawford with riding lessons, and borrows Fanny's horse to lead Mary and other members of the Mansfield community on four days of equestrian adventures, leaving his cousin at home (60). When he returns from his exhilarating outing, he inquires, "But where is Fanny?—Is she gone to bed?" (64). He now demonstrates great concern for the heroine, who has developed a headache from walking amidst roses. Edmund promptly chastises Mrs. Norris: "has [Fanny] been walking as well as cutting roses; walking across the hot park to your house, and doing it twice, ma'am?—No wonder her head aches" (65). Edmund "was still more angry with himself" and "was ashamed to think that for four days together [Fanny] had not had the power of riding" (67). He realizes that his undisciplined desire to pursue external stimulation with Mary has led him to neglect his pastoral responsibilities as a future aristocratic patriarch—specifically his familial (and national) duty to protect virginal women like his cousin. His selfish pursuit of pleasure has allowed a young English woman to become literally overheated and physically jeopardized.

Edmund quickly recalls his duties as a future male leader of the atrophying aristocracy and a caretaker of the wholesome heroine, as his insistence that Fanny join the Mansfield party to Sotherton demonstrates (69–70). At Sotherton, Edmund accentuates his Burkean identity by differentiating both his masculinity and his ideas about English culture from the other visitors, many of whom are intrigued by the proposed modernization of Rushworth's estate. During a tour of the grounds, Mary aggressively challenges Edmund to defend his choice to join the clergy by insisting that "[m]en love to distinguish themselves, and . . . distinction may be gained, but not in the church. A clergyman is nothing" (83). Mary's comments echo Godwin's radical assertion that humans are capable of "being continually made better [by] receiving perpetual improvement," and while Godwin's anti-hereditary mantra may have fueled aspiring modern men like Bingley and Willoughby, Edmund quickly dismisses such recent cultural thought (I: 93). He immediately responds to Miss Crawford's assessment by declaring:

A clergyman cannot be high in state or fashion. He must not head mobs, or set the ton in dress. But I cannot call that situation nothing, which has the charge of all that is of the first importance to mankind, individually or collectively considered, temporally and eternally—which has the guardianship of religion and morals, and consequently of the manners which result from their influence. No one here can call the *office* nothing. If the man who holds it is so, it is by the neglect of his duty, by foregoing its just importance, and stepping out of his place to appear what he ought not to appear. (83)[7]

Edmund insists that the church is essential to the well-being of the nation because ecclesiastical leaders provide models for proper individual behavior and protect the inherited values of the civic community.[8] He concludes that "it will . . . be every where found, that as the clergy are, or are not what they ought to be, so are the rest of the nation" (84). Edmund invests his role as a future administrator of the church with great significance to the state, describing his duties with the same national, social, and moral rhetoric employed by Burke in his *Reflections*.[9] His identity as a clergyman seemingly allows him to merge Burkean sentimentality with Burkean heroism, but Austen's novel reveals that he is not able to synthesize these masculine traits in modern environments such as the unorganized areas of Sotherton.

In such an unstructured environment, Edmund's sensitivity to Mary soon prompts him to dismiss again his role as a guardian of Fanny, as he leaves his cousin behind to continue walking and conversing with the modern woman. His career plans still amaze Mary, who reports that his drive reminds her of "some of the old heathen heroes, who after performing great exploits in a foreign land, offered sacrifices to the gods on their safe return" (97–98). She shockingly equates his adherence to duty with an archaic pagan offering rather than Christian national leadership. She completes her critique by adding that a "clergyman has nothing to do but to be slovenly and selfish—read the newspaper, watch the weather, and quarrel with his wife. His curate does all the work, and the business of his own life is to dine" (99). Mary strips the ecclesiastical profession of its sacrificial heroism, forcing Edmund to reconcile yet again the disparity between Burke's advocacy of the spirit of edifying religion and the spirit of a gentleman. Austen's hero must defend a traditionally valued English profession against Mary's indictment. Edmund confronts this difficult rhetorical challenge within the discursive context of other fictional clergymen such as Matthew Lewis's Ambrosio and Elizabeth Inchbald's Dorriforth—men who showcased the failures of the church to maintain its traditional existence in the changing modern world.

Lewis's *The Monk* (1796) details the dangers posed by physical sensations to even the most reverent young man, Ambrosio, who despite his public reputation as a "Man of Holiness" and "a present . . . from the Virgin," recognizes that he is but a man "whose nature is frail, and prone to error" (16–17; 40). Edmund, like Ambrosio, is a renowned young man devoted to the ecclesiastical life who struggles to negotiate physical desires; Ambrosio's trials are certainly more spectacular, but these promising youth essentially experience the problem of new sensations. Ambrosio's trial begins when Rosario identifies herself as a young woman named Matilda; Lewis reports that this formerly innocent man now experienced "the full vigour of Manhood. . . . He clasped her rapturously in his arms; He forgot his vows, his sanctity, and his fame:

He remembered nothing but the pleasure and opportunity" (90). Ambrosio's lascivious involvement with Rosario—who is, of course, the loyal servant of Satan—results in the demise of his ecclesiastical role and the subsequent collapse of society's religious and moral center. Edmund may not be tempted by the Prince of Darkness, but he is forced to negotiate the sensual charms of Mary Crawford that endanger both his stable clerical identity and the continued prosperity of his aristocratic family. Austen's hero must also shun the inappropriate example of Inchbald's Dorriforth, an older clergyman who "[becomes] a hard-hearted tyrant . . . [and] an example of implacable rigour and injustice" after he weds his former ward (A Simple Story 95). Inchbald notes that Dorriforth's "love to his lady had been extravagant—the effect of his hate was extravagant likewise" (197). Edmund learns to eschew such extreme and unbalanced modern sexualized subjectivities and instead crafts his ecclesiastical subjectivity after Burke's nostalgic model. He embraces an established clerical identity to deploy pastoral power, but Austen exposes his continued vulnerability to newfound physical pleasures as the Bertram household prepares for the domestic drama that concludes the novel's first volume.

The desire to stage a small drama, initiated by Mr. Yates and supported by Tom, Maria, and Henry Crawford, becomes Edmund's most trying challenge as the temporary Mansfield patriarch. Edmund "was determined to prevent it," and he initially attempts to dissuade the others from acting within an ancestral home by arguing that "if we are to act, let it be in a theatre completely fitted up with pit, box, and gallery" (112). Edmund appreciates the value of Mansfield, and he understands that such a domain cannot be allowed to devolve into a house of "acting"; he does not want homes like Mansfield or Pemberley—the physical foundations of the aristocracy and its inherited ideals—to become mere theatrical settings. And he is severely worried about women acting—or acting women; he is specifically anxious about his sister Maria, whom he considers committed to Mr. Rushworth.[10] Edmund is obsessed with directing the behavior of young females, and as a pastoral figure he is frightened they might assume various "play" identities that could distract them from their familial and national responsibilities as reproducers. Tom, however, rebukes Edmund's authoritative stance and momentarily reassumes his status as the impending patriarch of Mansfield. He announces, "I know my father as well as you do, and I'll take care that his daughters do nothing to distress him. Manage your own concerns, Edmund, and I'll take care of the rest of the family" (114). Edmund defers to the will of his lavish brother, recalling his instability as a temporary aristocratic leader. He may know what is right and proper according to his Burkean training, but this alone does not empower him to defuse the lure of modern drama.

Despite his failure to halt the plans to stage an intimate domestic drama, Edmund initially refuses to join the histrionics himself; he announces, "No, as to acting myself, . . . *that* I absolutely protest against" (115). His attitude toward the play, of course, takes a notable turn when he learns that Mary Crawford will participate. Austen narrates the scene carefully: "Maria gave Edmund a glance, which meant, 'What say you now? Can we be wrong if Mary Crawford feels the same?' And Edmund silenced, was obliged to acknowledge that the charm of acting might well carry fascination to the mind of genius" (116–17). He yet again succumbs to the temptation of an opportunity to experience moments of sensory exhilaration alongside Mary; he is to "play" a young clergyman beloved of Amelia, the character performed by Miss Crawford.[11] Edmund originally dismisses such typecasting, explaining that he "should be sorry to make the character ridiculous by bad acting. . . . and the man who chooses the profession itself, is, perhaps, one of the last who would wish to represent it on the stage" (131). He is both frightened and excited by the prospect of dramatically performing scenarios that might blur the distinction between reality and the stage, but his remarks also suggest his inability to act as both a responsible clergyman—an identity that he has defended despite its recent fictional representations—and a romantic lover. He may be conscious of the failings of ecclesiastics like Ambrosio and Dorriforth to balance their clerical responsibilities with sensual passions, and Edmund may even realize that his involvement in the drama risks his own demise, but he is tempted by the possibility of new and undisciplined sensations.

Edmund, in a scene that foreshadows the novel's closing wedding, again turns to Fanny for advice in resolving this tension between his heroic duties and his physical sensitivity. He initially adopts a rhetoric of crisis, asserting, "I do not know what to do. This acting scheme gets worse and worse you see. They have chosen as bad a play as they could; and now, to complete the business, are going to ask the help of a young man very slightly known to any of us. This is the end of all the privacy and propriety which was talked about at first" (138). Edmund embellishes his language, à la Burke, to emphasize the frightful consequences of a seemingly innocent and private Mansfield affair that might become public. He presents himself as a heroic figure who must now assume a dramatic role to preserve the integrity of his aristocratic family and its ancestral home. He proclaims, "There is but *one* thing to be done, Fanny. I must take Anhalt myself. I am well aware that nothing else will quiet Tom" (138). He explains "they will not have much cause of triumph, when they see how infamously I act. But, however, triumph there certainly will be, and I must brave it. But if I can be the means of restraining the publicity of the business, of limiting the exhibition, of concentrating our folly, I shall be well repaid" (139). He presents himself as a martyr who will perform the part of Anhalt only to contain the ridiculous performance.

His involvement forces him to confront volatile sensations that he is not well trained to negotiate, but Sir Thomas's return from Antigua on the night of the dress rehearsal halts the dramatic escapades before the hero becomes imperiled by his performance. The restored Mansfield patriarch briefly criticizes all the participants in the play, but Austen devotes special attention to his rebuke of Edmund. She carefully relates this scene through the eyes of her heroine: "Such a look of reproach at Edmund from his father [Fanny] could never have expected to witness; and to feel that it was in any degree deserved, was an aggravation indeed. Sir Thomas's look implied, 'On your judgment, Edmund, I depended; what have you been about?'" (166). Austen's subtle narration of Sir Bertram's reprimand reminds us of the father's, and indeed the nation's, expectation that Edmund would perform appropriate paternal duties; Sir Bertram looked to Edmund to maintain order in his stead, and Edmund has failed to prevent the ills of modernity from penetrating the ancestral family's domestic realm. Austen emphasizes that Fanny is likewise disturbed by Edmund's inability to perform as substitute aristocratic patriarch; the hero quickly renews his sense of moral propriety by isolating and upholding his cousin's behavior. He announces to his father, "We have all been more or less to blame . . . every one of us, excepting Fanny. Fanny is the only one who has judged rightly throughout" (168). Edmund is beginning to grasp Fanny's value as a pure woman, and she may reciprocate his appreciation as she now becomes more active in (re)constructing Edmund as a heroic male who remains sensitive. She even addresses Edmund's name, explaining to Mary Crawford that "the sound of *Mr.* Bertram is so cold and nothing-meaning—so entirely without warmth or character!—It just stands for a gentleman, and that's all. But there is nobleness in the name of Edmund. It is a name of heroism and renown—of kings, princes, and knights; and seems to breathe the spirit of chivalry and warm affections" (190). Fanny now demonstrates her value to the hero by portraying him as a legendary man who, despite his failings as a substitute patriarch, is still valorous, responsible, and sensitive.

Edmund's own earnest attempts to resecure his Burkean masculinity lead him to recall the importance of an ancestral home's integrity, and he voices such sentiments when discussing his own future dwelling. Although Henry Crawford claims that Edmund ought to consider multiple improvements to his living at Thornton Lacey, Austen's hero endorses the traditional architectural principles of his inherited home. Edmund indicates that he "must be satisfied with rather less ornament and beauty" (219); he upholds the relevance of archaic chivalric culture even to structural design. He adopts the conservative ideas of Jane West, whose *Letters Addressed to a Young Man on His First Entrance into Life* (1803) praises the importance of such historical precedent and announces that "our ancestors acted upon this plan for a long course of ages, and supported it by various civil and religious injunctions" (I: 56). Edmund greatly values and respects his nation's legendary customs, and he relates the importance of such practices to the construction and style of his home. He concludes that "the house and premises may be made comfortable, and given the air of a gentleman's residence without any very heavy expense, and that must suffice me; and I hope may suffice all who care about me" (219). Edmund, like Bingley, realizes that expensive modern updates cannot replicate the ancestral domain of a gentleman. Austen's hero appears pleased with the antiquated architecture of Thornton Lacey, even though he presents his contentment as something of a sacrifice—that is, he "must be satisfied" with a home inherited from an aristocratic family. Edmund's comments also suggest that the reconstruction of the Bertrams must begin internally; as a future clerical leader and sentinel of morality, he must first order his own house, remove modern distractions, and marry a woman willing and able to secure his hegemonic identity and reproduce the aristocracy.

Although Austen emphasizes Edmund's adherence to these ends, she also records his continued struggles to sustain such a dated aesthetic of existence in the post-Revolutionary nation. Austen notes that "Edmund was at this time particularly full of cares; his mind being deeply occupied in the consideration of two important events now at hand, which were to fix his fate in life—ordination and matrimony" (230). Edmund is a serious young man, and despite his prior difficulties as a substitute patriarch, he is committed to a future career as a morally edifying clergyman. And yet, he recognizes that he cannot achieve this clerical identity as an ethical leader of England by himself; he, like the other unmarried men of Austen's corpus, must acquire a wife to establish the hegemonic male social/sexual subjectivity required to participate fully in the national community. Austen explains that "his duties would be established, but the wife who was to share, and animate, and reward those duties might yet be unattainable. He knew his own mind, but he was not always perfectly assured of knowing Miss Crawford's" (230). Edmund appears as both a willing servant of the state who imagines his wife as a dutiful partner and a sentimental man who longs to know the true feelings of the sensually appealing Mary. He concludes that "the issue of all depended on one question. Did she love him well enough to forego what had used to be essential points—did she love him well enough to make them no longer essential?" (231). The hero is prepared to abstain from modern allurements, but he is not convinced that Mary is ready to make the same sacrifice. Edmund, as a well-trained Burkean man and future aristocratic leader, should simply dismiss Mary as a woman of the modern world who does not appreciate ancestral culture, but he is also a sensitive man, and he remains susceptible to Mary's sensual charms.

Austen carefully observes Edmund's continued fascination with Mary and treats her hero as she often does her heroines—excited for a ball and anxious about dancing partners. Austen remarks that "in every meeting" Edmund maintained "a hope of receiving farther confirmation of Miss Crawford's attachment; but the whirl of a ball-room perhaps was not particularly favourable to the excitement or expression of serious feelings" (232). Edmund becomes frustrated and desperate, and while he manages to reserve a dance with Miss Crawford, he explains to his passive cousin that Mary "says it is to be the last time that she ever will dance with me. . . . she never has danced with a clergyman she says, and she never *will*" (243). Edmund's future ecclesiastical duties again clash with his exploration of the sensual experiences Mary affords; she will not tolerate the hero's religious seriousness at a ball, and Edmund's clerical role precludes his reckless pursuit of pleasures beyond the controlled environment of a Mansfield dance floor. Austen's hero is anxious about the conflict between his heroic masculinity and his physical attraction to Mary, but he concludes, "it will all end right. I am only vexed for a moment" (243).[12]

Edmund also remains anxious about the current sexual vulnerability of young English females, and he now rededicates himself to the pastoral task of securing the cultural utility of the nation's unmarried women. He is especially concerned with Fanny, and he surprises his cousin by strongly advocating her marriage to Henry Crawford. After Sir Thomas fails to convince his niece of the beneficence of such a union, Edmund "came to [Fanny], sat down by her, took her hand, and pressed it kindly." The narration closely parallels their initial encounter when the hero comforted and consoled the frightened heroine; Edmund now exercises his ostensibly compassionate pastoral power to encourage Fanny to accept the identity of a well-married woman. Austen indicates that he "was, in fact, entirely on his father's side of the question," supporting Henry as a man and the potential benefits of the heroine's marriage to him (303). Edmund later explains to Fanny that Crawford "will make you happy, Fanny, I know he will make you happy; but you will make him every thing" (319). Edmund's comments reveal both his concern for his unmarried and dowryless cousin and his own understanding of the cultural value of such an innocent young woman. He recognizes that Henry will provide Fanny with the financial and domestic security she presently lacks, but it is Fanny who can provide Henry with an atavistic connection to an ancestral English culture and its aristocratic values. Edmund knows that Fanny's purity can cleanse Henry of the modern stains that hinder him from crafting a proper masculinity and obediently serving the nation.

Fanny's resistance to Edmund's advice indicates both her strong individual will and her adherence to ancestral rather than modernized ideals. She knows that the Crawfords are essentially altered by modernity, and Austen's heroine refuses to make such a cultural transition—or merge her purity with the perversity of outsiders. Sir Thomas, who does not yet understand Fanny's importance to his own aristocratic domain, chastises his niece and promptly returns her to her family at Portsmouth;[13] the subsequent demise of the Bertram family allows the patriarch and his son to develop an appreciation for the heroine's vital role in sustaining the aristocratic realm, its ideals, and its inhabitants. Edmund, for instance, continues to discuss his volatile feelings for Mary with Fanny, and in one of his letters to the heroine he reports that after a trip to London—the world of Mary—he "returned to Mansfield in a less assured state." He relates that his "hopes are much weaker," but he admits: "I cannot give her up, Fanny. She is the only woman in the world whom I could ever think of as a wife" (382; 384). He knows that he cannot exist as a responsible ecclesiastical figure alongside Mary's "influence of the fashionable world" and her "habits of wealth," but he is clearly still enamored of the modern woman. He reverts to a perverted version of chivalric heroism and announces, "I must bear it . . . I can never cease to try for her. This is the truth. The only question is *how?*" (384). He acts as a hopelessly devoted lover who will persist in his efforts to acquire the affections of a disinterested lady. John Wiltshire argues that in this lengthy letter, "Austen adopts, or rather adapts, the convention of the sentimental novel and Edmund . . . expose[s] his heart, his bleeding heart, to his correspondent . . . . by revealing with such naked sincerity the helplessness of his passion for Mary" (*Jane Austen and the Body* 104). Edmund's behavior is sentimental and seemingly heroic, reminding us of his Burkean training, but Austen again exposes the incompatibility of this masculine sexuality with modernity. Edmund constructs his sentimental pursuit of Mary as heroic, but *Mansfield Park* reveals that his heroic sensitivity actually endangers the stability of his family and the nation.

The impending collapse of the Bertram family reminds Edmund of the great peril of sensations produced by erotic desire, the vulnerability of the aristocracy and its values, and Mansfield's specific need of Fanny; in addition, the crises of Mansfield prompt Edmund to reassume his function as a familial savior. Lady Bertram tells Fanny of Tom's alcohol-induced illness and informs the heroine that "Edmund kindly proposes attending his brother immediately" (388). Lady Bertram's account echoes earlier depictions of her son as a hero, and Austen now overtly announces both the aristocratic family's and the heroine's desperate need for Edmund's valor. The narrator suggests that "Edmund was all in all. Fanny would certainly believe him so at least, and must find that her estimation of him was higher than ever when he appeared as the attendant, supporter, cheerer of a suffering brother" (391). Fanny is aware of Edmund's great importance to her, and she now also knows his significant role as a protector of the Bertrams and their ancestral cultural values. Mary Crawford is likewise conscious of Edmund's valiant position in his family, but she playfully constructs him as "Sir Edmund" and crassly questions whether Edmund "would not do more good with all the Bertram property, than any other possible 'Sir'" (396). Mary redefines Edmund's heroism as an indispensable practical skill for a modern man seeking to maximize possible improvement and advancement. Fanny, however, conceptualizes her cousin as an ancestral hero who can right wrongs, uphold a chivalric sense of duty, and remain sensible; and Edmund appears up to the task, as he willingly cares for his lavish brother who has tarnished the family's aristocratic legacy.

The next Bertram family scandals that Edmund must resolve involve the embarrassing escapades of his sisters; when he learns of Maria's improper relations with Henry Crawford and Julia's elopement with Yates, he quickly writes his wholesome cousin to discuss the affairs. He sounds like a vanquished knight who has failed in his quest, as he reports that "there is no end of the evil let loose upon us" (404). Edmund's rhetoric suggests that Burke's nightmare vision has come true, and the English nation now has "no compass to govern us" and consequently, can no longer "know distinctly to what port we steer" (129). The degeneration of England's aristocracy is metonymically represented by the errors of Edmund's family, whose individual members have failed to perform as dutiful and selfless participants of a larger cultural unit. And the ultimate breakdown of the Bertram aristocratic tradition is attributed to the public shame of young aristocratic women who could have culturally and biologically reproduced the nation. Edmund has failed to protect these members of his flock, and although he has consistently redefined himself as a sacrificial hero whenever he has encountered prior difficulties or dilemmas, he now acts as a Burkean man of feeling. When he arrives at Portsmouth to transport the heroine back to Mansfield, he proclaims, "My Fanny—my only sister—my only comfort now" (405). He emotionally announces his new appreciation for Fanny;[14] she may not be an adventurous heroine, but like Andromeda, she appears eager to offer her body for the good of her family and its culture. Edmund, however, is still not fully prepared to abandon his fascination with Mary.

When Edmund and Fanny finally arrive at Mansfield, he appears extremely confused, and Austen depicts the sensitive hero as "sunk in a deeper gloom than ever . . . with eyes closed as if the view of cheerfulness oppressed him, and the lovely scenes of home must be shut out" (408). As soon as he encounters Mary, he attempts to anesthetize his senses, preferring "to bury his own feelings in exertions for the relief of his brother's" (409). He can exist safely as a valorous yet sentimental man alongside Fanny, but he knows Mary threatens the stability of his identity as an impending leader of the aristocracy. Edmund instead numbs his senses and, much like the heroine, assumes a sacrificial role for the good of his family and the nation.[15] Still, he is able to renounce Mary Crawford only after her casual response to the news of his family's scandals. Edmund explains, "She reprobated her brother's folly in being drawn on by a woman whom he had never cared for. . . . To hear the woman whom—no harsher name than folly given!—So voluntarily, so freely, so coolly to canvass it!—No reluctance, no horror, no feminine—shall I say? no modest loathings" (414–15). Edmund is again nonplussed by Mary, but it is no longer her verbal impropriety that overwhelms the hero; he cannot stomach Mary's restrained reaction to the impulsive and irresponsible activity of his sisters.

Edmund realizes that Mary is not able to serve as his wife and partner, but he does not immediately forget her. Indeed, he actively attempts to represent her as an enjoyable illusion of his mind, claiming that it was not the physical person of Mary that excited his interest, but "the creature of my own imagination . . . that I had been too apt to dwell on for many months past. . . . [C]ould I have restored her to what she had appeared to me before, I would infinitely prefer any increase of the pain of parting, for the sake of carrying with me the right of tenderness and esteem" (418). Edmund's reflections echo the poetic speaker of Coleridge's "Kubla Khan," who imagines what might happen if he were able to revive the vision of an Abyssinian maid; like Coleridge's narrator, Edmund is obsessed, even though he recognizes the dangers of his obsession. Austen indicates that "time would undoubtedly abate somewhat of his sufferings, but still it was a sort of thing which he never could get entirely the better of; and as to his ever meeting with any other woman who could—it was too impossible to be named but with indignation" (420). Austen explicitly notes Edmund's continued fascination with Mary, but Austen has also shown that he is unable to reconcile his antiquated sexuality with the modern woman's lifestyle. And since no other woman could possibly fill the void her absence has left, Edmund is forced to abandon his desires for sensual exhilaration and instead accept the safety and reliability of an atavistic and benevolent marital union. The narrator indeed declares that "Fanny's friendship was all that [Edmund] had to cling to" (420).

Austen opens her final chapter by assuring her readers of satisfactory closure. She proclaims, "Let other pens dwell on guilt and misery. I quit such odious subjects as soon as I can, impatient to restore every body, not greatly in fault themselves, to tolerable comfort, and to have done with all the rest" (420). Austen self-consciously announces her intention to lighten this dark tale of the aristocracy's embarrassing demise; she promises to offer an ending replete with conjugal ceremonies, the necessary punishments, and "tolerable comfort." The heroic Edmund is, of course, unpunished, but he may be disciplined; or perhaps Austen's concluding remarks bespeak the requisite regulation of Burkean masculinity in modern England:

> Scarcely had [Edmund] done regretting Mary Crawford, and observing to Fanny how impossible it was that he should ever meet with such another woman, before it began to strike him whether a very different kind of woman might not do just as well—or a great deal better; whether Fanny herself were not growing as dear, as important to him in all her smiles, and all her ways, as Mary Crawford had ever been; and whether it might not be a possible, an hopeful undertaking to persuade her that her warm and sisterly regard for him would be foundation enough for wedded love. (428–29)

While Austen usually employs indirect speech to reveal the complex thought processes of her heroines, she uses this narrative strategy here to portray her hero's change of heart. She presents Edmund's burgeoning "romantic" interest in his cousin as a natural progression, but it is also essentially limited; his brotherly affection for Fanny may provide "foundation enough" for marriage.[16] Edmund has learned that his archaic Burkean masculinity simply cannot handle the excitement of modern women, and his cultural duty as a moral exemplar requires him to manage his sensitivity to their charms. He needs to marry a woman who is willing and able to reproduce both the next generation of the Bertram family and its aristocratic ideals, but his wife must also solidify his hegemonic social/sexual identity. Austen indicates that his regard for Fanny was "founded on the most endearing claims of innocence and helplessness, and completed by every recommendation of growing worth" (429). As a pure and willing woman, Fanny has all the traits Edmund now requires in a wife; she holds the latent potential to cleanse the aristocracy of its recent stains, bear and rear its future members, and secure Edmund's status as a future leader of the nation.

Austen reports that Edmund's marriage to Fanny permits the hero to continue "[l]oving, guiding, protecting her, as he had been doing ever since her being ten years old."[17] These disturbing comments suggest that Edmund views his marriage to Fanny as an extension of his closely monitored adolescent regard for the frightened girl; he reestablishes himself as her heroic guardian, and she, likewise, will remain his advisor and champion. Edmund renounces romantic sensibility in favor of innocent juvenile emotions, but his immature aesthetic of existence allows him to perform as a chivalric hero from bygone days, despite the turbulent culture of post-Revolutionary England. The narrator can only tersely observe, "what was there now to add, but that he should learn to prefer soft light eyes to sparkling dark ones" (429). The shift in Edmund's amorous interest appears shockingly casual and rather humorous, as he must simply eschew the "dark lady" for the subservient heroine who, not coincidentally, possesses the light eyes associated with England's supposed historical people. Austen adds one final discomforting note to the narrative, as we learn that with the death of Dr. Grant, Edmund acquires the Mansfield ecclesiastical living (432). The narrator indicates that the hero and heroine "removed to Mansfield" to live "within the view and patronage of Mansfield Park" (432). Edmund now physically and symbolically merges his marital union with both his clerical duties and his familial/national responsibilities as a future aristocratic patriarch. His marriage to Fanny stabilizes his masculinity, but it also enables him to ensure and direct the biological and cultural reproduction of the English aristocracy. He fulfills his role as a Perseus figure, coming to the rescue of the sacrificed heroine; and Fanny, as an Andromeda figure, fortifies the hero's masculinity. Edmund needs her feminine innocence and integrity to accomplish his Herculean task of maintaining the ancestral culture of England's past in the modernizing nation; moreover, Austen's corpus continues to suggest that English culture cannot risk the potential volatility of Deleuzian love or male lovers.

CHAPTER 6

Remaking English Manhood,
or Accepting Modernity

Knightley's Fused Finitude

◄◦►

*Before the end of the eighteenth century, man did not exist—any more than the potency
of life, the fecundity of labour, or the historical density of language. He is a quite recent
creature, which the demiurge of knowledge fabricated with its own hands less than two
hundred years ago. (Foucault,* The Order of Things *308)*

*We need to see how everyone, at every age, in the smallest things as in the greatest chal-
lenges, seeks a territory, tolerates or carries out deterritorializations, and is reterritorialized on almost anything. (Deleuze and Guattari,* What Is Philosophy? *67–68)*

Mr. Knightley does nothing mysteriously. (Emma Woodhouse in Austen, Emma *203)*

Emma's comment regarding Mr. Knightley's preference for deliberate behavior reminds us of the hero's effectiveness as a social organizer: he values
premeditated action, distrusts irrational spontaneous behavior, and carefully
plans his conduct to ensure the contentment of his community. Knightley
is a trusted civic leader who upholds the ideals of an ancestral English culture, and yet, like Darcy, he understands that the post-Revolutionary nation
is changing and must at least prepare for significant social shifts. *Pride and
Prejudice* depicts Darcy as a representative of a vanishing breed of romantic
aristocratic men, and the narrative outlines the development of ambitious bourgeois men; *Mansfield Park* documents the impending demise of
England's aristocracy, its families, and its male leaders; *Emma* dramatizes
Knightley's attempt to maintain qualities of Burke's ideal of aristocratic
English masculinity while directing the maturation of a modern commu-
nity and its young women and men. Knightley, unlike Edmund Bertram, is
neither afraid of modernity nor determined to preserve an archaic civiliza-
tion; Edmund shields himself from the growing dangers of contemporary
England to safeguard his masculinity and the future of the aristocracy, but
Knightley embraces the nation's new developments even as he remains

invested in the lore and structures of England's history. He understands that English males can no longer follow nostalgic models of sexuality, and while he performs important rituals of the nation's ancestral culture, Knightley also endorses the values of reason and industry championed by Enlightenment thinkers. *Emma* documents its hero's attempts to embody both traditional and modern modes of masculinity while preserving his sexual stability. He is neither an admired romantic figure like Darcy nor a Burkean cleric endowed with national import like Edmund Bertram; nonetheless, Knightley crafts a sexuality that serves as an archetype of modern masculinity: he fulfills both Burke's expectations for a chivalric male and the desires of post-Enlightenment thinkers for a virile man of reason. He realizes that he can secure his fused sexuality and his hegemonic social identity by marrying the heroine—a union that will neither engender Mr. Woodhouse's fear of the "break up [of] one's family circle" nor promote the volatile effects of Deleuzian love (11).

Austen's hero is self-consciously concerned with proper masculinity, and as Johnson points out, *Emma* "persistently asks how a *man* should behave and what he ought to do" (*Equivocal Beings* 197). She specifically argues that the novel "[diminishes] the authority of male sentimentality, and [reimmasculates] men and women alike with a high sense of national purpose" (*Equivocal Beings* 191). While Mr. Woodhouse represents an atrophied mode of aristocratic masculinity, Knightley, according to Johnson, is the paragon of a reimmasculated man; he models a new "humane" British masculinity, but he also recalls a pre-Burkean tradition of "gentry liberty, which valued its manly independence from tyrannical rule" (*Equivocal Beings* 199; 201). Knightley is a distinctive man because he engages in modern activities and relations without neglecting England's historical notions of maleness. He resists the tyranny of sentimentality, but he also recognizes that the sentimental masculinity of aristocratic men like Mr. Woodhouse, Edmund Bertram, and Sir Elliot were once important to the nation; as Johnson elaborates, it "guaranteed the continuation of the charm, the beauty, the hospitality, and the goodness of Old England itself, which liked its gallant old ways even if they did not make sense, and which won our love, veneration, and loyalty" (*Equivocal Beings* 198). But Knightley, like Darcy, recognizes that modern English culture must now embrace the realities of post-Revolutionary progress and train young men who can bridge the gap between the decay of an old society and the emergence of a new nation.

And while Darcy helps tutor aspiring men of/from trade to assume larger civic roles and responsibilities in the modern English nation, Knightley has (re)trained himself to adjust to the impending changes of England's modernizing culture. Johnson explains how he is both "impeccably landed, a magistrate" as well as "a farmer and a man of business." Knightley is "a gentleman of 'untainted' blood and judicious temper," but he is also "absorbed in the figures and computations Emma considers so vulgar"; he is "a man of energy, vigor, and decision, and as such emphatically not an embodiment of the stasis unto sluggishness Burke commended in country squires" (*Equivocal Beings* 201). Johnson is correct to highlight Knightley's accomplishment as a new kind of English male who embodies a humane model of independent manliness; his sexuality, however, is nonetheless calculated and structured. His well-disciplined and functional aesthetic of existence requires him to remain deliberate in his activity, rationalize potentially uncontrollable emotions like love, and reconfigure marriage as the culmination of logical feelings. Knightley synthesizes qualities of Burkean maleness, Enlightenment masculinity, and gentry independence, creating a new male subjectivity that becomes vital to the nation's transition from a preindustrial rural society to a modern state.[1]

His fused masculinity is crucial to the successful negotiation of his changing local and national community. The world of *Emma*, like the nation of the early nineteenth century, experiences important social shifts that alter its organizational structure; moreover, *Emma* is a novel preoccupied with the status of the nation and the idea of "Englishness." Highbury's inhabitants consistently return to Englishness as a tool for describing their everyday experiences and encounters; they employ national adjectivals to name and evaluate their community and its residents, demonstrating the novel's investment in the traditions of England's past and marking the village as a domain of native English people. Mr. Knightley claims, "Mrs. Weston is the very best country-dance player, without exception, in England" (221); upon learning of Frank and Jane's engagement, Emma offers Mr. Weston congratulations "on the prospect of having one of the most lovely and accomplished young women in England for [his] daughter" (363); and Mrs. Elton cannot prevent herself from declaring the strawberries of Donwell Abbey are "the best fruit in England" (324). The people of Highbury also continually broach national issues such as citizenship and the Empire. When Frank tours Highbury with the heroine, he shows himself "to be a true citizen of Highbury" and displays his "*amor patriæ*" by buying gloves at Ford's (179); in order to dismiss the annoying Mrs. Elton, Jane Fairfax enters into a strange but historically accurate glorification of the English postal service as "a wonderful establishment" (266); and even Miss Bates references the difficult Irish question of the early nineteenth century, as she almost distinguishes Ireland from the British Empire (141).[2] Peter Smith argues that "the principal topic in *Emma*, as in *Mansfield Park*, is England, England's weaknesses, the dangers inherent in those weaknesses, and the choices that might still be made to secure the nation's future" (221). Austen emphasizes Knightley's sustained interest in the future prosperity of Highbury and the nation; moreover, she illustrates how his concern with the development of young English men will be essential to continued civic contentment.

Austen presents Highbury as a microcosm of England's reconfigured post-Revolutionary culture; it is a "large and populous village" that is growing quickly and experiencing notable social changes (5). Julia Prewitt Brown points out that "the novel is peopled with upwardly and downwardly mobile individuals." She adds that the community of *Emma* "is viewed not from the perspective of frozen class division but from a perspective of living change" (114). Unlike the aristocratic inhabitants of Mansfield Park, the citizens of Highbury accept the inevitability of social transformation as a reality of the modernizing nation; consequently, individuals like Mrs. Weston, Frank Churchill, and Jane Fairfax enjoy significant social ascensions, the Bateses experience a steady fall, and tradesmen like the Coles are now hosting members of ancestral families like Knightley and Emma. In addition, Austen's text indicates that members of aristocratic families, like John Knightley and Isabella, can explore new urban professional lifestyles. *Emma* is a novel that reveals definite cultural shifts, but as Peter Smith notes, it is not a tale of apocalyptic despair but a narrative that considers various strategies for adjusting to the progressions of modernity—progressions that appalled and stultified the worlds of *Pride and Prejudice* and *Mansfield Park*. Miroslav Hroch theorizes that "the basic precondition of all national movements—yesterday and today—is a deep crisis of the old order, with the breakdown of its legitimacy, and of the values and sentiments that sustained it" (75). The culture of *Emma* is slowly accepting the collapse of traditional systems of order, such as the aristocracy and its archaic mode of masculinity; the inhabitants of Highbury have not forgotten about historical structures of power, but they also allow new cultural possibilities.

Knightley, as a new English man who accepts that English society must adjust to a post-Revolutionary nation, manages to preserve some traits of the past culture. Unlike Sir Bertram, Austen's hero shows little ambition to suspend the modernization of England, but he is not merely resigned to or ambivalent about impending transformations. He is aware of Burke's desire for the perpetuity of England's aristocratic male leaders, and he appears throughout much of the novel as a feudal lord for Highbury who keeps the community organized, content, and free from significant disturbances. For example, when Knightley discusses his project to renovate the path to Langham, he points out that he "should not attempt it, if it were to be the means of inconvenience to the Highbury people" (97). Knightley may appear to plan upgrades for his own estate, but he is also concerned with improving the quality of public roadways for the residents of the burgeoning village who need safe and convenient routes to participate in the modern national economy.[3] When he later arrives at the Coles' party, Emma observes that he has traveled in his carriage and commends him: "This is coming as you should do . . . like a gentleman" (191). It is at this party, moreover, that we learn that Knightley has gallantly sent his carriage for the Bateses and Jane Fairfax (200). He knows how to act as a chivalric man, and his charitable deeds prove his status as a noble and genteel figure. His compassion for the citizens of Highbury recalls Charlotte Smith's depiction of *Desmond*'s Montfleuri, a rational landed patriarch who "made it the business of his life to make his vassals and dependents content, by giving them all the advantages their condition will allow" (I: 82). Like Montfleuri, Knightley retains the duties of a concerned feudal administrator who, as Duckworth claims, "continually [brings] into the daily life of Highbury the spirit of chivalry" (156). Knightley is invested in both the social improvement of his community and the sustenance of ancestral customs, but for Knightley, cultural updates are not necessarily frightening, and the hero does not revert solely to archaic modes of masculinity.

Donwell Abbey is integral to Knightley's fused sexuality as it provides a nexus to England's chivalric culture and allows the hero to demonstrate his adherence to Enlightenment dictates such as reason and industry. Austen highlights Knightley's affinity for the Abbey throughout the novel, as he is continually concerned with his stewards and crops, but the narrator pays special attention to his estate following the announcement of his plan for a strawberry-picking expedition. Mrs. Elton attempts to assume control of the arrangements and declares, "It is to be a morning scheme, you know, Knightley; quite a simple thing. . . . There is to be no form or parade—a sort of gipsy party.—We are to walk about your gardens, and gather the strawberries ourselves, and sit under trees;—and whatever else you may like to provide, it is to be all out of doors. . . . Every thing as natural and simple as possible" (320–21). Knightley promptly dubs Mrs. Elton's plans as both irrational and unnatural; he has no intention of allowing his friends to perform the antiquated behavior of a premodern culture or adopt the exoticized guise of a racial stereotype. He replies, "My idea of the simple and the natural will be to have the table spread in the dining-room. The nature and the simplicity of gentlemen and ladies, with their servants and furniture, I think is best observed by meals within doors" (321). Knightley's idea of the natural is pointedly rational, even though he proposes traditional dining conventions and the use of servants. He will not allow sentimental aggrandizements or unreasonable behavior to taint his ancestral lands.

When Mrs. Elton later expresses her desire to travel to Donwell by donkey, he also notes the irrationality of this fancy by explaining that donkeys are unnecessary since "Donwell-lane is never dusty, and now it is perfectly dry"; however, he allows her to "come on a donkey . . . if you prefer it. You can borrow Mrs. Cole's" (321). He highlights the modern accessibility of his estate, but as a humane and desentimentalized English man, he allows Mrs. Elton's idiotic desire for a donkey, much as he continually tolerates the archaic behavior of Mr. Woodhouse. He even manages to accommodate the heroine's father during the Donwell expedition, arranging care for the ante-diluvian patriarch within the ancestral Abbey. Knightley is routinely respect-ful of Mr. Woodhouse, whom Johnson accurately describes as "the ideal of sentimental masculinity described throughout this book" (*Equivocal Beings* 198). The hero is not ignorant of the nation's chivalric lore and its corre-sponding models of masculinity, and he is not motivated to rid the nation of such representatives. He is not a diehard disciple of Godwin, committed to demonstrating that a "generous blood, a gallant and fearless spirit is by no means propagated from father to son" or insisting that "the descendants of a magnanimous ancestry" are "the legitimate representatives of departed heroism" (*Enquiry* I: 41). Knightley is in no hurry to precipitate modernity, but he is also not frightened by progress, and his maintenance of Donwell is indicative of this attitude. The hero, unlike the Bertrams, has successfully integrated his ancestral home into his community's changing culture, but he has also managed to maintain the Abbey's historical grandeur.

When Emma arrives at Donwell for the strawberry-picking expedition, she reflects, "It was just what it ought to be, and it looked what it was—and Emma felt an increasing respect for it, as the residence of a family of such true gentility, untainted in blood and understanding" (323). She adds, "It was a sweet view—sweet to the eye and the mind. English verdure, English culture, English comfort" (325).[4] Donwell is an evocative pastoral world reminiscent of a mythologized medieval England, replete with steward-like figures such as William Larkins and Robert Martin; but while the hero's realm may appear nostalgic and romanticized, he remains an active partici-pant in the daily duties of the land. He is undoubtedly a genteel man, but he is also a man with "a great deal of health, activity, and independence" (191). The narrator also notes that Knightley, "as a farmer, as keeping in hand the home-farm at Donwell . . . had to tell what every field was to bear next year" (90), and during a tour of the grounds with Harriet, he offered "informa-tion as to modes of agriculture, &c" (326). He still plays a major part in the business of the Abbey, following the model of the assiduous farmers of the late-eighteenth-century utopian novels by Jacobin writers such as Charlotte Smith, Elizabeth Inchbald, and Gilbert Imlay. His agricultural planning specifically reminds us of Imlay's Captain Arl-ton, who spent his mornings "laying out his grounds, and planting the several fruits, and other things necessary to the comfort and pleasure of living." Imlay adds that Arl-ton "not only attends to this business, but he does a great part of it with his own hands, which gives him that exercise so necessary to invigorate the constitution" (313). Knightley could leisurely enjoy his grand estate, but he adopts the behavior of the Jacobin farmers, who commit themselves to working the soil with vigor.

His exceptional status as an aristocratic man who has adapted to post-Enlightenment modernity is not lost on the citizens of Highbury; even Miss Smith recognizes the hero's impressive qualities, and after she introduces Emma to Robert Martin, Harriet admits that her young admirer "certainly . . . is not like Mr. Knightley." Emma quickly explains to her friend that "Mr. Knightley's air is so remarkably good, that it is not fair to compare Mr. Martin with *him*. You might not see one in a hundred, with *gentleman* so plainly written as in Mr. Knightley" (28). The heroine's comment emphasizes both the rarity and the grand social reputation enjoyed by the administrator of Donwell, who seems to reek gentility and nobility despite his commitment to rationality and industry. And yet, Emma is not necessarily enamored of the hero's "downright, decided, commanding sort of manner"; she explains that "it suits *him* very well; his figure and look, and situation in life seem to allow it; but if any young man were to set about copying him he would not be sufferable" (30). Emma suggests that Knightley's social standing enables him to fuse chivalric and modern masculinity, but her remarks also indicate that the consequences of the hero's mechanized identity are rather unappealing. Knightley is deliberate, structured, and imposing; he embodies the paradox that Foucault associates with the development of modern subjectivity in the early years of the nineteenth century.

Foucault argues that in the decade following the French Revolution, the modern individual emerges and is defined by its accordance with natural laws, scientific dictates, and cultural customs for the purpose of becoming finite and naturalized (*Order of Things* 310).[5] Foucault concludes that "the experience taking form at the beginning of the nineteenth century situates the discovery of finitude not within the thought of the infinite, but . . . as the concrete forms of finite existence" (316). The post-Enlightenment human subject, according to philosophers like Godwin and Thomas Paine, is endowed with the ability to improve and diversify her/his mode of being, but as Foucault theorizes, this potential is always already contained by the "natural" potential of man's physical body.[6] Knightley is a compelling example of this Foucauldian modern subject; he furnishes his finite sexual subjectivity with both Burkean and Enlightenment standards for masculinity, but even after this impressive achievement, his capacity is essentially finite. Deleuze and Guattari discuss the modern individual's relationship to powerful social forces, such as the post-Revolutionary discourses on English masculinity, in terms of a tri-fold process of territorialization, deterritorialization, and reterritorialization (*Anti-Oedipus* 10). The different late-eighteenth-century dictates for proper maleness mark Knightley, and Austen illustrates how he is territorialized by chivalric and rational guidelines; but she also demonstrates how his modern faculty to reason and adapt permits Knightley to deterritorialize himself by exposing the artifice and irrationality of anachronistic customs. *Emma*, however, suggests that he is consistently reterritorialized as a disciplined man who reverts to a synthetic yet finite subjectivity that allows him to make a successful and secure transition to a modern English culture. He ultimately seeks a safe and predictable marital union, free from the multiplicity of Deleuzian love, which will ensure his mechanic masculinity.

Austen accentuates Knightley's well-organized sexuality by distinguishing him from both the archaic Mr. Woodhouse and yeomen like Robert Martin, but she devotes far more attention to the important differences between the hero and Frank Churchill. Austen traces the hero's running commentary on Frank, and Knightley's remarks reveal both his anxiety about the future of the nation's undisciplined young men and his own conceptions of proper masculinity. He initially becomes upset when he learns that Frank has again postponed, because of the Churchills' claims on his time, a planned visit to his father and new bride at Randalls. Austen's hero claims that he "cannot believe that [Frank] has not the power of coming, if he made a point of it. . . . A man at his age—what is he?—three or four-and-twenty—cannot be without the means of doing as much as that. It is impossible" (131). Knightley then instructs Emma that "there is one thing . . . which a man can always do, if he chuses, and that is, his duty; not by [maneuvering] and finessing, but by vigour and resolution"; he adds that "a sensible man would find no difficulty" in dutifully visiting his father and Mrs. Weston (132). Knightley upholds both duty and sensibility as essential features of the proper English man, and while his advocacy of responsibility employs sentimental rhetoric reminiscent of Burke's *Reflections,* his emphasis on the vigor and resolution of men recalls Wollstonecraft's call for industrious and accountable men. Knightley concludes his assessment of the Churchills' influential guidance by charging that "as [Frank] became rational, he ought to have roused himself and shaken off all that was unworthy in [the Churchills'] authority" (134). The hero insists that the dismissal of irrational authority is a marker of a mature man, and Knightley later directly addresses the effects of this unreasonable tutelage upon Frank. While discussing the young man's letter of apology with Emma, Knightley insists that "[h]e knows he is wrong, and has nothing rational to urge.—Bad" (404). Knightley allows the archaic sentimentality of Mr. Woodhouse and the silly ideas of the ineffectual Mrs.

Elton, but he cannot countenance the irrational behavior of modern young men who will become the leaders of the modern English nation.

Knightley consistently treats Frank's immature behavior as a severe deficiency that prevents him from becoming a leader in his community. After witnessing the young man's manipulation of a child's game, he declares, "these letters were but the vehicle for gallantry and trick." The hero derides Frank as a "gallant young man, who seemed to love without feeling, and to recommend himself without complaisance" (314). Knightley, as an industrious man of labor who maintains an ordered sexuality and a well-planned agricultural estate, remains consistently perturbed by Frank's pursuit of useless sensations; he cannot allow Frank's laziness, charges him with being "a very weak young man," and concludes that he is "leading a life of mere idle pleasure" (133–34).[7] Knightley knows that the men who will guide England through its transition must be noble and active, chivalric and industrious, and he informs Emma that Frank "can be amiable only in French, not in English. He may be very 'amiable,' have very good manners, and be very agreeable; but he can have no English delicacy towards the feelings of other people" (134–35). Knightley's scorching rebuke marks Frank as a French effete who has followed only Burke's call for a hypersensitive man of lore; Frank clings to the antediluvian masculinity modeled by Mr. Woodhouse, but, as Knightley continually indicates, the young man has received inappropriate training as a misplaced sentimental English male. For example, upon his initial tour of Highbury, Frank "begged to be shewn the house which his father had lived in so long, and which had been the home of his father's father; and on recollecting that an old woman who had nursed him was still living, walked in quest of her cottage from one end of the street to the other" (176). Frank's intemperate fondness for nostalgia leads him on a ridiculous quest for a mysterious woman of whom he has little knowledge. He upholds an extravagant and irrational fondness of the past, recalling Mr. Woodhouse's futile desire to preserve the continuity of his "family circle" and Willoughby's earnest wish to recollect his experiences at Barton Cottage as fixed (11).

Frank also shares Willoughby's fondness for dancing, and when the topic of a ball is broached, he "argued like a young man very much bent on dancing" (177–78). In addition, Frank is a devoted singer, who is later "accused of having a delightful voice" (204)—a skill he is all too happy to exhibit. Knightley once more criticizes Frank's enthusiasm for sensory pleasures, and the hero differentiates himself from the younger man by advocating calculated and regulated sensibility. Knightley knows he is "no dancer in general," and he angrily charges, "That fellow . . . thinks of nothing but shewing off his own voice. This must not be" (207; 206). Frank, according to Knightley, is egotistical and does not understand how to relate proper feeling. The hero's response to Frank's late letter, in which he offers an apology and explanation to the heroine, accentuates his rationalized discipline in opposition to Frank's careless behavior. He observes, "Mystery; Finesse—how they pervert the understanding! My Emma, does not every thing serve to prove more and more the beauty of truth and sincerity in all our dealings with each other" (404). Knightley's comment invites us to speculate on the mechanical order of his future life with Emma, but it also elaborates his idea of proper feeling. He equates appropriate sensibility with exposed sincerity and the absence of any unreasonable or potentially disruptive mystery. He is especially bothered by Frank's gift of the pianoforte to Jane and argues "that was the act of a very, very young man, one too young to consider whether the inconvenience of it might not very much exceed the pleasure" (405). Knightley criticizes Frank's anonymous gift as an example of his underregulated affection. Austen's hero is concerned with the sustained contentment of his civic community, and he appears extremely anxious about its future male leaders like Frank, who are drawn to both volatile emotions and an anachronistic mode of masculinity.

Knightley has no interest in mysterious or irrational activities and instead maintains that proper sentimentality requires appropriate restraint and careful planning. Even when Knightley broaches the proposal of moving to Hartfield to live with Emma and the needy Mr. Woodhouse, Austen observes that the administrator of Donwell spoke "in plain, unaffected, gentleman-like English, such as [he] used even to the woman he was in love with" (407). Knightley is always already regulated, even when he discusses—with the woman he ostensibly loves—the radical idea of abandoning Donwell Abbey for Hartfield, the realm of the heroine.[8] Austen exposes his move to Hartfield as a strategic decision intended to ensure his regulation rather than as a result of his strong passion for Emma. Indeed, the text demonstrates Knightley's restraint from passionate love—a desire that Deleuze claims can engender "a plurality of worlds." Deleuze explains that "the pluralism of love does not concern only the multiplicity of loved beings, but the multiplicity of souls or worlds in each of them" (*Proust* 7). Modern sexual subjects, according to Deleuze, have the ability to exceed our finitude and experience new relations through sexual desire and erotic love—relations that could allow us to appreciate infinite possibilities of sensations, subjectivities, and sexualities. *Emma* suggests that Knightley cannot tolerate such desires or relations; they would destabilize his mechanized masculinity and prevent him from providing the leadership his national community desperately needs during its modernization. For Deleuze, love allows an individual to unsettle the order of his/her territorialization, but Knightley instead relies upon his reterritorialization as a finite subject to merge new and old models of English masculinity. Julia Prewitt Brown claims that save the influence and enthusiasm of the heroine, "Mr. Knightley is a dull and predictable English gentleman" (109). Knightley is indeed deliberate and disciplined, but his "love" for Emma represents not an anomaly in his structured subjectivity, but the insurance of his stability.

Despite his close self-management, Knightley is aware of amorous emotion, its signs, and its ramifications; in order to maintain the stability of his sexuality, he rationalizes "love" as a negotiated transaction and treats overwhelming amorous emotion as a hazard to be avoided. And while Knightley never accepts love as a romantic passion associated with sexual desire, he is, nonetheless, conscious of how others practice love. He is especially concerned about immature young men like Frank Churchill and Robert Martin, who are susceptible to irrational emotions that risk irresponsible behavior and severe depression. His early conversations with Emma about Robert Martin and Harriet Smith reveal his fears of such unmanaged passions. The hero specifically recalls how he had attempted to dissuade his young steward from pursuing the engagement because of the woman's low social position, but he knows that love can engulf a man and admits he "could not reason . . . to a man in love" (55). Emma also recognizes the irrational tendencies of male lovers, and she explains that "till [men] do fall in love with well-informed minds instead of handsome faces, a girl, with such loveliness as Harriet, has a certainty of being admired and sought after, of having the power of choosing from among many" (57). The heroine challenges Knightley's view of Mr. Martin's sacrificial proposal to Harriet and quickly reminds the hero that it would be "very much mistaken" to suggest that "your sex in general would not think such beauty, and such temper [as Harriet's], the highest claims a woman could possess" (57). Emma's comment recalls Mrs. Arlbery's explanation of men's approach to marriage in Burney's *Camilla* (1796). She asserts: "O, intolerably, with the men! They are always enchanted with something that is both pretty and silly; because they can so easily please and so soon disconcert it; and when they have made the little blooming fools blush and look down, they feel nobly superior, and pride themselves in victory. . . . A man looks enchanted while his beautiful young bride talks nonsense" (254).[9] Emma shares Mrs. Arlbery's belief that men pursue beautiful women even if they are silly, and the heroine's charge exposes both the cultural expectation that young English men will treat women's physical attractiveness as the primary impetus for amorous emotion and the exception of Knightley to this rule.

Although Knightley earlier informed Mrs. Weston that he "[loves] to look at [Emma]," his persistent observation of the heroine resembles a close surveillance rather than an admiration of her physical appearance (34). Still,

Knightley is not ignorant of the machinery of love, and Austen tells us that he specifically "felt the disappointment of [Robert Martin], and was mortified to have been the means of promoting it" (60).[10] The administrator of Donwell can recognize the pathological effects of romantic desire when he sees them, and he even behaves as an inquisitive detective seeking to prevent other youth from engaging in the perilous activities of love. In the latter third of the novel, Austen pays increasing attention to the hero's "detection" of the secret relationship between Frank Churchill and Jane Fairfax. The narrator informs us that Mr. Knightley initially "began to suspect [Frank] of some double dealing in his pursuit of Emma. That Emma was not his object appeared indisputable" (309). Austen adds that he "began to suspect [Frank] of some inclination to trifle with Jane Fairfax. He could not understand it; but there were symptoms of intelligence between them" (310). The narrator's comments provide a telling analysis of the hero's notion of love: it is, for Knightley, an "inclination" or mystery whose clues can be diagnosed and studied but not fully comprehended. He has seen Jane and Frank reciprocate glances and gestures at a dinner party, which "brought him yet stronger suspicion of there being a something of private liking, of private understanding even, between Frank Churchill and Jane" (310). Austen's description is ultimately quite humorous; Frank and Jane are, of course, engaged in a love relationship, but Knightley can only fathom this as a mysterious "private liking." He does not—and perhaps cannot—associate this "liking" with sexual desire, but he knows not to take such strange visual exchanges and inexplicable partiality lightly.

Knightley thus endorses a notion of "love" and marriage that is logical and controlled. When he speaks to Emma early in the novel about her purported matchmaking success with Mr. and Mrs. Weston, Knightley corrects her by stating that "a straight-forward, open-hearted man, like Weston, and a rationally unaffected woman, like Miss Taylor, may be safely left to manage their own concerns" (11). He is convinced that men and women do indeed acquire strong sentiments for each other, and yet, he speaks about these feelings as neither mysterious nor turbulent. Instead, Knightley imagines love relationships as rational associations that can be reasonably negotiated.[11] He specifically informs Mr. Woodhouse and the heroine that he cannot regret Mrs. Weston's departure from Hartfield "when it comes to the question of dependence or independence!—At any rate, it must be better to have only one to please, than two" (8). Knightley openly supports the marriage of Emma's former attendant not because of her strong love for Mr. Weston but because the union promises to reduce Mrs. Weston's domestic workload; it is, according to the hero, eminently logical for Mrs. Weston to marry, as she will now have fewer people to serve. He announces a similar view of marriage when he discovers Emma's plan to match Elton with Harriet. Knightley instructs the heroine that "men of sense, whatever you may chuse to say, do not want silly wives" (58). He adds that Elton specifically is "a very good sort of man . . . not at all likely to make an imprudent match. He knows the value of a good income as well as anybody. Elton may talk sentimentally, but he will act rationally" (59). Knightley upholds marriage as a rational endeavor with prominent financial implications, and he recognizes, per the discourses of Wollstonecraft and other Enlightenment feminists, that male lovers make unreasonable husbands.[12]

Knightley's regulated approach to love prevents his deterritorialization and thus allows him to maintain a fused finitude throughout the novel, but this rational view of such emotion also leads him to misunderstand impassioned behavior. For example, late in the novel, the hero incorrectly construes Frank's mysterious actions as indicators of the young man's strong feelings for the heroine. Once he convinces himself of Frank's courtship of Emma, he plans a trip to London to visit his brother, but before leaving he stops at Hartfield to confront the heroine. Austen reports that Knightley "looked at [Emma] with a glow of regard. . . . He took her hand . . . and certainly was on the point of carrying it to his lips—when, from some fancy or other, he suddenly let it go" (349).[13] Austen carefully portrays this scene to provide a glimpse of possible reciprocated feelings between Knightley and Emma, but she also highlights the hero's reluctance to voice his sentiments or pursue physical desire. The narrator concludes that Knightley and Emma "parted thorough friends, however; [Emma] could not be deceived as to the meaning of his countenance, and his unfinished gallantry;—it was all done to assure her that she had fully recovered his good opinion" (350). Emma interprets the hero's actions as a reassuring sign of his pseudo-fraternal friendship; and upon reconsideration, she views his behavior not as an indication of strong amorous feeling but as a reassurance of his benevolent approval. Knightley reverts to his identity as a fraternal guardian of the heroine and quickly departs her company to prevent any spontaneous amorous exchanges. Knightley may leave Highbury to remove himself from impulsive interactions with the heroine that could destabilize his mechanic masculinity, but his trip to London actually serves to show the hero how modern marital relations can allow a structured man to ensure his continued stability in the tumultuous culture of the nineteenth century.

Upon his return, Knightley "accidentally" meets Emma on her walk, and "for a moment or two nothing was said . . . till she found her arm drawn within his, and pressed against his heart" (385–86). After attempting to console Emma for the disappointment he assumes she must feel following the announced engagement of Frank and Jane, he speaks of his own interests and asks the heroine, "Tell me, then, have I no chance of ever succeeding?" (389–90). Austen repeats this pathetic image of the supplicant Knightley as she narrates his endeavor to propose to the heroine, "I cannot make speeches, Emma. . . . If I loved you less, I might be able to talk about it more. But you know what I am.—You hear nothing but truth from me" (390). Nancy Armstrong argues that Knightley's proposal speech "is a renunciation of the conventional language of love" (151). But Knightley renounces nothing; his truncated attempt to express his sentiments is instead a manifestation of his disciplined sexuality that cannot risk deploying the destabilizing powers of love. Austen's mechanized hero cannot follow Deleuze's instruction to "[open himself] up to love and desire (rather than the whining need to be loved that leads everyone to the psychoanalyst)" ("A Letter to a Harsh Critic" 10). Knightley accepts the ordered finitude that ensures his modernity. He becomes an influential example of the diluted yet structured modern male. Knightley values security, familiarity, and continuity; his disciplined sexuality restricts his potential to love, and his close regulation allows him to craft a fused masculinity to bridge the gaps between Burke's ancestral model of maleness, the Enlightenment conception of the proper English man, and the needs of the modernizing nation.

Emma understands the ramifications of Knightley's mechanical sexuality, and rather than forcing her longtime companion to enunciate his regard, she quickly responds to his feeble entreaty. Austen narrates that the heroine "spoke then, on being so entreated.—What did she say?—Just what she ought, of course. A lady always does.—She said enough to show there need not be despair—and to invite him to say more himself" (391). Austen's witty commentary circumvents the need to discuss openly a proposal and subsequent acceptance. This scene, moreover, details Emma's careful management of the cautious hero; she encourages her "lover" and convinces him of his inevitable success. The narrator quickly explains that "within half an hour, [Knightley] had passed from a thoroughly distressed state of mind, to something so like perfect happiness, that it could bear no other name" (392). Austen portrays our hero as an obsessive intellectual who has successfully managed to resolve tensions in his mind; Knightley is allowed to be happy, but Austen is careful to note that "no other name" could be applied to the hero's experience. Austen adds to the strangeness of this aborted proposal scene when she informs us that Knightley had traveled to London "to learn to be indifferent.—But he had gone to a wrong place. There was too much domestic happiness in his brother's house; women wore too amiable a form in it; Isabella was too much like Emma" (392). These comments imply that Knightley finally decided to voice his long-established feelings for the heroine not because he experienced a romantic epiphany, but because of the striking likeness he recently observed between Emma and Isabella. His "love" for Emma is reignited by a desire for a woman like Isabella—and the hegemonic stability she promotes for the modern English man. Knightley convinces himself that if his brother—a man from the same ancestral family—can exist safely as a married man in the modern urban world of London, he might certainly enjoy security in Highbury—as long as he marries a woman who will protect his continued sexual security by valuing ancestral customs and prevent any destabilizing eruption of desire.

Once Knightley has persuaded himself of the safety of a marriage to Emma, he does directly declare his love for her. Indeed, he announces, "[I] have been in love with you ever since you were thirteen at least" (419).[14] This comment is troubling for many reasons. First, if this claim is true, Knightley developed his affection for the heroine when she was likely still a prepubescent, reminding us of the hero's disassociation of romantic love from sexual desire. His shocking declaration, moreover, demonstrates his perpetual inability to act on his emotions, as it has taken him eight years to vocalize his ostensibly strong feelings. Knightley's long-term relationship with Emma and the Woodhouse family reduces the potential volatility of his "love," and as marriage will cause little to no change in his relationship with the heroine, he should be able to maintain indefinitely his well-ordered masculinity. Emma also reflects on their lengthy relationship and notes that Knightley "had loved her, and watched over her from a girl." She adds, "let him but continue the same Mr. Knightley to her and her father, the same Mr. Knightley to all the world; let Donwell and Hartfield lose none of their precious intercourse of friendship and confidence, and her peace would be fully secured" (376–77). Emma wants to preserve Knightley as stable and finite, and her comments suggest her understanding that his stability is indeed vital to the continued contentment of their society.

Late in the story, Emma iterates her concern with Knightley's secured identity. Following the hero's request that Emma "call [him] something else," the heroine insists, "Impossible!—I never can call you any thing but 'Mr. Knightley'" (420). He must remain the same Mr. Knightley to placate his wife, but his deliberate consistency also allows him to craft and sustain a regulated sexuality that fuses traditional and modern features of hegemonic English masculinity, eschews the destabilizing emotions of erotic love, and serves as a poignant example of the disciplined modern man. Austen ends her tale by reporting that "the wishes, the hopes, the confidence, the predictions of the small band of true friends who witnessed the ceremony, were fully answered in the perfect happiness of the union" (440). Austen emphasizes not the love between the hero and heroine but the fulfilled expectations of the friends who attended the wedding. Love is absent, while social desires are satisfied, modernity is accepted, and Knightley's finite masculinity is secured.

CHAPTER 7

Imagining Malleable Masculinity and Radical Nomadism in *Persuasion*

—◄o►—

History is always written from the sedentary point of view and in the name of a unitary State apparatus, at least a possible one, even when the topic is nomads. What is lacking is a Nomadology, the opposite of history. (Deleuze and Guattari, A Thousand Plateaus *23)*

Revolutionaries often forget, or do not like to recognize, that one wants and makes revolution out of desire, not duty. (Deleuze and Guattari, Anti-Oedipus *366)*

There is a new element in Persuasion. *[Austen] is beginning to discover that the world is larger, more mysterious, and more romantic than she had supposed. (Woolf 204)*

Virginia Woolf's comment on *Persuasion* has prompted numerous critics to explore the novelty of Austen's final completed narrative.[1] This scholarly emphasis on the freshness of *Persuasion* has in turn encouraged readers of Austen to view her prior five tales as familiar stories that commemorate the stability of England. Austen's novels, however, persistently question the security of the nation's ancestral order, and as we have seen, she exposes one feature of this social insecurity by dramatizing a crisis of English masculinity. Her works reveal a cultural anxiety about both England's future male leaders and the decay of its ostensibly established men. *Northanger Abbey* depicts the consequences of Henry Tilney's disciplined adherence to Enlightenment dictates of rationality and the tyrannical behavior of General Tilney. *Sense and Sensibility* narrates the inability of Mr. John Dashwood to sustain the unity of his landed family following the death of his father and details the struggles of Brandon and Willoughby to train their sensibilities. *Pride and Prejudice* highlights the final exemplar of the crumbling English aristocracy, but it also prefigures a newly emerging class of men associated with trade, upon whom England must now depend for important civic contributions. *Mansfield Park* offers perhaps the most powerful image of the collapse of ancestral conventions; this dark novel prefigures the fall of the Bertram family and portrays Edmund's incestuous efforts to maintain some sense of religious integrity, genteel masculinity, and an inherited cultural structure. *Emma* presents a world that has begun to accept the impending social transformation of the post-Revolutionary nation and illustrates how even Burkean men can successfully adapt to modernity. Austen's corpus has been concerned with England's transition to modernity throughout, and, thus, her last text is not a radically new direction for Austen; *Persuasion* continues Austen's depiction of this cultural shift that marks the early decades of the nineteenth century, but the novel also offers a portrait of a new kind of English man—a man who dismisses conventional modes of masculinity developed by Burke and Enlightenment thinkers in favor of a malleable sexuality that embraces the radical fluidity and social/sexual instability engendered by Deleuzian love and desire.

Wentworth, like Knightley, adapts conventional modes of English masculinity to the culture's recent innovations, but unlike the hero of *Emma,* Wentworth eventually relinquishes his reliance on the security of modern finitude to pursue volatile sensations. Knightley understands that he must adjust his aristocratic masculinity to participate actively in a post-Revolutionary culture. In *Persuasion,* Wentworth ultimately realizes that English society must necessarily become disciplinary as it continues to modernize; the naval captain opts to seek an alternative maritime existence characterized by movement and deregulation. His love for Anne exposes the disordered diversity of his masculinity, and with the heroine he seeks out a nautical lifestyle that does not depend upon the customs, organizational systems, or philosophical dictates upheld by post-Revolutionary discourses. The marriage between hero and heroine that ends *Persuasion* imagines a new world in which individuals prefer the complexity and dynamism of themselves and others to the stability and security sought by Austen's other men. The marital union of Anne and Wentworth does not negate their identities as sailor and wife; they remain subjects of early-nineteenth-century England, and their social/sexual identities as sailor and wife are integral to the success of the modernizing nation. Their marriage is, however, both a reaction to and a revolution against the antiquated world of England's ancestral culture, represented by the eroding world of Mansfield, the inertness of Mr. Woodhouse, and the decadent lifestyle of Sir Walter. The hero and heroine are not interested in the egoism and predictability of a stable hall of mirrors; they search out alterity and perpetual change. Wentworth's volatile love for Anne enables him to pursue what Deleuze and Guattari term "nomadic waves or flows of deterritorialization" (*A Thousand Plateaus* 53). While Knightley's reliance on the unifying effect of modern subjectivity necessitates his reterritorialization, Wentworth's passion for the heroine allows him to evade the regulatory forces of post-Revolutionary civilization and embrace the waves and flows of the sea—even as he remains on land.[2]

Wentworth's dynamic and malleable masculinity is especially prominent because of the pathetic status of other men in the novel; the ancestral English society that has been faltering throughout Austen's works has now reached the critical stage of decadence, and the male leaders of this society in *Persuasion* are marked by such decay. Austen may foreground the atrophy of aristocratic masculinity at the novel's start, as Sir Walter begins the narrative by reading from the Baronetage of "a still-born son, Nov. 5, 1789" (9). This "still" death of the potential Elliot heir symbolizes both the cessation of the integral family line and the demise of an ancestral masculinity cherished by Burke, the Bertrams, and Sir Elliot. Burke's vision of a sustained connection to the nation's heritage has failed; the Elliot heritage must now accept external influences, as its men literally and metaphorically have become still and impotent. Burke's worst fears are now realized; as he muses in his *Reflections,* "all is to be changed. All the pleasing illusions, which made power gentle, and obedience liberal, which harmonized the different shades of life, and which, by a bland assimilation, incorporated into politics the sentiments which beautify and soften private society, are to be dissolved" (128). The powerful yet gentle aristocratic English men who administered the nation's inherited hegemonic culture are putrefying. Austen's text specifically demonstrates the inability of Sir Elliot and his heir to accept modern social developments, including new kinds of identities and relations. *Persuasion* portrays the ancestral man of England in a state of decay that is distinct from the desperate nostalgia of the Bertram males and the benign idiocy of Mr. Woodhouse; moreover, the traditional culture that had buttressed such archaic men is now itself deteriorating, exposing the crass artifice that once solidified the hegemonic function of aristocratic men.

Austen immediately prefigures the death of Burke's model of the English man with her character sketch of the novel's extant practitioner of such archaic male sexuality. Sir Walter is the paragon of this decaying masculinity, and as the narrator explains, "vanity was the beginning and the end of [his] character, vanity of person and of situation" (10). He is only able to navigate the world through his own egotistical concerns, and his egoism prevents him from appreciating alterity. His ignorance in isolation even threatens the sustainability of the domestic domain that secures his aristocratic standing.[3] When his decadent lifestyle leads to a substantial debt that forces him to have action taken, he allows his lawyer to rent his ancestral home to Admiral and Mrs. Croft, who have recently returned from the war with France.

Lady Russell reflects on this decision and offers an informative comment on both Sir Walter and post-Revolutionary England's aristocratic community. She muses, "what will he be doing, in fact, but what very many of our first families have done,—or ought to do?—There will be nothing singular in his case" (18). Lady Russell's remarks reveal the publicly recognized demise of England's traditional culture; it is no longer anomalous for aristocratic families to rent their estates to individuals of new money. The ancestral domestic sphere that once symbolized the historical power of England's elite, à la Permberley, has been abandoned and transformed into an equity-producing investment. And unlike Knightley's move from Donwell to Hartfield, the Elliots are forced to leave their ancestral home out of financial exigencies and must now assume rented quarters.

The impending heir of Kellynch, Sir William Walter Elliot, initially appears to share Sir Walter's disinterest in preserving the cultural legacy of the family estate.[4] He married a woman of new money prior to the start of the narrative, but the narrator indicates that he is now interested in renewing his connections with his relations by marrying one of his single cousins. Anne, his presumed choice as a second wife, provides a prominent commentary on her cousin, explaining that he "was rational, discreet, polished,—but he was not open. There was never any burst of feeling, any warmth of indignation or delight, at the evil or good of others." The narrataor concludes that "this, to Anne, was a decided imperfection" (152). Austen continually highlights Mr. Elliot's ability to perform standard Enlightenment rationality and predictable Burkean gallantries, but like Knightley his behavior is hackneyed and mechanical—devoid of dynamism and spontaneity. Mr. Elliot appreciates the utility of both chivalric and rational activities as strategies that enable him to achieve egotistical ends. Austen presents Mr. Elliot as the future of the male aristocracy. Her portrayal of the territorialized Kellynch heir reveals how social dictates for appropriate English maleness have disciplined his body and desires. His pursuit of new money only promoted his reterritorialization, as he now must return to his ancestral family to acquire new monetary resources through a sanctioned marriage.

The narrator's initial portrait of Wentworth appears strikingly similar to her sketch of Mr. Elliot: Wentworth is ambitious and industrious, and he focuses his energies around the pursuit of Anne. In Austen's retrospective account of Wentworth and Anne's early relationship, the narrator casts her hero as a charming romantic figure who is both confident and enthusiastic; however, *Persuasion*'s account of the early trials of Wentworth reminds us that fabulously romantic men like Darcy are no longer viable. We learn that almost eight years ago, Wentworth, "not immediately employed, had come into Somersetshire. . . . He was, at that time, a remarkably fine young man, with a great deal of intelligence, spirit and brilliancy" (29). Austen notes that Anne and Wentworth "were gradually acquainted, and when acquainted, rapidly and deeply in love" (30). The narrator momentarily adopts the style and narrative technique of Sir Walter Scott's popular romances: Wentworth is a mysterious yet common man who has ingratiated himself to a wealthy and powerful family; he is "a young man, who had nothing but himself to recommend him, and no hopes of attaining affluence, but in the chances of a most uncertain profession, and no connexions to secure even his farther rise in that profession . . . a stranger without alliance or fortune" (30). Austen casts her hero as a humble man with lofty aspirations who, like Mr. Elliot, eagerly seeks advancement. Not surprisingly, Wentworth auditions various conventional modes of English masculinity in order to achieve hegemonic social/sexual security.

Despite his mundane and fortuneless status, Wentworth adopts the optimism advocated by Enlightenment thinkers like Godwin and embodied by men like Gardiner and Bingley; at other times, it is tempting to view Wentworth as a devoted man of reason like Henry Tilney. Wentworth indeed initially appears to support Godwin's claim that "fortitude is a habit of mind that grows out of a sense of our independence." Austen's hero, like Godwin, believes in the preeminence of the independent man, and he is confident of his ability to advance himself by "consulting and providing for his own subsistence" (*Enquiry* II: 10). Austen, likewise, explains that "Captain Wentworth had no fortune. . . . But, he was confident that he should soon be rich;—full of life and ardour, he knew that he should soon have a ship, and soon be on a station that would lead to every thing he wanted." He follows the model of Jacobin heroes who remain convinced in the efficacy of their individual desires and efforts. While Anne is attracted to this impressive young man and specifically admires his "confidence," Lady Russell, the heroine's trusted advisor, translates Wentworth's "confidence" as a "sanguine temper, and fearlessness of mind"; she concludes that although he "was brilliant, he was headstrong" (30–31).[5] The same brash enthusiasm that Godwin champions and lures Anne frightens the cautious Lady Russell, who persuades our heroine to dismiss the ambitious but financially insecure sailor. Wentworth promptly "[leaves] the country in consequence," but he does not immediately abandon his commitment to conventional modes of English masculinity (31). He no longer appears as a mysterious romantic hero, but Austen continues to present her hero as an industrious man who has earned his wealth and merit.

Austen's stereotypical early depictions of Wentworth have led critics like Andrew H. Wright to argue that the hero is often obsessed with "over-conventionality" (151). He appears briefly as a romantic figure and soon adopts Enlightenment dictates of self-improvement; Jocelyn Harris even dubs Wentworth the descendant of the archetypal conservative patriarch, Sir Charles Grandison. Harris explains that Wentworth's "dashing naval career displays the martial hero," and "his rescue of Anne from the suffocating embraces of the child or his concern for her fatigue are knightly and gentle enough" (204). Wentworth can perform and adopt various conventional masculine behaviors, and Austen's early portraits of the young man demonstrate how he benefits from such hegemonic male identities. Indeed, Wentworth enjoys the success promised by the Enlightenment's advocacy of individual industry and improvement. Austen announces that "all his sanguine expectations, all his confidence had been justified. His genius and ardour had seemed to foresee and to command his prosperous path. . . . He had distinguished himself, and early gained the other step in rank—and must now, by successive captures, have made a handsome fortune" (33).[6] Wentworth, like the farmers of Jacobin novels, has labored to garner his success, but unlike such agricultural men and Austen's own aspiring men like Bingley, Gardiner, and Mr. Weston, Wentworth has achieved his accomplishments while serving in the navy, and the national importance of his service enhances the value of his body and industry. Wentworth has obtained access to the national community by serving the national community, and the turbulent instability of the war-ridden seas proves vital to his social/sexual subjectivity.

While his active duty in the military involved great efforts and industrious labor associated with the Enlightenment ideal of English masculinity, Wentworth reverts to hyper-conventional chivalric behavior upon his return to England. During his visit to Uppercross, Austen casts her hero as a chivalric figure who can behave gallantly and perform noble deeds. The Miss Musgroves are promptly enamored of Wentworth. They speak of his "pleasant manner" that they believe demonstrated how "he felt all the motive of their attention just as he ought," and they observe that "he had looked and said every thing with such exquisite grace" (55). The Miss Musgroves conceive of our hero as an elegant man, and their family finds "charming manners in Captain Wentworth, no shyness or reserve" (59). The Miss Musgroves' comments remind us of Harris's assertion that Austen presents Wentworth as the next Grandison; moreover, the young women's remarks also recall Burke's model of a gallant and sensible man. Wentworth's charming early behavior at Uppercross more closely resembles Burke's portrait of an effete military man whom Wollstonecraft rebukes than the virile man idealized by the feminist thinker. Austen's portrayal of her hero suggests that he is both knowledgeable of Burke's model of masculinity and is capable of rehearsing chivalric behavior; he even joins Charles Musgrove on various gentlemanly shooting expeditions. He also maintains this chivalric persona when he encounters Anne. During a visit with the Crofts, Wentworth apologizes to Anne for almost assuming her chair, reciting, "I beg your pardon, madam, this is your seat." Austen reports that "though [Anne] immediately drew back with a decided negative, he was not to be induced to sit down again." Wentworth rehearses conventional chivalric masculinity, and even persists in the appropriateness of his actions, but the narrator explains that "Anne did not wish for more of such looks and speeches. . . . [his] cold politeness, his ceremonious grace" (72). Anne's reflections indicate both her dislike of gallant rituals and the visibly artificial nature of Wentworth's performance.

Austen's most explicit comment on Wentworth's hyper-conventional behavior follows her hero's eager announcement of his intentions to marry. Austen relates: "it was now [Wentworth's] object to marry. He was rich, and being turned on shore, fully intended to settle as soon as he could be properly tempted . . . ready to fall in love with all the speed which a clear head and quick taste could allow" (62). He presents his impending marriage as the final step in confirming his hegemonic status as a stable and successful English man. Wentworth informs his sister that he is "quite ready to make a foolish match. Any body between fifteen and thirty may have me for asking. A little beauty, and a few smiles, and a few compliments to the navy, and I am a lost man" (62). Wentworth appears willing to behave irrationally, but he is nonetheless methodical in his planning. He will act foolishly for the purpose of acquiring the wife who will secure his standing as an established English man; moreover, the qualities he desires in his future wife reveal the conflicted and synthetic nature of his own masculinity. Wentworth explains to his sister that he seeks a woman who will have "a strong mind, with sweetness of manner" (62). Austen's naval hero imagines his appropriate wife as a hybrid female who is not only confident and intellectual but also tender and sensitive. His insistence that his spouse should be firm of mind recalls the male behavior advocated by Wollstonecraft, while his belief that a woman must be tender and sensitive reflects Burke's investment in female delicacy. Johnson points out that Wentworth "is in fact caught within highly charged tensions about women's manners, and his description of the ideal woman is oxymoronic, because however much he may desire 'strength' in women, he considers it essentially inconsistent with the sweetness he also exacts" (*Jane Austen* 150). Johnson is correct to emphasize Wentworth's "oxymoronic" expectations for a future wife; and while such expectations demonstrate the contrarieties of proper English femininity, they also allow Austen to highlight Wentworth's adherence to diverse models of conventional English maleness.

Wentworth rearticulates his chivalric attitudes toward women when he asserts that he "would never willingly admit any ladies on board a ship of his" because he believes it is impossible "with all one's efforts, and all one's sacrifices, to make the accommodations on board, such as women ought to have." Wentworth affirms an archaic notion of fragile femininity and responds to his brother-in-law's harsh rebukes by asserting that "there can be no want of gallantry . . . in rating the claims of women to every personal comfort *high*" (68). Wentworth defends the actions of a chivalric man who protects and pampers elegant women, but his sister promptly critiques his antiquated views. Mrs. Croft chides Wentworth, dubbing his ideas about women's need for elaborate accommodations as "all idle refinement" (68). She instructs him, "I hate to hear you talking so, like a fine gentleman, and as if women were all fine ladies, instead of rational creatures" (69). Mrs. Croft's comments directly address the hero's conventional behavior; he has been acting like a fine gentleman, and his sister identifies this performance as artificial. Admiral Croft concludes that when Wentworth "has got a wife, he will sing a different tune. When he is married. . . . we shall have him very thankful to any body that will bring him his wife" (69). Wentworth will not allow such patronizing predictions and immediately declares, "Now I have done. . . . When once married people begin to attack me with, 'Oh! you will think differently, when you are married,' I can only say, 'No, I shall not;' and then they say again, 'Yes, you will,' and there is an end of it." (69–70). Wentworth's closing remarks in this discussion may appear trite, but they effectively illustrate the artificiality of his sexual identity; he knows he is rehearsing established modes of masculinity, and his comments expose the routine he must execute. And yet, while Austen's other heroes learn to accept such territorialized roles and the disciplined existences they ensure, Wentworth eventually recognizes the inherent discipline of his territorialization and learns to deterritorialize himself from such social/sexual regulations.

But Wentworth is able to accomplish his deterritorialization only because of his love relationship with Anne, and in the early portions of the narrative the hero is still a bitter individual who appears as a stereotypical melancholic man; the narrator notes that "he had not forgiven Anne Elliot. She had used him ill; deserted and disappointed him" (62). Anne is also conscious of Wentworth's resentment, and Austen relates that her heroine "felt the utter impossibility, from her knowledge of his mind, that he could be unvisited by remembrance any more than herself. There must be the same immediate association of thought, though she was very far from conceiving it to be of equal pain" (63). Anne is certain that Wentworth maintains strong memories of their earlier romance, and her belief proves true when Wentworth unexpectedly encounters the heroine at her sister's home. Austen narrates, "the surprise of finding himself almost alone with Anne Elliot, deprived his manners of their usual composure" (78). This scene serves as our first indication of Wentworth's extant feelings for the heroine; his sensations overwhelm his composed behavior, revealing cracks in his sexuality that well-regulated men like Knightley or Mr. Elliot would never allow to become visible. Wentworth is discomposed because of his powerful amorous emotions for the heroine—emotions that Deleuze and Guattari suggest prompt individuals to divulge "the multiplicities [the beloved] encloses within himself or herself which may be of an entirely different nature. To join them to mine, to make them penetrate mine, and for me to penetrate the other person's" (*Thousand Plateaus* 35). Wentworth's passions for the heroine enable him to unveil and accept the diversity of Anne *and* disclose his own multiplicity. The artificial singularity and crafted security of his subjectivity become engulfed by the malleability he comes to embrace within himself and his lover.

Wentworth is indeed susceptible to the potency of amorous emotions, and while he clings to conventional male behavior early in the novel, Austen soon presents him acting as neither a Burkean man nor a coldly rational individual. For example, when he finds Anne hampered by her ill-tempered nephew, he removes the young boy from her back. Austen relates that Anne "found herself in the state of being released from [the child]; some one was taking him from her." She is surprised to find that Wentworth has been her "rescuer," and the narrator stresses both "his kindness in stepping forward to her relief" and "the silence in which it had passed" (79). Wentworth's benevolent action does not follow the conventions of chivalric heroism or sentimental masculinity; rather, his is a quiet deed of concern. He behaves in a similar manner during the return from their lengthy walk to the Hayters. Anne relates that "she saw how her own character was considered by Captain Wentworth; and there had been just that degree of feeling and curiosity about her in his manner, which must give her extreme agitation" (87). His feeling leads him to arrange for Anne to ride home from the outing with the beneficent Crofts. Austen informs us that "Captain Wentworth, without saying a word, turned to her, and quietly obliged her to be assisted into the carriage." Anne is clearly affected by this gesture of kindness and reflects, "Though condemning her for the past . . . he could not see her suffer, without the desire of giving her relief. It was a remainder of former sentiment" (89). Wentworth's gestures are marked by neither virility nor heroism; he does not carry Anne or provide her with a pristine transportation. And yet his actions are also not the result of rational deliberations; he instead demonstrates compassion for Anne. Wentworth's behavior reminds us of Foucault's theory of the aesthetic of the existence, which "implies complex relationships with others insofar [that] this *ethos* of freedom is also a way of caring for others" ("The Ethics" 287). Austen prefigures how Wentworth's aesthetic is ultimately not egotistically organized around chivalric or Enlightenment conventions of hegemonic masculinity; his social/sexual subjectivity instead revolves around his care for others—a compassion that enhances his ability to appreciate diversity in himself, others, and new physical locations.

The artifice of Wentworth's early masculine performances deteriorates prominently during the expedition to Lyme, where he reunites with his nomadic naval colleagues. His behavior becomes notably less conventional at this seaside locale, and as Wentworth acts more freely he becomes more receptive of his own feelings for Anne. Indeed, the atrophy of the hero's rote masculinity appears to mirror the landscape of Lyme, whose "principal street [is] almost hurrying into the water" (93). This mingling of earth and sea emblematizes Austen's depiction of the naval community and its ability to transfer the values of a maritime existence to a domestic setting. Anne is very impressed by the hospitality of Wentworth's naval friends, and the heroine indicates that "nothing could be more pleasant than their desire of considering the whole party as friends of their own, because the friends of Captain Wentworth" (95). She is drawn to the unaffected charm of the Harvilles, noting how different it is from "the usual style of give-and-take invitations, and dinners of formality and display" (96). The domesticated naval community, unlike Anne's antiquated family, is not interested in elaborate social gatherings; moreover, Wentworth acts with a cordial simplicity and a sincere concern for others when he is surrounded by his naval colleagues. The men and women of the navy are not able to abandon social identities and regulations, but as Roger Sales argues, "the naval officers . . . inhabit a world which values comradeship or partnership" (182). Wentworth's friends, unlike Bingley or the Coles, are not concerned with sustaining their recently elevated social positions; they instead, as Tony Tanner points out, "reconstitute a meaningful domesticity, re-create the idea of home, [and] ultimately redefine the notion of society itself" (224). Austen's portrayal of the navy anticipates both a new kind of domestic life and new social possibilities that Austen's corpus had not earlier imagined. The naval community revises the standard hegemonic function of the domestic sphere. The men of the navy have already solidified their importance in the nation; thus, they have no need to establish their sexual stability by maintaining hegemonic control at home. And while Harville and Benwick cling to various conventional conceptions about men and women, Austen highlights the geniality of the men and women of the naval community.

Austen favorably presents the naval community as nomadic packs; its members are not tied to specific domestic settings or tethered to structured social identities. Deleuze and Guattari theorize that nomads exist and move as packs in which they enjoy "absolute movement." They explain that "nomads have no points, paths, or land, even though they do by all appearances" (*Thousand Plateaus* 381). Austen's portrayal of Wentworth's naval comrades emphasizes their versatility and acceptance of diverse experiences and people; they welcome unknown visitors without reservation, and do not conceive of their "home" as a fixed point of stasis. This radical flexibility and open reception of others displayed by the navy accentuates the conventionality of Wentworth's earlier actions. Moreover, his reunion with the Harvilles also allows us to appreciate Wentworth's compassion for his maritime friends. We learn, through Anne's conversation with Captain Harville, of the hero's dutiful and empathetic service to the melancholic Benwick.[7] Following the death of Benwick's fiancée, Fanny Harville, Wentworth offered to inform his friend of the deplorable news. Harville tells Anne that "Nobody could do it, but that good fellow, (pointing to Captain Wentworth). . . . [He] travelled night and day till he got to Portsmouth, rowed off to the Grappler that instant, and never left the poor fellow for a week" (105). Harville's story suggests the hero's knowledge of the tradition of male sentiment, but this account also reminds us how Wentworth's care for others in the nomadic naval pack is an integral feature of his aesthetic of existence. Wentworth's care of his self involves his concern for others, and his time in Lyme prompts him to reconsider the care he has displayed toward Louisa Musgrove.

Louisa's near-tragic fall from the Lyme Cobb encourages Wentworth to reevaluate his relationship with the young woman as well as his conventional and contradictory expectations for women. He previously informed Louisa that his "first wish for all, whom I am interested in, is that they should be firm," but when the young woman announces her intention to jump a second time from the seaside wall, the hero "advised her against it, [he] thought the jar too great" (86). Louisa, however, persists, and jumping "too precipitate by half a second . . . was taken up lifeless!" Wentworth is shocked by Louisa's fall and looks upon her "with a face as pallid as her own, in an agony of silence" (106). The hero endures an overwhelming emotional experience, while Anne illustrates her resourcefulness by calling for a surgeon. Wentworth "caught the word; it seemed to rouse him at once, and saying only 'True, true, a surgeon this instant'" (107). Louisa is not well served by Wentworth's conflicting desires for female firmness and delicacy—neither her strength nor her fragility prevents her fall. Anne's adaptability, however, enables the heroine to manage this moment of crisis and disruption. Her actions simulate the versatility required of the naval community, and Wentworth appreciates her flexibility. He even requests that Anne remain with the Harvilles to assist in the care of Louisa, explaining, "if Anne will stay, no one so proper, so capable as Anne! . . . You will stay, I am sure; you will stay and nurse her'; cried he, turning to her and speaking with a glow, and yet a gentleness, which seemed almost restoring the past" (111). While the visit to Lyme begins with Anne's admiration of Wentworth's naval community, by the end of their outing Wentworth observes the maritime values of the heroine. The lovers had earlier ceased their relations because of severe class distinctions, but Anne and Wentworth now appear comfortable with the social/sexual subjectivities allowed by a nomadic lifestyle.

Austen highlights the effects of Wentworth's sustained affection for Anne following his arrival in Bath.[8] When he first encounters the heroine in Bath, the narrator records that "he was more obviously struck and confused by the sight of [Anne], than she had ever observed before; he looked quite red." Austen adds that "[t]ime had changed him, or Louisa had changed him. There was consciousness of some sort or other. He looked very well, not as if he had been suffering in health or spirits . . . yet it was Captain Wentworth not comfortable, not easy, not able to feign that he was" (166). Wentworth is again discomposed by Anne; the "multiplicities of multiplicities" that, according to Deleuze and Guattari, become manifest in a love relationship, inhibit the hero from sustaining himself as a stable man. The familiar conventions of male behavior upon which Wentworth had previously relied to orchestrate his conduct are no longer functional. His passion for Anne overwhelms such models of hegemonic English masculinity; he suddenly lacks an organizing mechanism around which to order his sexuality, and while he offers Anne his umbrella to protect her during a walk in the rain, he does not protest when she refuses. He quickly abandons his chivalric routine, as he does when Anne later spots the hero amongst a group of naval officers.

The narrator relates that he "was preparing only to bow and pass on, but [Anne's] gentle 'How do you do?' brought him out of the straight line to stand near her, and make enquiries in return, in spite of the formidable father and sister in the back ground" (171). His feelings for Anne prevent him from reverting to secure/securing modes of English masculinity like Austen's other men; he has allowed love "to abolish [the] subjectification" that Deleuze and Guattari claim leads individuals to assume territorialized modes of disciplined behavior (*Thousand Plateaus* 134).[9] Deleuze and Guattari argue that "every love is an exercise in depersonalization on a body without organs yet to be formed" (*Thousand Plateaus* 35). Austen emphasizes Wentworth's disavowal of conventional masculine artifice that would establish him as a hegemonic social/sexual subject in favor of the malleable masculinity devoid of regulatory structures like machines or organs. The narrator reports that the heroine "was expecting him to go every moment; but he did not; he seemed in no hurry to leave her" (172).[10] He again demonstrates his sustained care for Anne—a concern that remains integral to the development of his own aesthetic of existence. The heroine recognizes his compassion and concludes that "all, all declared that he had a heart returning to her at least; that anger, resentment, avoidance, were no more; and that they were succeeded, not merely by friendship and regard, but by the tenderness of the past; yes, some share of the tenderness of the past. She could not contemplate the change as implying less.—He must love her" (175). Anne, unlike Emma and Fanny, does not imagine her husband as a guardian or friend; Anne presents the hero as a committed and passionate lover who risks his security by revealing his emotions. Wentworth is sensitive to the depersonalizing forces of desire and their effects upon both him and his beloved. While Anne is confident of Wentworth's love, the hero must negotiate one final obstacle before he can enunciate his feelings for the heroine.

Mr. Elliot's inconsistent courtship of Anne causes Wentworth notable anxiety during the latter portion of the novel. The hero initially observes a strange familiarity between the heroine and her family heir during the Lyme outing, but his concern escalates following the concert in Bath.[11] During intermission, the narrator reports that Anne and Wentworth were engaged in a cordial dialogue, and the hero "even looked down towards the bench, as if he saw a place on it well worth occupying"; however, "at that moment, a touch on her shoulder obliged Anne to turn round.—It came from Mr. Elliot." Mr. Elliot's ill-timed request for an Italian translation greatly affects Wentworth, who offers the heroine "a reserved yet hurried sort of farewell. 'He must wish her good night. He was going—he should get home as fast as he could. . . . [T]here is nothing worth my staying for'" (180). Wentworth's recent expressions of sincere emotions have left him vulnerable to destabilizing experiences, including envy, which threaten his tenuous aesthetic of existence. He has exposed himself to a diversity of powerful feelings, and Mr. Elliot's interruption compels the hero to revert to established models of masculine propriety to save face. Anne is not long in discerning the reason for her lover's abrupt departure: "Jealousy of Mr. Elliot! It was the only intelligible motive. Captain Wentworth jealous of her affection!" (180). Wentworth's conveyance of affection will prove essential to his efforts to deterritorialize himself from the social dictates for appropriate English maleness, but this brief scene illustrates how jealous sentiments easily encourage him to become reterritorialized by conventional modes of English masculinity.

Wentworth does not immediately dismiss the ceremonious male behavior that once again inhibits his ability to express emotions.[12] Austen brilliantly positions her hero struggling with envy while he quietly remains within ear-shot of Anne's discussion with Harville on the duration of amorous feelings. Wentworth takes this opportunity to author his climactic love letter in which he reveals the volatility of his passions for the heroine:[13]

> I can listen no longer in silence. I must speak to you by such means as are within my reach. You pierce my soul. I am half agony, half hope. Tell me not that I am too late, that such precious feelings are gone for ever. I offer myself to you again with a heart even more your own, than when you almost broke it eight years and a half ago. Dare not say that man forgets sooner than woman, that his love has an earlier death. I have loved none but you. Unjust I may have been, weak and resentful I have been, but never inconstant. You alone have brought me to Bath. For you alone I think and plan. . . . I am every instant hearing something which overpowers me. (223)

Wentworth adopts the language of a lover, using a vocabulary of passion unprecedented in Austen's earlier narratives. He announces the power of his extant feelings for Anne—feelings that he claims have remained constant. He acknowledges his weak and embittered behavior that engendered resentment, but he also explains that Anne—and not a post-Revolutionary social discourse on appropriate maleness—serves as the sole motivation for his recent actions. He willingly admits that he is overwhelmed by his emotions for the heroine, and he again offers himself as a vulnerable lover. Wentworth's powerful revelation exposes the breadth of his emotions, and his exposure is both potent and dangerous: it illustrates the sincerity of his feelings, but it also promotes the instability and pliability of his sexuality.

His letter is the most open disclosure of amorous emotion by any man in Austen's corpus, and his passionate expression proves vital to his deter-ritorialized, nomadic lifestyle. The narrative immediately foreshadows this unplanned movement when the hero, soon after delivering his letter, approaches Anne and Charles Musgrove. Charles inquires about Went-worth's intended direction, thinking he may be able to relinquish the duty of escorting Anne; when Charles asks, "Captain Wentworth, which way are you going? only to Gay-street, or farther up the town?" Wentworth promptly responds, "I hardly know" (226). Wentworth's lack of knowledge about his future plans prefigures his impending domestic life with Anne—a life that will not be structured around definitively ordered plans or dictated by a decaying social system. Immediately following Wentworth's announcement of undirected movement, Austen relates that the lovers "exchanged again those feelings and those promises which had once before seemed to secure every thing, but which had been followed by so many, many years of division and estrangement. There they returned again into the past . . . more tender, more tried, more fixed in a knowledge of each other's character, truth, and attachment; more equal to act, more justified in acting" (226–27). Anne and Wentworth renew their amorous emotions, but they are now more "tender" and "tried." Wentworth's letter has clearly affected his lover, and the hero maintains that "of what he had then written, nothing was to be retracted or qualified. He persisted in having loved none but her." Wentworth even references his attempt to mask his passion for Anne with artifice; he announces that "he had meant to forget her, and believed it to be done. He had imagined himself indifferent, when he had only been angry" (227). Wentworth exposes both his constancy and his prior pretense. He openly declares his perpetual desire for the heroine, but he also admits his earlier efforts to obscure his volatile desire.

Wentworth is self-conscious about his earlier dependence upon conventional versions of English masculinity to shield himself from the diverse experiences engendered by love; moreover, he now willingly acts upon his desires for Anne. Wentworth explains that he traveled to Bath so that he "could at least put [himself] in the way of happiness." He adds that in Bath "[he] could exert [himself], [he] could do something" (229). Austen's hero deliberately acts to pursue his own amorous desires, prominently distinguishing himself from other men of Austen's corpus who happen upon love. His behavior is governed by love—not by Enlightenment notions of rationality or Burkean conceptions of chivalry. He abandons such models of English masculinity and opens himself to the unpredictable flows of amorous desires when he questions, "Was it unpardonable to think it worth my while to come? and to arrive with some degree of hope? You were single. It was possible that you might retain the feelings of the past, as I did" (229–30). Wentworth identifies himself as lover of Anne, and his Deleuzian love allows him to reveal his own diversity, experience the multiplicity of his beloved, and evade the modern cultural discipline that urges men to create finite social/sexual subjectivities.

Wentworth's openness even allows him to revisit his former feelings of bitterness toward the heroine. He tells Anne that for many years he "could think of [her] only as one who had yielded, who had given [him] up, who had been influenced by any one rather than by [him]" (231). His confession reminds us of the hero's prior reliance upon Enlightenment notions of individual responsibility that instructed men and women to act as independent agents and earn their successes by laborious effort. He could fathom Anne's obedience to her family only as weakness, but he now admits, "I did not understand you. I shut my eyes, and would not understand you, or do you justice" (233). Wentworth's earlier strategy for managing his strong passions for Anne required him to dismiss her behavior as irrational and unworthy, effectively protecting himself from his emotions for the heroine. He again discusses his past adherence to conventional Enlightenment notions of merit and industry when he explains that he "[had] been used to the gratification of believing myself to earn every blessing that I enjoyed. I have valued myself on honourable toils and just rewards" (233). Austen's hero, like the farmers of Jacobin novels, felt that he could earn his rewards through toil, but as he concludes, he "like other great men under reverses . . . must endeavour to subdue my mind to my fortune. I must learn to brook being happier than I deserve" (233). Wentworth's emotional language illustrates the conventionality of his previous mindset and behavior, but his love for Anne negates the relevance of such cultural dictates. He realizes that he will now experience more happiness than either his individual industry merits or his rational capacity justifies. Wentworth accepts an aesthetic of existence free from the regulations of Enlightenment or Burkean codes of masculinity. He is nonetheless an established man, "with five-and-twenty thousand pounds, and as high in his profession as merit and activity could place him" (234). He is a professional sailor, and this social status ensures his participation in the nation; yet, unlike the other men of Austen's corpus, Wentworth no longer depends upon a hegemonic social/sexual identity. His elastic aesthetic of existence instead revolves around a nautical lifestyle marked by nomadic flows and the care of himself and his lover.[14]

Austen may prefigure such a migratory way of life by not placing Anne and Wentworth within a stable and permanent domestic setting. Prewitt Brown notes that "*Persuasion* is the only one of [Austen's] novels that ends with a vague ignorance of where the hero and heroine are going to live, and even of what the years will bring for them" (140). Austen does not install Anne and Wentworth in a secure domain, but she does acknowledge the power of amorous emotions to guide their behavior. In classic Austenian style, she questions, "Who can be in doubt of what followed? When any two young people take it into their heads to marry, they are pretty sure by perseverance to carry their point" (233). Austen's comment may appear strikingly similar to the witty quips that close many of her narratives, but this closing remark actually accentuates the potency of Anne and Wentworth's desires. Unlike the "lovers" of *Northanger Abbey* and *Emma*, Anne and Wentworth "carry their point"; they are not stalled by belated parental approval. In addition, Austen does not qualify Anne and Wentworth's happiness as she does for many of the marriages that close *Sense and Sensibility, Mansfield Park,* and *Pride and Prejudice.* The future of *Persuasion*'s lovers is strikingly ambiguous, and the lack of their definitive plan reminds us of the undulations inherent in their maritime relationship.

Austen's closing remarks highlight both the radical movement and the powerful desires involved in Wentworth and Anne's marriage. The narrator concludes that "Anne was tenderness itself . . . [and] the dread of a future war all that could dim her sunshine. She gloried in being a sailor's wife, but she must pay the tax of quick alarm for belonging to that profession, which is, if possible, more distinguished in its domestic virtues than in its national importance" (237). Anne and Wentworth accept the realities involved in their nautical existence, and according to Austen, the values associated with this lifestyle are more important in the domestic sphere. Wentworth and Anne, however, are not rooted to a single domicile; they must instead accept the wisdom of Mrs. Croft's prophecy that "none of us expect to be in smooth water all our days" (69). Anne and Wentworth's acceptance of inevitable motion—and the radical malleability it requires—allows them the opportunity to seek a nomadic life, removed from the territorializing structures of a nation that is experiencing both decay and modernization. Unlike Austen's prior couples, Anne and Wentworth do not uphold the relevance of an ancestral culture or attempt to advance Enlightenment doctrines; they are always already prepared to leave the discipline of post-Revolutionary England. Austen suggests throughout the novel that the lovers' feelings for each other engender personal insecurity, and the close of the novel may anticipate the radical impact of their relationship upon English society. Deleuze and Guattari point out that "love and desire exhibit reactionary, or else revolutionary, indices . . . where persons give way to decoded flows of desire" (*Anti-Oedipus* 366). Anne and Wentworth do not, of course, organize aggressive countercultural movements, but they do embody potentially revolutionary desires for each other. They model a Deleuzian existence that encourages men and women to pursue the multiplicity of love and the complexity of packs rather than hegemonic relationships and the organized discipline of modern England.

Austen does not provide us with a complete Nomadology as theorized by Deleuze and Guattari, and yet she does offer an image of what such a nomadic life might entail, especially for sexualized lovers in a modern nation. Deleuze and Guattari explain that the "nomad can be called the Deterritorialized par excellence, . . . because there is no reterritorialization *afterward*" (*Thousand Plateaus* 381). Wentworth and Anne serve as compelling examples of this migratory concept, as they avoid the reterritorizalization inherent in the acceptance of a stable domestic life. Austen's lovers resist the lure of social security in favor of the mobility of the sea, and as Deleuze and Guattari conclude, "the maximum deterritorialization appears in the tendency of maritime and commercial towns to separate off from the backcountry, from the countryside" (*Thousand Plateaus* 432). Anne and Wentworth achieve such separation from the reterritorializing forces of modern capitalism and post-Revolutionary nationalism that encourage men and women to accept individualized and functional civic roles. Wentworth and Anne embrace both the dynamism of their malleable lifestyle and the destabilizing power of their love. Wentworth specifically allows himself to experience amorous passions, exposing the diversity of his masculinity; unlike Austen's other men, he does not fix his sexuality—it remains in flux and perpetually nomadic. He reveals, by expressing his amorous emotions for Anne, the variety involved in his social/sexual subjectivity, and his awareness of this multiplicity enables him to live a nomadic existence with his wife, pursuing potentially revolutionary desires.

CONCLUSION

Austen's initial portrait of Wentworth highlights his masculine conventionality, but the naval hero's Deleuzian love for Anne ultimately allows him to
accept his own multiplicity as well as the diversity of others. Wentworth is an
anomaly in Austen's fiction, as her other heroes strive to develop aesthetics
of existence that are stable and closely regulated. Her male figures navigate
the post-Revolutionary discursive field that produces divergent desires
for appropriate English masculinity; they attempt to establish themselves
as hegemonic national men by negotiating the dictates of Burkean and
Enlightenment thinkers. And her men ensure their social/sexual security by
eschewing the overwhelming complications engendered by love. Anne and
Wentworth, however, disregard the hegemony of early-nineteenth-century
domesticity in favor of the dynamism of a nautical existence characterized
by compassionate reciprocity, turbulence, and a proximity to the sea. The
modern English society desperately attempts to reinstall structure, order,
and discipline following the Napoleonic Wars, and correspondingly, the
nation promotes fixed yet conflicting versions of organized masculinity to
develop a new generation of disciplined and responsible male leaders. Wentworth circumvents such discipline, as he and Anne embark on a maritime
journey that is sure to include fluctuations and instability.

The England in which Austen wrote understandably sought to return to
a mythical organic community of safety and stability that supposedly existed
sometime prior to the turbulence of the French Revolution—and her stories
are still upheld as fictional visions of such a culture. She portrays characters
who mold themselves as static social/sexual subjects in order to help sustain
the unity of the nation, its nexus to the past, and its future prosperity. While
criticism has concentrated on the representations of her female characters
and their struggles to negotiate various social expectations, she, as we have

seen, also documents the efforts of her men to pursue secure social/sexual identities. Austen's male figures strive to follow different instructions for crafting masculinities that will reputedly ensure the future prosperity of the English nation, but her narratives also reveal the consequences of such attempts. Her male characters discipline themselves by dismissing the volatile possibilities of love to achieve a stable mode of hegemonic masculinity preferred by the nation, but their suppression of amorous desires also inevitably leaves them mechanized and reterritorialized. *Persuasion* narrates the collapse of England's ancestral culture, and Austen, rather than positioning Anne and Wentworth in a rebuilt domestic domain, sends her hero and heroine to the sea, where they will accept a new life rooted in movement, malleability, and multiplicity. Wentworth and Anne model a Deleuzian love relationship and embody features of Deleuze and Guattari's deterritorialized nomad; Austen's lovers resist the reterritorialization of modern capitalism by embracing the complexity produced by their powerful amorous emotions and avoiding the stasis of a permanent domestic dwelling.

Austen continues her literary journey to the sea in her final work, the unfinished comic tale *Sanditon*. She returns to a maritime setting to relate the strange tale of a prospective resort town that accentuates the exceptional nomadism imagined in *Persuasion*. Sanditon is a coastal settlement, but we should not expect to find naval packs or Anne and Wentworth spending much time in the company of Lady Denham and the Parker family. Austen presents Sanditon as a maritime experiment that has failed to embrace the undulations of the sea; the village has instead become reterritorialized by modernity. Upon Mr. Parker's return from his failed effort to acquire a surgeon, he rides through the older section of town and announces, "Civilization, Civilization indeed! . . . Look my dear Mary—Look at William Heeley's windows.—Blue Shoes, and nankin Boots!—Who would have expected such a sight at a Shoemaker's in old Sanditon!—This is new within the Month.—There was no blue Shoe when we passed this way a month ago.—Glorious indeed!" Mr. Parker is thrilled with the economic growth of the community; he revels in this burgeoning mercantilism and reflects, "Well, I think I *have* done something in my Day. Now, for our Hill, our health-breathing Hill" (339). He takes great pride in the financial maturation and impending future of the town—a great success that is symbolized, according to Mr. Parker, by the arrival of fashionable new shoes. He and his business partner, Lady Denham, are speculators who have invested in Sanditon; rather than allowing their intimacy with the sea to deterritorizalize themselves from the regulations and organ(izing) structures of a modern industrializing nation, Parker and Denham desperately hope and scrupulously plan to bring order and commercialism to the sea.

Mr. Parker announces his enduring confidence in the continuing success of Sanditon to Mr. Heywood early in the narrative when he announces that "everybody has heard of Sanditon . . . the favourite spot of all that are to be found along the coast of Sussex" (325). Mr. Heywood acknowledges that he has "heard of Sanditon," but he is not convinced of the continued prosperity of such communities. He explains that "every five years, one hears of some new place or other starting up by the Sea, and growing the fashion.—How they can half of them be filled, is the wonder! *Where* people can be found with Money or Time to go to them! Bad things for a Country;—sure to raise the price of Provisions and make the poor good for nothing" (325). This dialogue between Mr. Heywood and Mr. Parker illustrates the emerging popularity of the nomadic maritime lifestyle, but it also suggests the attempts of some to reterritorialize this nautical existence by transferring modern venture capitalism to the coast. And Mr. Heywood is especially concerned about the social viability and utility of such maritime communities that invite individuals to escape the daily routines of England's industrializing society; he finds these settlements detrimental to the sustenance of the state economy and hazardous to the management and utility of the lower classes. His remarks remind us of England's burgeoning industrial economy that Adam Smith suggested would require the efficient use and organization of mass human resources.[1] Mr. Heywood is seriously worried that communities like Sanditon are encouraging irresponsible behavior and promoting the decline of the individual's social utility.

Parker acknowledges the validity of Heywood's concerns, but the former upholds Sanditon as a valuable asset to the nation. Parker also agrees that the English coast has become overpopulated; indeed, he announces, "our Coast is abundant enough; it demands no more [settlements]. . . . And those good people who are trying to add to the number, are in my opinion excessively absurd, and must soon find themselves the Dupes of their own fallacious Calculations" (325–26). Parker sympathizes with Heywood's criticism of these sundry seaside communes that he identifies as bad financial ventures, but he presents Sanditon as a necessary complement to a prosperous English state—with just the requisite amount of modernity thrown in to guarantee new commodities, propriety, and discipline. And yet, despite Parker's and Heywood's criticism, the nation has, according to Austen's text, witnessed a proliferation of these colonies on the ocean. This dialogue may occupy only a small section of Austen's final work, but it suggests the author's keen knowledge of a growing number of coastal cooperatives—groups of people who have disregarded modern security in favor of the fluctuations and fluidity of the sea. Wentworth and Anne will not be found in the reterritorialized village of Sanditon, but you may spot them in the streets of one of the many smaller underdeveloped encampments. Austen's Deleuzian lovers could not remain radically dynamic and malleable in Sanditon, but these smaller communities, viewed by Parker and Heywood as political and economic liabilities, might embrace Anne and Wentworth's social/sexual flexibility.

Sanditon has tamed the turbulence of the sea and replaced the volatility of a nautical setting with a stagnant elegance reminiscent of Sir Elliot and Mr. Woodhouse. Two of the tale's male figures, Sir Edward and Arthur Parker, continue the legacy of such a decaying mode of masculinity as they crave convention and stasis. Sir Edward appears fond of the ocean, but the nephew of Lady Denham speaks of the sea and the shore by using "all the usual Phrases employed in praise of their Sublimity, and descriptive of the *undescribable* Emotions they excite in the Mind of Sensibility.—The terrific Grandeur of the Ocean in a Storm, its glassy surface in a calm, its Gulls and its Samphire, and the deep fathoms of its Abysses, its quick vicissitudes" (351). Sir Edward, like Benwick, is a man who "had read more sentimental Novels than agreed with him"; he displays a hackneyed sensibility by mechanically employing conventional Burkean expressions of sublimity (358). He recites an appreciation for the sea, but he is not interested in experiencing its turbulent fluctuations. Likewise, Arthur Parker, a self-proclaimed invalid, insists upon stability while residing in Sanditon—along with plenty of strong cocoa and heavily buttered toast (369). Austen notes that "Mr. Arthur P.'s enjoyments in Invalidism were very different from his sisters—by no means so spiritualized.—A good deal of Earthy Dross hung about him" (370). Arthur may represent the antithesis of Wentworth; the convalescent abhors movement and builds his aesthetic of existence around inactivity. Both Arthur and Sir Edward can manage nicely in Sanditon; they have access to a lending library replete with sentimental novels, and they receive plenty of afternoon refreshments. These men may have gone to the sea, but instead of embracing its fluctuations they have sought out stultifying proprieties to ensure their reterritorialization.

Wentworth ultimately disregards the security or reterritorialization promised by conventional propriety; he organizes his aesthetic of existence around the care of himself and others—allowing him to appreciate the complex flows and lines of flight that enmesh him with his relations and surroundings. His malleable social/sexual subjectivity enables him to remain deterritorialized and explore new ways of stylizing himself and relating to others. He remains outside the disciplinary structures of modern society that Foucault claims limit our possible relational experiences. Foucault explains that in the modern "institutional world . . . the only relations possible are extremely few, extremely simplified, and extremely poor" (158). He adds that "society and the institutions which frame it have limited the possibility of relationships because a rich relational world would be very complex to manage." Wentworth and Anne confront the challenges of these modern relational restrictions that Foucault argues regulate individuals; Austen's lovers, however, refuse to accept such regulation as they pursue potentially revolutionary desires that allow them to "imagine and create a new relational right that permits all possible types of relations to exist" ("The Social Triumph" 158). Wentworth and Anne remain fluid, and this fluidity allows them to embrace a diversity of relations and audition a Deleuzian nomadic lifestyle. Deleuze explains that nomads have the potential to explore new cultural possibilities because they "aren't part of history; they're excluded from it, but they transmute and reappear in different, unexpected forms in the lines of flight of some social field" ("On Philosophy" 153). Anne and Wentworth have the capacity to pursue new lines of flight that do not iterate historical conventions but instead facilitate new becomings. And Deleuze shamelessly announces that "men's only hope lies in a revolutionary becoming" ("Control and Becoming" 171). He theorizes that nomads evade the territorializing effect of regulatory forces that aim to organize our desires by creating our lacks; Austen's dramatization of Wentworth and Anne's marriage provides a glimpse of such a nomadism, and her mention of the many smaller coastal settlements in *Sanditon* indicates that this nomadic ambition is growing.

The new "becoming" sought by Anne, Wentworth, and other aspiring nomads is undoubtedly dangerous, both to the stability of the post-Revolutionary nation and their individual subjectivities, but it also promotes a social/sexual status that enables them to love and be loved. Anne and Wentworth's expressed amorous emotions are crucial to their nomadic fluidity. Their undisciplined love exposes them to multiple flows of passion and desire; indeed, Deleuze and Guattari conclude that "making love is not just becoming as one, or even two, but becoming as a hundred thousand" (*Anti-Oedipus* 296). Anne and Wentworth's amorous sincerity allows them to embrace the unpredictability of the sea, and their maritime existence continually augments the dynamism of their relationship. Austen's other lovers strive to purge their lives of volatile passions and sensations to create socially secure identities, but her presentation of Anne and Wentworth highlights the potent diversity engendered by their love. And yet, modern civilization invariably prefers sexualities that are regulated and stable; organized culture has little patience for radically fluid nomadic lifestyles and instead encourages responsible social agents who are static and safe. Critics of the mid-1990s Austen craze identified Austen's novels as a site of such social/sexual security. Laurie Morrow even went so far as to juxtapose Austen to "moral relativism," claiming that the early-nineteenth-century author "believes in moral absolutes" (263). Morrow presented Austen as an ethical absolutist who offers us definitive strategies to ensure social progress, cultural stability, and self-improvement.[2]

The late-millennial Austen vogue, as I noted in my preface, corresponded with the emergence of popular mid-1990s men's movements that also promised self-improvement and social contentment. While Morrow upheld Austen as a panacea for the ills of (post)modernity and moral decomposition, Bly and the Promise Keepers promoted strict sexual separation and social hegemony as the necessary conditions for strong men and a stable culture. Gary R. Brooks and Glenn E. Good addressed the late-millennial crisis of masculinity announced by Bly and the Promise Keepers in their *New Handbook of Psychotherapy and Counseling with Men* (2001). Brooks and Good note that "everywhere we look we see signs of deeply dissatisfied contemporary men" (3). They add that "for many, the past few decades have ushered in a period that has eroded traditional male values and damaged the image of masculinity itself" (4). Bly and the Promise Keepers offered various strategies for recovering traditional notions of masculinity and manliness, and the central tenet of both movements was the strict social and sexual separation of men and women. This fundamental step was designed to eradicate the problems that Brooks and Good note; male values were to be defined in opposition to female values, and the image of masculinity was to be codified in opposition to femininity. The mid-1990s men's movements proposed to reestablish sexual certainty and stability as the initial step in reordering a confused culture.

Despite the successes of these men's movements, the late-twentieth-century Austen vogue offered a more amenable plan for maintaining the sexual security of men and the social security of the nation. The updates of Austen's narratives showed us attractive men who lived with women in endearing relationships. The modern men of Austen's works did not need to exclude themselves from women because they disciplined their susceptibility to desire. While Bly and the Promise Keepers urged confused men to let loose their emotions amongst other men, the late-millennial revisions of Austen's stories reminded us how men and women could comfortably coexist *if* men regulated their emotions. The men and masculinity envisaged by Austen's tales are at once more appealing and more socially productive than Bly's Wild Man or the Promise Keepers' Christian husband. Austen's men do not need to remove themselves from women to preserve their social/sexual stability, and their relations with women ensure the biological and cultural reproduction of the nation. The late twentieth century, like the post-Revolutionary years, was a time of turbulent cultural uncertainty, and masculinity was just one of many social markers in doubt. But as Abigail Solomon-Godeau concludes, "masculinity, however defined, is, like capitalism, *always* in crisis. And the real question is how both manage to restructure, refurbish, and resurrect themselves for the next historical turn" (70). Austen's men serve as useful early examples of our ongoing modern attempt to manage a disciplined masculinity that is sexually safe and socially useful. Her men are neither feeble nor inefficacious, but they are also not emotionally overbearing figures; they are well-managed social/sexual subjects whose hegemonic identities promote both the order of sexual relations and the organization of the modernizing nation.

NOTES

—◀◯▶—

Notes to Preface

1. American society has long been fond of Austen and her works; ever since the 1870 publication of James Edward Austen-Leigh's *A Memoir of Jane Austen,* the novelist has remained popular in America. Ian Watt, however, argues that it is in the mid-twentieth century when American literary criticism became particularly interested in Austen and her novels. The American academy, not coincidentally, developed this interest in Austen following a time in which the American public was fascinated with the early-nineteenth-century author. While Americans endured the many cultural, economic, and personal tragedies of World War II, Austen enjoyed great popular appeal through the Metro-Gold-wyn-Mayer (MGM) production of *Pride and Prejudice.* This film, as Kenneth Turan points out, was accompanied by a conscious attempt to "sell" Austen to the American public, leading MGM to "launch its greatest book promotion in years, with no less than five popular-priced editions of the book getting into print as a result of the film" ("*Pride and Prejudice*" 142). The American press did not ignore this promotion of the early-nine-teenth-century novelist.

As Americans tired of the misery and mud of the battles overseas, Harold Hobson and others "advertised" Austen as a peaceful and sanguine author of educational tales. Hobson announces that "Jane Austen took little account of war. No one would guess from her novels that she lived through the most perilous time Great Britain endured until 1940 brought a new and more dangerous enemy even than Napoleon." Hobson adds that "Miss Austen neglected war; and, in return, war has passed her by. Not only are her homes unharmed, but the very streets through which her characters moved on their morning walks are little touched" (6). Hobson's romanticized view of a safe Austen is echoed by Henry Seidel Canby, an associate editor of *The Saturday Review of Literature.* Canby claims that "the greatest novels (in English at least) written in wartime are unquestion-ably Jane Austen's"; and yet, Canby declares that throughout Austen's tales, "the war, if we remember correctly, is never mentioned except in the last" (26). Even as late as 1959, an anonymous review in *Time* suggests that "Jane Austen grew up in the world of the French and American Revolutions, and showed no trace of interest in either. The world of her six novels is simply and finally that of genteel young women gunning for husbands" ("Jane Extended"). The mid-twentieth-century American media capitalized upon Austen's established cultural popularity and (re)constructed her as the proprietor of a safe domestic world that served as a relief from the horrors of war. America's love affair with Austen, however, did not end with the fall of Hitler. For a lengthy discussion of the significance of Austen-Leigh's *Memoir,* see B. C. Southam's introduction to *Jane Austen: The Critical Heritage, Vol. 2,* 1–12. For a further consideration of the American reception of Austen in the nineteenth century, see John Halperin, "Jane Austen's Nineteenth-Century Critics: Walter Scott to Henry James." See Ian Watt's discussion of the rise of American literary criticism on Austen in his introductory essay to *Jane Austen: A Collection of Critical Essays.*

2. Bly, for example, addresses a loss of heroic models and myths; he claims that we must listen again to "the old myths," in which we hear "of Zeus' energy, that positive leadership energy in men." Bly explains that "from King Arthur we learn the value of the male mentor in the lives of young men; we hear from the Iron John story the importance of moving from the mother's realm; and from all initiation stories we learn how essential it is to leave our parental expectations entirely and find a second father or 'second King'" (ix–x). Bly calls on men to recall ancient models of masculinity that once served to order Western civilization. And both Bly and the Promise Keepers echo the 1790s concern with social transformation. Messner notes that Bly's movement "[believes] that industrial society has trapped men into straitjackets of rationality, thus blunting the powerful emotional communion and collective spiritual transcendence that they believe men in tribal societies typically enjoyed" (20). The Promise Keepers blame the growth of this modern society and its social movements for the demise of the traditional family and its stable gender roles. Messner explains that "Promise Keepers is more apt [than Bly] to blame feminism, gay liberation, sexual liberation, and the 'breakdown of the family' for men's problems" (17). These 1990s movements, like the post-Revolutionary discourses of the late-eighteenth and early-nineteenth century, offer explanations (or at least justifications) for the respective crises of masculinity, and their plans to repair fragile or vulnerable men inevitably involve a clear conceptual and physical separation of men from women.

3. John Gray's *Men Are from Mars, Women Are from Venus* (1992) and Anne and Bill Moir's *Why Men Don't Iron: The Fascinating and Unalterable Differences Between Men and Women* (1999) attempted to outline intrinsic differences between the sexes that help to justify the ostensibly redemptive male-only gatherings *and* hegemonic social systems that depend upon a clear cultural distinction between the sexes.

4. Laurie Morrow, for example, upholds Austen's fiction because it "provides an escape from an unattractive present" (262). Morrow insists that Austen's narratives "hold the promise that bad behavior can be limited and provide hope that the world can be a better place" (263). Morrow invests Austen's work with the salutary ability of improving culture by improving individual behavior; and Morrow specifically credits Austen with documenting the pleasures and comforts of a hegemonic society based upon a strictly divided system of gendered identity. She writes: "Austen presents favorably intelligent women who seek traditional roles and who are content in them and respected; she does not portray such women as witless, helpless victims, yearning to discover themselves. She doesn't ridicule them as stay-at-home cookie-bakers. Austen plays to a desire for domesticity today's women often feel but dare not admit, sometimes even to themselves" (262–63). Austen, according to Morrow, shows us a pleasant, well-mannered, and ordered culture in which women eagerly accept domestic regulations; and late-twentieth-century America clearly saw Austen as a champion of security and stability.

Notes to Introduction

1. Deleuze and Guattari believe that "sexuality is the production of a thousand sexes, which are so many uncontrollable becomings" (*Thousand Plateaus* 278). A sexual subject, according to Deleuze and Guattari, has the potential to experience a vast diversity of sexes, sexualities, and sexual sensations.

2. Deleuze theorizes that "To love is to try to *explicate*, to *develop* these unknown worlds which remain enveloped within the beloved" (*Proust and Signs* 7). For a further discussion of Deleuze's theory of love and the subject, see Ronald Bogue, *Deleuze and Guattari* (1989), 43.

3. As I have suggested elsewhere, American society has specifically credited Austen with the ability to teach men and women proper gendered behavior. See specifically Kramp, "The Potency of Jane, or the Disciplinary Function of Austen in America," 19–32. This popular conception of Austen, moreover, derives from a long-standing scholarly tradition that emphasizes Austen's assent with her own culture's conceptions of gender propriety. Philip Mason effectively illustrates the critical basis for this popular perception of Austen. While he admits that "it is as novels that Miss Austen's books should be read," he claims "they are social history too." He continues: "They are minute and exact sketches . . . of the way her people thought about marriage, property, social differences, and the kind of behaviour which was proper for ladies and gentlemen" (70–71). Mason's argument has more recently been echoed by Penelope Joan Fritzer who, in *Jane Austen and Eighteenth-Century Courtesy Books* (1997), suggests that Austen's novels dramatize proper behavior for men and women as outlined in eighteenth-century courtesy books. See especially 3–9.

4. Johnson traces this obsession with educating young women through the works of F. R. Leavis, D. W. Harding, and Wayne Booth; she specifically indicates that Austen scholars in the 1960s began to highlight the heroines' premarital training by presenting the marriage plots as the "telos towards which the narrative[s] . . . moved since the first page" ("Austen Cults and Cultures" 221). She concludes that "critics as diverse as Mark Schorer, Lionel Trilling, Ian Watt, Arnold Kettle, Marilyn Butler, Tony Tanner, Patricia P. Brown, and Mary Poovey" view such premarital regulation of women as a vital component of both their character development and their preparation for marriage (222). See also, Johnson's "The Divine Miss Jane: Jane Austen, Janeites and the Discipline of Novel Studies."

5. Tyler declares that "Jane Austen has taught me how to read the world and has given me more guidelines and examples on how to behave than the combined efforts of Emily Post, psychoanalysis, and a lengthy stay at the Betty Ford Clinic possibly could" (xvii–xviii). Tyler's comments are, of course, reminiscent of the long tradition of Janeitism that has transformed Austen into an angelic figure who is simultaneously salutary and omniscient.

6. The work of Sedgwick has been extremely influential in identifying this heteronormalizing strand in Austen criticism. Sedgwick announced that "[a] lot of Austen criticism sounds hilariously like the leering school prospectuses or governess manifestoes brandished like so many birch rods in Victorian S-M pornography" ("Jane Austen" 315). Clara Tuite has recently observed that the canonical authority of Austen rests upon an unquestioned "heterosexist investment" in the novelist's works as manuals for proper romantic love; Tuite, moreover, explains that "the heterosexual investment in the natural-

ness of these marriage endings underwrites Austen's canonicity" (17). This heterosexist investment and the emphasis on Austen's authority as a marriage/love advisor is clearly apparent in Tyler's work; she insists that "in all of Austen's novels the lovers face a challenge and in every case the lessons of maturity, correct conduct, and rational thought are mastered;" she concludes that "in every case the novel ends happily as eventually the declaration and offer are made and accepted" (61; 58).

7. While there have been few critical discussions of heterosexual men in Austen's corpus, there is a rich scholarly tradition within Austen studies that considers the importance of the novelist to historical and contemporary queer cultures. Johnson points out that "one of the biggest open secrets of the literate world, after all, is that Austen is a cult author for many gays and lesbians" (Editorial Response 4). For further discussion of this tradition, see such important recent works as D. A. Miller's *Jane Austen, or The Secret of Style* (2003) and Clara Tuite's *Romantic Austen: Sexual Politics and the Literary Canon* (2002).

8. Virginia Woolf's famous comments on Austen, which certainly aided the writer's entrance into the literary canon, may also have institutionalized this scholarly practice that has sharply focused Austen scholarship. Woolf announced in 1925 that Austen was "the most perfect artist among women, the writer whose books are immortal" (206). Woolf upholds the creative and imaginative genius of the novelist, but she also specifically identifies Austen as *the* elite female artist. Woolf's proclamation undoubtedly elevated Austen's position in the academic study of English literature, and it likely helped to generate numerous important feminist discussions of the nineteenth-century author throughout the 1980s.

9. Such works directed our attention to the personal, familial, and national importance of the maturation, marriage, and sexuality of Austen's young women. These studies enhanced our knowledge of English women's social experiences in the years following the French Revolution; this critical trend to focus on the stories and depictions of women in Austen's corpus culminated with the publication of Deborah Kaplan's *Jane Austen among Women* (1992). Kaplan shifted the focus of traditional Austen criticism from the disciplinary approach that Sedgwick identified and instead insisted the novelist's texts were marked distinctively by a women's culture. Kaplan still emphasized the primacy of the heroines in the novels, but she also firmly asserted that "Austen found crucial support for her writing career not from her sister alone but also from the women's culture that Austen's female friends made." Kaplan employs her concept of a "women's culture" to theorize the presence of "an independent, self-assertive female" in Austen's texts (*Jane Austen* 3–4). She claims that, unlike "feminist and nonfeminist postmodern literary critics [who] deconstruct the subject, the concepts of women's culture . . . grant selfhood to women" (5). Kaplan's project positions Austen as a significant progenitor of a feminist theory of subjectivity that conceptualizes the female as an independent entity who emerges from an integral women's culture. In addition, Kaplan's criticism aligned Austen with the objectives of second-wave literary feminism, specifically the goal to concentrate on the fictional representation of women.

10. Gerald I. Fogel offers a helpful summary of Freud's theory of male sexual development. Fogel explains:

> Freud's view of male sexuality is often summarized in a few sentences. The recognition of the differences between the sexes is one of the crucial events that accompanies and influences the phallic-oedipal phase, which is characterized in

the boy by a wish to obtain exclusive sexual possession of the mother by defeating and eliminating the father. Under the threat of castration by his powerful, forbidding rival, the little boy renounces his incestuous infantile claims and solves his dilemma by identifying with his father, who is internalized as the psychic agency of the superego. Castration anxiety and the importance of the relation to the father is central. Successful oedipal resolution correlates with a strong, healthy sexual identity and the consolidation of a more mature, autonomous psychic structure. (6–7)

11. Gilles Deleuze and Félix Guattari announce that "[p]sychoanalysis is like the Russian Revolution; we don't know when it started going bad. We have to keep going back further" (*Anti-Oedipus* 55).

12. Deleuze's theory of the folded subject, like Foucault's concept of the aesthetic of existence, involves the subject's efforts to craft a unique space of identity within and through powerful social forces. Deleuze theorizes that human subjects construct a fold to function effectively in society, explaining that "subjectivation is created by folding" (*Foucault* 104). Individuals, for both Foucault and Deleuze, must negotiate the discourses and demands of culture as they create modes of existence. Deleuze employs the metaphor of the fold to explain this process in which the subject navigates and records multiple social desires for her/his "self," and as Deleuze notes, "the multiple is not only what has many parts but also what is folded in many ways" (*The Fold* 3). For a further discussion of Deleuze's theory of the fold, see Alain Badiou's "Gilles Deleuze, *The Fold: Leibniz and the Baroque*" and Constantin V. Boundas, "Deleuze: Serialization and Subject-Formation." Boundas, in his analysis of Deleuze, indicates that "the subject is the individual who, through practice and discipline, has become the site of a bent force, that is, the folded inside of an outside" (115).

13. This participation of the individual in discursive power relations is key to Foucault's understanding of ethical behavior and the subject. He explains that he "wanted to try to show . . . how the subject constituted itself." He "had to reject a priori theories of the subject in order to analyze the relationships that may exist between the constitution of the subject or different forms of the subject and games of truth, practices of power, and so on" ("Ethics" 290).

14. While each of these theorists has written extensively on masculinity, see especially, R. W. Connell's *Masculinities* (1995), Michael Kimmel's *The Politics of Manhood: Profeminist Men Respond to the Mythopoetic Men's Movement (And the Mythopoetic Leaders Answer)* (1995), Kimmel's *Manhood in America* (1996), Kimmel's *The Gendered Society* (2000), and Robyn Wiegman's *American Anatomies: Theorizing Race and Gender* (1995). See also Judith Kegan Gardiner's collection, *Masculinity Studies and Feminist Theory: New Directions* (2002), and Rachel Adams and David Savran's *The Masculinity Studies Reader* (2002).

15. Olliver's thesis, "Jane Austen's Male Characters" has not garnered significant critical attention. The 1996 JASNA meeting, however, produced an important issue of *Persuasions*. In Looser's contribution to the conference (and later the journal), she refers to "the groundbreaking recent work interrogating masculinities in Austen's writings" (161). This work, like Joseph A. Kestner's "Jane Austen: Revolutionizing Masculinities" and Joseph Litvak's "Charming Men, Charming History," offers intelligent readings of Austen novels that encouraged scholars to pursue critical book-length studies of her men. This has not happened; instead, scholars have tended either to follow Kestner's model of focusing on

the latter novels' depictions of masculinity or pursue uncritical and ahistorical readings of Austen's men. Feminist scholars, including the writers I have previously mentioned, have consistently and effectively addressed Austen's men in critical assessments of the novelist's women; I will discuss specific critics in my treatments of the individual novels. This scholarship, like much feminist scholarship, opened the possibility of studying gender relations and gender identity in Austen's corpus.

16. Fulford's recent articles have been extremely helpful to my work on Austen's men. See especially "Romanticizing the Empire: The Naval Heroes of Southey, Coleridge, Austen, and Marryat" and "Sighing for a Soldier: Jane Austen and Military Pride and Prejudice."

17. Many of these well-managed male figures, including Mr. Darcy and Mr. Knightley, have long-enjoyed popular appeal. The mid-1990s Austen movies solidified and perhaps advanced the lure of such men as romantic figures; as Deborah Kaplan points out, "the casting of the film's heroes was instrumental in achieving the on-screen-romance-ification of Austen's work" ("Mass Marketing" 174). See also Lisa Hopkins, "Mr. Darcy's Body: Privileging the Female Gaze," which explores the presentation of Colin Firth's body in the BBC Television production of *Pride and Prejudice.*

18. As I mentioned earlier, Fulford's work has been especially helpful in explaining new cultural developments engendered by the glorious return of the military from the Napoleonic Wars; Fulford specifically notes that *Persuasion* ushers in a new model for the gentry based upon professionalism. He explains: "Austen's navy redefined gentility in terms of professional activity and discipline" ("Romanticizing the Empire" 188).

Notes to Chapter 1

1. The late eighteenth century has long served as a convenient marker for the emergence of European nationalism, and this period specifically demonstrates the importance of textual dissemination to the creation of a national culture. Scholars of nationalism have traditionally pointed to the post-Revolutionary years as the age in which the modern European nation develops. Ernest Renan announces that "France can claim the glory for having, through the French Revolution, proclaimed that a nation exists of itself" (46). Benedict Anderson theorizes the nation as "an imagined political community" and argues that "print-language is what invents nationalism" (6; 134). In the decade following the French Revolution, English writers produced numerous texts that created alternative visions of imagined national communities. These works constructed England's modern national identity through a dialogic process, both likening itself to and differentiating itself from France. Seamus Deane explains that "France . . . provided a useful contrast in highlighting what was distinctive about England's experience and its constitutional and cultural forms" (2). England's discussions about the Revolution throughout the 1790s questioned the validity and justness of the French experiment while they simultaneously established the principles and parameters for the various envisioned future English states. Prasenjit Duara argues that "nationalism is best seen as a relational identity" (163). A nation secures its status as unique and sovereign by isolating itself from other states, but a national culture, as Paul Gilroy notes, is "conceived along ethnically absolute lines, not as something intrinsically fluid, changing, unstable, and dynamic, but as a fixed property of social groups rather than a relational field" (355). The method for creating a modern nation is dialectical and relies upon the juxtaposition with an "other" state, but the end

product is assumed to be independent and unique.

2. Although Austen did not publish her novels until the second decade of the nineteenth century, many critics have effectively demonstrated the importance of the 1790s to her tales. See, for example, Claudia Johnson's *Jane Austen: Women, Politics, and the Novel* (1988) and Marilyn Butler's *Jane Austen and the War of Ideas* (1975).

3. Gary Kelly agrees with Kadish's claim. Kelly examines the turbulent post-Revolutionary period and notes that "in this conflict of loyalties, identities and distinctions, gender difference was increasingly important and complex" (*Revolutionary Feminism* 5).

4. This presumed certainty regarding gender was particularly important in this period because of the cultural uncertainty surrounding knowledge and identity that scholars such as Foucault identify in this period. Foucault explains that "[t]he last years of the eighteenth century are broken by a discontinuity similar to that which destroyed Renaissance thought at the beginning of the seventeenth; then, the great circular forms in which similitude was enclosed were dislocated and opened so that the table of identities could be unfolded; and that table is now about to be destroyed in turn, while knowledge takes up residence in a new space" (*Order of Things* 217).

5. Linda Colley notes that "defeat in America, revolution in France, and war with both, together with the expanding volume and diversity of domestic and imperial government, imposed a massive strain on the lives, nerves and confidence of the British élite." Colley points out that "in all, nineteen Members of Parliament are known to have committed suicide between 1790 and 1820; more than twenty lapsed into what seemed like insanity, as did their monarch George III" (151–52). Colley adds that this stress was compounded by the lack of aristocratic heirs; she explains that "many landowners did not marry," and "for nearly a century, landed families were thus not reproducing themselves" (156).

6. For further discussion of the development of the domestic sphere in post-Revolutionary England, see *Women, Privilege, and Power: British Politics, 1750 to the Present*, edited by Amanda Vickery (2001); Kathryn Gleadle, "British Women and Radical Politics in the Late Nonconformist Enlightenment, c. 1780–1830"; Harriet Guest, *Small Change: Women, Learning, Patriotism, 1750–1810* (2000); and Robert B. Shoemaker, *Gender in English Society, 1650–1850: The Emergence of Separate Spheres?* (1998).

7. This process should not be surprising, but important scholarship such as Nancy Armstrong's *Desire and Domestic Fiction* (1987) has failed to account for the role of the domestic sphere in the construction of post-Revolutionary English middle-class male subjectivity. While Armstrong treats the domestic sphere as a new power for "the domestic woman . . . through her dominance over all those objects and practices we associate with private life," I emphasize the role of the domestic sphere in establishing both sexually and politically powerful men and the modern hegemonic structures that perpetuate such power (3). Finally, I believe it is important that such men seek sexual stability and the subsequent membership in the national citizenry as the traditionally dominant male aristocracy atrophies.

8. I treat the various texts of this public discussion as part of what Foucault identifies as "a steady proliferation of discourses concerned with sex" that he describes as "a discursive ferment that gathered momentum from the eighteenth century onward" (*History of Sexuality, Vol. 1* 18). Foucault's work has been instrumental in the study of the deployment of sexuality from the late eighteenth to the end of the nineteenth century; indeed, his assertion that "the history of sexuality—that is, the history of what functioned in the nineteenth century as a specific field of truth—must first be written from the

viewpoint of a history of discourses" invites us to re-read England's textual responses to the Revolution in terms of their commentaries on the nation's conception of proper male sexual identity (69). Foucault adds that "it is not simply in terms of a continual extension that we must speak of this discursive growth; it should be seen rather as a dispersion of centers from which discourses emanated" (34). The discourses of the 1790s are diverse and complex. They are not simply extensions of one another but divergent disseminations that develop "a complex machinery for producing true discourses on sex" (68). Foucault's use of the term *sexuality* incorporates much more than sexual organs, sexual preference, or gender identification. Armstrong explains that for Foucault "sexuality includes not only all those representations of sex that appear to be sex itself—in modern culture, for example, the gendered body—but also those myriad representations that are meaningful in relation to sex" (11).

9. Catharine Macaulay also speaks of the polarization of British politics following the French Revolution. She indicates in 1790 that "two parties are already formed in this country, who behold the French Revolution with a very opposite temper: to the one, it inspires the sentiments of *exultation* and *rapture;* and to the other, *indignation* and *scorn*" (*On Burke's Reflections* 6). This dialectic, of course, involved much manipulation, as the individual participants in the debates of the late eighteenth century exaggerated both their limited knowledge of the Revolution and the arguments of their counterparts. Hedva Ben-Israel Kidron investigates how English historians respond to the Revolution; she points out that "[i]n England, knowledge of the events could not be so readily assumed as in France" and concludes that "the story, therefore, had to be told" (5). English writers' strategic retelling of the history of the French Revolution solidified a polarized political landscape in England that helped to delineate distinct visions of the future nation and its man.

10. Burke's discourse of the chivalric male is both prevalent and powerful throughout the late eighteenth and early nineteenth century. L. G. Mitchell points out that Burke's *Reflections* was "an immediate best seller" and suggests that "never has a book been so widely read and so widely spurned" (vii–viii).

11. The English writers of the 1790s soon discovered that their respective narratives of the activity in France were particularly important because "the Revolution had created a wider reading public for political affairs and that there was a need to control the subject" (Kidron 5). England's respondents to the Revolution such as Burke and Wollstonecraft, encouraged by this new audience for political texts, attempted both to support their plans for a revised nation and its man while simultaneously denigrating the proposals of their opponents. They read and responded to each others work, creating a complex and tumultuous debate in which the initial arguments quickly become lost and perverted in favor of rhetorical attempts to sway public opinion.

12. Foucault explains that such writings did not prohibit sex; rather, sex was "managed, inserted into systems of utility, regulated for the greater good of all, made to function according to an optimum" (*History of Sexuality, Vol. 1* 24). This production of a true concept of sex leads Foucault to conclude that "sexuality must not be thought of as a kind of natural given which power tries to hold in check, or as an obscure domain which knowledge tries gradually to uncover. It is the name that can be given to a historical construct" (105).

13. Richard Price's *A Discourse on the Love of Our Country* (1789) initiates this tempestuous dialogue by calling for a prominent reconfiguration of English duty. Price insists that he must explain to men "the duty we owe to our country, and the nature, foundation,

and proper expressions of that love to it which we ought to cultivate" (1–2). Price's call for national love creates a desire for men to maintain strong amorous feelings for their country, but his text actually precipitates additional socially produced desires throughout the late eighteenth century that limit English men's ability to love. He conceptualizes amorous patriotism as essential to the liberty enjoyed by a nation and its residents, and he denounces monarchy and ancestral descent as impediments to this pursuit.

14. Although I will talk about Burke as the leading voice of the conservative camp in this debate, his ideas on revolution are far more complex than many Jacobin writers suggest. While Burke was clearly opposed to the French Revolution and actively spoke out against this event, he was not simply a conservative thinker who disavowed all revolutionary activity. As he makes clear in his *Reflections,* Burke supported the Glorious Revolution and the American Revolution. For an extended discussion of Burke's ideas on revolutionary activity, see Peter J. Stanlis, *Edmund Burke: The Enlightenment and Revolution,* 195–215. Stanlis points out that "in social and political affairs, Burke was not a determinist and insisted that man is, to a great extent, a creature of his own making, and when made as he ought to be made, is destined to hold no trivial place in the universe" (196). Burke supports revolutionary action that helps men arrive at their "proper" place, but he does not believe the French Revolution pursued this end.

15. Gillian Skinner adds that "[i]n Burke's view, absolute equality was not only unattainable but also undesirable; inequality was part of the natural order of things" (160).

16. Susan Khin Zaw indicates that "Burke sees the state in the image of the family: much as subordinate members of a household must love, honour and obey its head if there is to be peace, security and prosperity within the family, so the lower orders must love, honour and obey their rulers if there is to be peace, security and prosperity within the state" (128).

17. This romantic remembrance involves class demarcations, even though these markers are becoming less clear. Stephen K. White indicates that Burke was primarily addressing "the aristocracy and gentry of England," and "the appeal to chivalry was aimed at the 'second nature' of these classes" (67). Burke speaks to the socially powerful and elite and incites their fears of potential rebellion.

18. She added later that "nature has given woman a weaker frame than man" and concluded that "bodily strength seems to give man a natural superiority over woman" (*Vindication of the Rights of Woman* 97–98; 108).

19. For further discussion of the literary precedents for the sentimental hero, see Ann Jessie Van Sant's *Eighteenth-Century Sensibility and the Novel: The Senses in Social Context,* 98–110.

20. Van Sant discusses how the very concept of sensibility or proper feeling was "related to immediate moral and aesthetic responsiveness" (5). Indeed, both conservative and radical writers will uphold their perspectives on emotion as moral concerns.

21. See especially 125–27.

22. Sapiro points out that in *Reflections,* "Burke relayed his moral and political message as a nightmare teller would: not merely through a chronological story or a logical argument but by invoking the horror of it all through tone and imagery" (189). Burke's rhetoric attempts to evoke fear in his readers, consequently encouraging them to dismiss nightmarish revolutionary passions.

23. Thomas Paine is perhaps the most ardent supporter of a strict devotion to rationality as a means of improving the English nation and its men. Paine, in the first part of his *Rights of Man* (1791), outlines a historical process that moves from the "government

of priestcraft" to the time of "conquerors," and finally to the reign of reason, which he understands to pursue "the common interests of society, and the common rights of man" (120–21). Eleanor Ty explains that "[Paine's] own work [emphasized] fact and common sense, using a 'vulgar' and plain rather than a decorous and refined style, [appealing] to a great mass of the common people" (9). Paine distinguishes his envisioned nation from the English aristocratically ordered community of Burke by imagining a pseudo-egalitarian civilization of rational men.

Virginia Sapiro claims that for Wollstonecraft, "[t]he powers of reason and understanding must be developed for virtuous social relations to exist—and vice versa. This was the basis of her vision of history" (225).

24. Barker-Benfield points out that Wollstonecraft "criticizes [Burke] throughout for affecting sensibility rather than being genuinely a man of feeling" (107).

25. Zaw relates that "Wollstonecraft believes that someone who, like Burke, merely feels and does not reason cannot be virtuous. But she also believes that someone who reasons without feeling cannot be good. Her solution to this conundrum is her concept of feeling informed by reason" (135).

26. For an extensive discussion of Burke's chivalric gender system, see Johnson, *Equivocal Beings,* 1–19; see also Zaw 123–30.

Notes to Chapter 2

1. Austen's juvenile writings, like her novels, are comedies, and she works with/in the conventions of this literary genre. To this extent, the vast majority of her youthful tales end in marriages, albeit often quite humorous and absurd marital unions. For a lengthy consideration of Austen's use and manipulation of literary conventions within her juvenile writings, see Lois A. Chaber, "Transgressive Youth: Lady Mary, Jane Austen, and the Juvenilia Press," and Julia Epstein, "Jane Austen's Juvenilia and the Female Epistolary Tradition."

2. The frustrations experienced by the men of the juvenilia certainly anticipate the struggles endured by the men of Austen's mature fictions; and yet, critics have historically disregarded the importance of her juvenile writings. The publication of *Jane Austen's Beginnings: The Juvenilia and* Lady Susan (1989), a collection of essays on Austen's early writings edited by J. David Grey, ostensibly announced the arrival of her juvenile productions within the field of academic literary study. Margaret Drabble explains in her foreword to this anthology that "one does not need a degree in English literature to appreciate [the juvenilia's] wit and their extraordinary narrative confidence," but they do "repay study." Drabble adds that "a good case is made here for both studying and teaching some of the juvenilia" (xiii). While it is now possible to teach Austen's youthful writings because of two well-edited affordable versions of this literature, Grey's critical text remains an anomaly in Austen studies as the sole full-length critical work devoted to her early tales, although many scholars have briefly examined Austen's juvenilia to inform their discussions of the author's later works. This became a popular trend throughout the 1980s, as numerous writers, especially second-wave feminist critics, looked to the author's early narratives to frame their readings of Austen's mature corpus. This critical tendency helped to legitimate the juvenilia as literature that merited scholarly attention.

Sandra Gilbert and Susan Gubar's *The Madwoman in the Attic: The Woman Writer and the Nineteenth-Century Literary Imagination* (1979) solidified both second-wave academic feminism within English studies and the place of the juvenilia within Austen studies. Gilbert and Gubar asserted that "it *is* shocking how persistently Austen demonstrates her discomfort with her cultural inheritance, specifically her dissatisfaction with the tight place assigned women in patriarchy and her analysis of the economics of sexual exploitation" (112). Gilbert and Gubar insist that Austen is continually concerned with the position of women in society and argue that throughout her juvenile writings she critiques and parodies societal conventions that "have inalterably shaped women's lives" (114). Gilbert and Gubar identify women and women's issues as the primary subject of Austen's work and the appropriate subject of Austen criticism, leading to numerous feminist studies of her corpus throughout the 1980s. *The Madwoman in the Attic* also revealed the importance of the juvenilia to the critical approach of second-wave feminist scholars—a critical approach that neglected the depiction of Austen's masculine figures. LeRoy W. Smith followed the lead of Gilbert and Gubar, suggesting that in the world of the juvenile writings "the female's life is much more difficult than the males." Smith concludes that in these works "Austen already understood how individuals are affected by patriarchal values" (49). Deborah J. Knuth likewise dismisses the prominent struggles experienced by Austen's male characters throughout her early fictions and believes that these tales offer a "logical point of departure for a study of Jane Austen's women's relationships" (66). And Claudia Johnson, in her essay, "'The Kingdom at Sixes and Sevens': Politics and the Juvenilia," indicates that "Austen was well aware of the way in which her presentation of female characters in the juvenilia was politically coded" (52–53). These critics accurately highlight the importance of the female subject within Austen's juvenilia, but these tales ultimately dramatize various tensions of the English gender system in the post–French Revolutionary years, including a cultural anxiety about the insecure young man. For an extensive discussion of the relative critical neglect of Austen's juvenilia, see Margaret Anne Doody's Introduction to *Catharine and Other Writings*.

3. Joseph Litvak argues that "men like Henry Tilney become increasingly troubling for their 'perverse' combination of cockiness with complaisance" ("Charming Men" 269). Litvak's comment recalls the strange composite quality of Henry's subjectivity and sexuality, but I will argue that the hero's "troubling" appearance is ultimately the result of his rational efforts to fulfill his society's distinct yet specific expectations for proper masculinity. He seems cocky to many readers because of his ability to satiate the desire-producing machine; moreover, he seems complaisant because his subjectivity is extremely well organized and will not allow the development of any irrational sensation or experience. This incongruous permutation of accomplishment and ambivalence is essential to the comic quality of Austen's depiction of Henry.

4. He is a superior man, reminiscent of Samuel Richardson's famous hero, Sir Charles Grandison. Margaret Anne Doody argues that "behind this Charles Adams—a most un-fallen son of Adam (in his own opinion)—we can see not only Richardson's Sir Charles, but whole sets of Enlightenment concepts of self-improvement and self-approval" (xxviii). Like Grandison, Adams is a grand and beloved male character who continually tries to ameliorate himself.

5. Frances Beer argues that "Jack and Alice" ridicules the "slippery equivocation" of women like Lady Williams, a character described as a "[study] in corruption" (11).

6. "Three Sisters," another pithy novel included in the initial volume of Austen's juvenilia, traces the trials of Mr. Watts, who, unlike Adams, maintains no pretensions about either his perfection or his future spouse. Watts actively pursues a wife throughout this tale, and he focuses his energy on a family of three sisters. He initially proposes mar-

riage to Mary Stanhope who proclaims: "I do not intend to accept it. . . . He is quite an old Man, about two and thirty, very plain so plain that I cannot bear to look at him. He is extremely disagreeable and I hate him more than any body else in the world" (55). When the letters of Miss Georgiana Stanhope assume narrative control of the novel, Watts remains a notably anxious and unattractive figure uninterested in amorous emotions. Georgiana describes Watts as "rather plain to be sure" and questions, "but then what is Beauty in a Man; if he has but a genteel figure and a sensible looking Face it is quite sufficient. . . . Mr. Watts's figure is unfortunately extremely vulgar and his Countenance is very heavy" (59). Georgiana's reflections remind us of Watts's deplorable appearance; but her remarks also imply that male beauty is unnecessary if a man is genteel. Watts is not a comely man, but like Charles Adams he displays little ability to pursue effectively romantic relations with women. He is an obnoxiously authoritative figure, who, as Mary Stanhope relates, "talks a great deal of Women's always Staying at home and such stuff" (56). Watts upholds a patriarchal gender system that requires separate sexualized spheres, and he believes he must marry a woman whom he can control and detain at home. He is not picky about who this woman may be, and Mary understands that if she does not accept his proposal, he will extend his offer to her sisters, but "he won't be kept in suspense" (57). Watts's behavior suggests his realization that he needs a domesticated woman to be a socially proper man, but he has no desire for a particular woman.

When Mary and Watts begin discussions about their "desired" marriage, both attempt to exercise control. Mary demands a new blue and silver chaise, but she reports that "the old Fool wants to have his new Chaise just the colour of the old one, and hung as low too." Watts will not tolerate the ubiquitous prenuptial demands of a woman, and he tells Mary, "as I am by no means guided by a particular preference to you above your Sisters it is equally the same to me which I marry of the three" (61). His honest statement certainly affects Mary, who agrees to marry the stubborn man. She then proceeds to list her various "needs" as his wife, including jewels, balls, a greenhouse, travel, and a private theatre; and Mary informs her future husband that all he can expect from his acts of generosity is "to have me pleased" (62). Watts is not at all interested in this masculine role, and when Mary's sister Sophia iterates these standards for her future husband, Watts asserts: "These are very odd Ideas truly, young Lady. You had better discard them before you marry, or you will be obliged to do it afterwards" (63). Watts will not tolerate such requests, and he is perfectly willing to sacrifice any personal romantic desires for the benefit of an easily placated domestic partner. He is still concerned that he ought to marry, but he will not, and perhaps cannot, play the role of the emotionally overwhelmed lover who succumbs to the excessive demands of a "beloved."

Austen concludes her short novel in a comically mundane manner. After agreeing to a compromise regarding the colors and height of the new chaise, Mr. Watts actively affects the persona of a lover before Mary. He announces: "I am come a courting in a true Lover like Manner" (66). Watts's overt proclamation of his altered status emphasizes the artifice involved in this new identity. His artificial amorous behavior, however, ironically leads to troubling consequences, as he is now offended by Mary's comments concerning Mr. Brudenell, an attractive man who appears near the story's close. Mary expounds: "Watts is such a Fool! I hope I shall never see him again. . . . Why only because I told him that I had seen a Man much handsomer than he was this Morning, he flew into a great Passion and called me a Vixen" (67). Watts is unable to handle the undisciplined passions of a love relationship. While he had earlier insisted upon his unattachment to any specific woman, now that he has become a "lover," he will not allow his wife to express desires or even admiration for any man except himself. Like many gothic villains, he becomes a jealous man who must control his domesticated female partner. Mary's mother intervenes to calm the frustrated lover; he now "met Mary with all his accustomed Civility, and except one touch at the Phaeton and another at the Greenhouse, the Evening went off with a great Harmony and Cordiality" (67). He appears to abandon his role as a lover, reverting to the safe masculine identity that guarantees him a wife, the necessary domestic machinery, and the ubiquitous domestic squabble. Austen presents Watts as a humorous male figure who is perfectly capable of acquiring a female counterpart and achieving a secure aesthetic of existence. His accomplishment comically allays a social anxiety about unmarried men, but Austen's juvenile text also illustrates the inability of young men to express and embrace sincere amorous emotions that might destabilize their sexual subjectivities.

7. Austen draws immediate attention to Stanley's exposure to French fashion and culture, experiences that inform his character throughout the story as he remains extremely conscious of his dress and his social activity. He is reported to be "as handsome as a Prince," and he is appropriately forthcoming (206).

8. Despite this great length of time that he devotes to his toilet, Stanley emerges and announces, "have not I been very quick? I never hurried so much in my Life before" (209).

9. Stanley continues to rehearse earlier models of appropriate masculinity when he escorts Kitty to the ball. Upon arriving at the social event, Austen relates that he, "forcibly seizing [Kitty's] arm within his, overpowered her voice with the rapidity of his own" (211). He now reverts to a ridiculous form of chivalry that parodies "gallant" male behavior. It is at the ball, moreover, when we learn from Stanley's family about his other personal traits and ambitions. His sister Camilla, who is also the confidant of Kitty, informs the heroine that her brother has returned from France because "his favourite Hunter . . . was turned out in the park on his going abroad, [or] somehow or other fell ill" (213). Stanley's fondness for hunting, like his concern with his personal appearance, has tremendous influence on his activity, and except for these two overwhelming undertakings, we discover the young man is still relatively uncommitted. Unlike his politically active father, the younger Stanley "was so far from being really of any party, that he had scarcely a fixed opinion on the Subject. He could therefore always take either side, and always argue with temper" (221). He seems to be committed to nothing but his toilet and horse, and the elder Stanley also reports that his son is "by no means disposed to marry" (219). Edward knows how to dress and hunt, but he is still a young man who remains uninterested in either political stances or long-term love relationships. John Halperin describes Edward Stanley as possessing a "peculiar combination of gallantry toward women and egregious self-absorption" (39). Austen highlights Stanley's "peculiar combination" of masculine attributes, and this odd synthesis demonstrates the insecure status of the (new) modern young men of England.

10. LeRoy Smith argues that "Stanley's abrupt departure brings an embarrassing recognition that a young woman should not expect seriousness from a socially privileged young man" (48).

11. See John Davie's explanatory note on this sentence for an extended discussion of Austen's use of the word "nice" (383).

12. Austen's early works do include the occasional romantically inclined man who takes great pride in disregarding parental authority. Edward Lindsay, the hero of "Love and Friendship," is an amusing male character who is perhaps the most memorable lover

of Austen's juvenile writings. Indeed, Lindsay may be the most amorously eloquent and expressive man in Austen's entire corpus. He is initially described as "the most beauteous and amiable Youth," and Laura, the narrator of the tale, indicates that she "felt that on him the happiness or Misery of [her] future Life must depend" (*Catharine* 78, 79). He is a physically attractive man on whom are placed extremely high expectations, but Lindsay is also a comically rebellious figure who has acted against his father's plans for his future wife. Lindsay explains: "My Father, seduced by the false glare of Fortune and the Deluding Pomp of Title, insisted on my giving my hand to Lady Dorothea. No never exclaimed I. Lady Dorothea is lovely and Engaging; I prefer no woman to her; but Know Sir, that I scorn to marry her in compliance with your Wishes. No! Never shall it be said that I obliged my Father" (79). Lindsay's abrupt stance in opposition to his father demonstrates the hero's ridiculous sense of independence. He openly admits to his strong feelings for Lady Dorothea, but he resists a potential marital union with her because it would accord with his father's wishes. Austen's early characterization of Lindsay highlights both his nubile appearance and his fierce obstinacy toward his father. He is a radical beauty, and he is determined to express and act upon his ideas concerning love.

Lindsay proposes to Laura after relating his history with much romantic sensibility. He asks: "[M]y Adorable Laura . . . when may I hope to receive that reward of all the painfull sufferings I have undergone during the course of my Attachment to you, to which I have ever aspired? Oh! when will you reward me with Yourself?" (80). He is a very effective rhetorician who knows how to express both a dramatic story and amorous emotions. And he is also successful, as Laura informs us that they "were immediately united by [her] Father, who tho' he had never taken orders had been bred to the Church" (80). Austen's comic wit suggests the ridiculous quality of Lindsay's romantic language. He believes in the potency of love, and he appears content to live on and through his passion, even if his marriage is not official. Lindsay chides his sister: "[D]id you then never feel the pleasing Pangs of Love. . . . Does it appear impossible to your vile and corrupted Palate, to exist on Love? Can you not conceive the Luxury of living in every Distress that Poverty can inflict, with the object of your tenderest Affection?" (82). Lindsay is committed to his amorous emotions and takes great pleasure in the sensations promoted by his love relationship with Laura. He is a man of great sensibility and sensitivity who remains extremely resistant to the regulatory measures of paternal authority.

When Lindsay later encounters his father, he proclaims that it is his "greatest boast that I have incurred the Displeasure of my Father!" and describes his words and actions as manifestations of "his undaunted Bravery" (83). Lindsay constructs himself as a rebel who is apparently uninterested in both his family's and his society's concern about his future marital plans. While he briefly fashions himself as a courageous and stern man, his actions upon the surprising reunion with his old friend, Augustus, reveal a notably different sensibility. When Lindsay encounters his old companion, he declares, "My Life! my Soul!"; Augustus responds, "My Adorable Angel!" and Austen reports that these passionate men then "flew into each other's arms" (82). Lindsay and Augustus certainly appear comic, but Austen's depiction of their emotional display also emphasizes their powerful passions. They are important anomalies in Austen's corpus: male characters who are able and willing to express feelings and sensations. After Augustus is forced into debtor's prison for his indulgent postmarital lifestyle, Lindsay follows his friend to offer his assistance and comfort, and the men return to the action of the narrative only to die in a fatal phaeton accident. Lindsay manages to survive the crash for a moment, and his wife "was overjoyed to find him yet sensible" (97). He is sensitive and committed to love until his death; he disregards the authority and anxieties of his society in favor of his own passionate desires, including his amorous interests. He denounces the disciplinary measures of his own culture, choosing instead to pursue his sensations and amorous emotions. The post-Revolutionary English nation, however, cannot tolerate such men, and Austen depicts Lindsay's efforts to pursue a life lived on love as frustrated, ridiculous, and tragic.

13. For a further discussion of Lady Susan's radical prominence in Austen's corpus, see Julia L. Epstein, "Jane Austen's Juvenilia and the Female Epistolary Tradition"; Barbara J. Horwitz, "Lady Susan: The Wicked Mother in Jane Austen's Work"; Beatrice Anderson, "The Unmasking of Lady Susan"; and Hugh McKellar, "*Lady Susan:* Sport or Cinderella?"

14. He tells his sister, Mrs. Vernon, that Lady Susan has disturbed the peace of multiple households through her scandalous activity. Reginald respects the cultural importance of the domestic realm, and he views Lady Susan as a threat to this vital domain. Reginald reports to his sister: "By [Lady Susan's] behaviour to Mr. Manwaring, she gave jealousy and wretchedness to his wife, and by her attentions to a young man previously attached to Mr. Manwaring's sister, deprived an amiable girl of her Lover" (211).

15. Lady Susan adds: "[Reginald] is lively and seems clever, and when I have inspired him with greater respect for me than his sister's kind offices have implanted, he may be an agreeable Flirt" (217).

16. Reginald attempts to alleviate his father's fears about the seductive powers of Lady Susan, reporting that he "can have no view in remaining with Lady Susan than to enjoy for a short time . . . the conversation of a Woman of high mental powers." While he does believe that "the World has most grossly injured that Lady, by supposing the worst," Reginald assures his father that he maintains only trivial interests in the elder woman (226). Reginald presents himself as a free-spirited man who is simply enjoying the company of Lady Susan.

17. Reginald's sentimentality is not isolated to his "love" for Lady Susan, as he is also susceptible to Frederica, the heroine's daughter. Frederica appeals directly to the passionate man, requesting his assistance in her efforts to avoid her mother's authority. While Reginald does act on behalf of Frederica, asking Lady Susan to relinquish her plans for the marriage of her daughter to Sir James, he is quickly again enamored of the older woman, declaring that he had "entirely misunderstood Lady Susan" (247). Mrs. Vernon advises her mother that her son is once more under the controls of Lady Susan, warning, "Prepare my dear Madam, for the worst. The probability of their marrying is surely heightened. He is more securely her's [sic] than ever" (251). Mrs. Vernon's reflections highlight the familial concern over the marital plans of Reginald. Austen also suggests an anxiety about his insecure sexual and social subjectivity. Reginald seems conscious of the powerful desires produced for his masculinity, but he is also very nervous. Lady Susan describes him as "a Man whose passions were so violent and resentful," and following their discussion about Frederica's potential marriage to Sir James, she adds that it was easy "to see [in Reginald] the struggle between returning Tenderness and the remains of Displeasure." While Lady Susan finds "something agreable in feelings so easily worked on," Reginald's turbulent emotions demonstrate his personal instability, as he remains susceptible to Lady Susan's charms and unable to revert to a stable masculine sexuality (252–53).

18. Imlay's novel shares many of the Enlightenment sentiments voiced by William Godwin's *Enquiry Concerning Political Justice* (1793), published the same year as *The Emigrants.* Godwin argues that "the actions and dispositions of men are not the offspring of any original bias that they bring into the world in favour of one sentiment or character

rather than another, but flow entirely from the operation of circumstances and events acting upon a faculty of receiving sensible impressions" (I: 26–27). Godwin adds that "the enquirer that has no other object than truth, that refuses to be misled, and is determined to proceed only upon just and sufficient evidence, will find little reason to be satisfied with dogmas which rest upon no other foundation, than a pretended necessity impelling the human mind to yield its assent" (I: 29).

19. Lok's influence on Waldorf, the hero of the novel, is significant; nevertheless, King closes her novel by documenting Waldorf's realization that "the true philosopher seeks the good of mankind; he foregoes his own interests to promote their good, and never hurts them willingly" (II: 61).

20. Hamilton presents Delmond as her hero, who considers honor to be "the inspiring motive of the great and noble" and cherishes "the sentiments of honour" that he learned reading childhood romances of the "lives of those illustrious heroes" (I: 150; 124).

21. Claudia Johnson argues that "Henry categorically denies the gothic any legitimately mimetic provenance" (*Jane Austen* 35).

22. Maria Jerinic argues that "[t]he object of Austen's parody and the real threat to women, however, is not the gothic novel but it is men, particularly men who wish to dictate to women what they should and should not read. Austen does not want to reshape or reform men, but her text does insist that women be allowed the same opportunities as men to choose what they read" (138). Henry, of course, fancies himself an expert critic on literary texts and certainly participates in the authoritative stance described by Jerinic.

23. Henry's commitment to Enlightenment reason specifically affects his attitudes about language. When Catherine refers to Radcliffe's *Mysteries of Udolpho* as a "nice" book, Henry responds: "The nicest;—by which I suppose you mean the neatest. That must depend upon the binding" (83). Henry is a student of Samuel Johnson's *Dictionary of the English Language,* and thus he is convinced that words have definitive meanings that can be ascertained and protected. Eleanor tells Catherine that Henry "is for ever finding fault with me, for some incorrectness of language, and now he is taking the same liberty with you. The word 'nicest,' as you used it, did not suit him; and you had better change it as soon as you can, or we shall be overpowered with Johnson and Blair" (83). Eleanor describes her brother as a man obsessed with the proper and fixed meanings of words, and while Henry's fondness for Johnson and Blair may not appear to demonstrate his commitment to rationality, his desire to demarcate appropriate definitions illustrates his participation in the Enlightenment project to delineate and enforce specific categories of knowledge and experience. Henry explains that "originally perhaps ['nice'] was applied only to express neatness, propriety, delicacy, or refinement;—people were nice in their dress, in their sentiments, or their choice. But now every commendation on every subject is comprised in that one word" (84). He is very frustrated that words are no longer used in the "correct" manner, and his attitude implies that they indeed have *a* proper usage. By calling for specified semantics, our hero demonstrates his commitment to a dichotomous understanding of language and thought as either reasonable or unreasonable. Johnson argues that "because Henry dictates the parameters of words, the kind of control he exercises extends to thought itself" (*Jane Austen* 38). For a further consideration of this scene, see Johnson, *Jane Austen,* 39. For a more extensive discussion of Henry's attitudes on language, see Tara Ghoshal Wallace, "*Northanger Abbey* and the Limits of Parody," 264.

24. For more discussion on the General's interests in domesticity, see Hoeveler, 129–30.

25. General Tilney uses his gallantry to exercise authority and control, but he eventually acts in a notably nongallant manner when he turns Catherine from Northanger "without any reason that could justify, any apology that could atone for the abruptness, the rudeness, nay, the insolence of it" (183). See Tanner 65 for a consideration of the General's gallantry.

26. Austen introduces Henry as "a very gentlemanlike young man" who was "rather tall, had a pleasing countenance, a very intelligent and lively eye, and, if not quite handsome, was very near it" (11). The narrator's initial description announces the hero to be a gentleman, but her qualifying statements immediately draw attention to the construction of such a chivalric man of gentility.

27. For further consideration of this frequently discussed conversation, see Diane Hoeveler's "Vindicating *Northanger Abbey*," 125–26 and David Monaghan, *Jane Austen: Structure and Social Vision*, 20–21.

28. For an extensive consideration of the implications involved in Henry's comments on marriage, see Johnson, *Jane Austen*, 38, and Tanner 63.

29. Austen quickly invites us to laugh at such social propriety, however, as Henry informs Catherine: "Take care, or you will forget to be tired of [Bath] at the proper time.—You ought to be tired at the end of six weeks" (58). The narrator again displays Henry's awareness of the irrational conventions associated with "proper" chivalric social activity, allowing us to laugh at the knowledge and performance of the impressive hero.

30. Marvin Mudrick offers a compelling reading of John Thorpe. Mudrick claims that Thorpe is "importunate and unscrupulous enough to carry the Gothic role; but there is nothing sinister about him. He is simply exasperating, vulgar, rude, and foolish" (46). Mudrick concludes that that Thorpe does not "[abduct] or [torture] Catherine when she declines his attentions; he does not even connive with her father at marrying her against her will. His world and his talent are too limited for spectacular achievements; but he does as much mischief as he can" (47).

31. Henry's comments are ironic not only because of the General's later tyrannical activities, but also because of the country and the age in which this novel was written. Austen's language reminds readers of the Napoleonic Wars and the larger post-Revolutionary turmoil that racked the English nation. Tony Tanner points out that "Henry tries to evoke an England which is a kind of phantasm of peaceful life from which the possibility of horror and violence has been eradicated" (71). Johnson's work has been instrumental in drawing attention to the political overtones of Austen's language. For a consideration of the language employed by Henry in this scene, see *Jane Austen* 40.

32. Joseph Litvak acknowledges Henry's knowledge of literary texts but insists that Henry disciplines the literary quality of novels. See "Charming Men, Charming History," especially 255–56.

33. Henry's rationality also guides his attitude and behavior toward women; he appears conscious of the social debates about women's intellectual abilities, but he is also aware of hackneyed conceptions of the young female. For example, Henry announces his fear to Catherine that he "shall make but a poor figure in your journal tomorrow," demonstrating his knowledge of women's supposedly compulsory habit (12). He explains: "My dear madam, I am not so ignorant of young ladies' ways as you wish to believe me; it is this delightful habit of journalizing which largely contributed to form the easy style of writing for which ladies are so generally celebrated. Every body allows that the talent of writing agreeable letters is peculiarly female. Nature may have done something, but I am sure it must be essentially assisted by the practice of keeping a journal" (13).

Henry's comment is both humorous and presumptuous, as he presumes that Catherine must keep such a daily account. He is also aware of the trends and maintenance of female attire, and he informs Mrs. Allen that he purchased a gown for his sister "the other day, and it was pronounced to be a prodigious bargain by every lady who saw it." Henry is an apparent expert in women's clothing and can even spot a deal. He can purchase fashionable clothing, locate economical garments, and even evaluate the durability of fabric. When Mrs. Allen asks him about Catherine's gown, Henry replies: "It is very pretty, madam . . . but I do not think it will wash well; I am afraid it will fray" (14). He is comfortable and confident demonstrating his knowledge of women's dresses so long as he restricts himself to rational remarks. For a discussion of Henry's skill as a tailor, see Hardy, *Jane Austen's Heroines*, 3–6 and Morgan, *In the Meantime*, 67.

34. Many critics have drawn attention to Henry's condescending attitude toward women. See especially Jerinic 144; Johnson, *Jane Austen*, 37–38; Cohen 222–24; and Litvak 267.

35. Castle adds that "Henry does not so much tell Catherine *what* to think as show her that she *can* think" (Introduction xxii). Henry appears to know Wollstonecraft's *Vindication,* but as Johnson argues, he often behaves as "a self-proclaimed expert on matters feminine, from epistolary style to muslin" who "simply believes that he knows women's minds better than they do" (*Jane Austen* 37). Johnson's criticism recalls the perception of Henry as an arrogant individual. He is a confident man who can participate in many discussions and perform various masculine roles, and he is even willing to instruct women in matters "feminine." Henry is a performer, and he can play a variety of parts, but he is also exposed as a self-conscious comic character who is aware of the artifice involved in his composite masculine social/sexual subjectivity.

36. Mark Loveridge, for example, argues that "Henry is sophisticated," and "has his own, rather unnerving, analytical attitude to the world, to Catherine, and to the idea of character" (6). And Mudrick points out that "Henry prides himself on his worldliness and his lack of sentimentality" (43). Loveridge, Mudrick, and others are correct to emphasize our hero's sophisticated analytic approach, but the report of his brother's impending marriage and the corresponding collapse of James Morland's engagement threaten to shatter Henry's worldview and his understanding of love. He cannot comprehend these events, and Johnson's *Dictionary* is unable to explain them clearly. Various critics have linked Henry's sophistication to the novelist's own sophisticated persona. For a discussion of this interesting topic, see Mudrick 43 and Wallace, "*Northanger Abbey* and the Limits of Parody," 262.

37. Henry's immediate response to this moment of personal instability is to leave Northanger. He announces to Catherine and Eleanor: "I am come, young ladies, in a very moralizing strain, to observe that our pleasures in this world are always to be paid for, and that we often purchase them at a great disadvantage, giving ready-monied happiness for a draft on the future, that may not be honoured" (170). As he prepares to leave for his other home at Woodston, he reflects upon the sacrifices he has and must make. Austen again emphasizes her hero's self-consciousness, allowing her hero to invoke an edifying tone and adopt the discourse of Dr. Johnson. Henry seems aware of the consequences he has had to accept because of his efforts to develop a complete masculine subjectivity and sexuality. His duties at Woodston force him to leave Northanger and the heroine, but before he departs he offers Catherine a "gratified look on being told that her stay was determined" (178). This is the most overt expression of affection that Austen allows Henry in the novel.

38. Susan Morgan claims that Henry, "in the finest spirit of romance, defies his father for the sake of true love" (68). Margaret Kirkham echoes Morgan, suggesting that Henry "learns to see in Catherine's unaffected character qualities which inspire true affection" (88). And LeRoy Smith argues that "the qualities that have attracted Henry Tilney to Catherine from the first—spontaneity of feeling and expression, honesty and openness, natural taste—are unchanged by her disillusioning experience. They move Henry to propose in spite of his father's objections" (59). These critics neglect Austen's self-consciousness as a novelist and ignore the absence of any indication that Henry "loves" Catherine. He does rehearse certain aspects of the romantic male role, but his dogmatic rationality prevents him from expressing sincere amorous emotions. His esteem stems from an assurance of Catherine's affection, and even the narrator does not attempt to define this union as a love relationship.

39. Austen discusses the hero's complex story about the General's misunderstanding of Catherine's potential wealth and announces: "I leave it to my reader's sagacity to determine how much of all this it was possible for Henry to communicate at this time to Catherine" (201). Austen again openly acknowledges her own narrative artifice, and she also elaborates on the self-consciously rebellious activity of Henry.

40. Austen's depiction of the General recalls the behavior of Radcliffe's Marquis of Mazzini, the villain of *A Sicilian Romance* (1790). Radcliffe's novel details how the Marquis loses his rational faculties and becomes "successively the slave of alternate passions" (184). Late in the story, the narrator notes that the Marquis's "head grew dizzy, and a sudden faintness overcame him . . . [he] found himself unable to stand" (189). General Tilney is likewise overcome by the emotions engendered by his daughter's marriage and loses control of his rational faculties.

Notes to Chapter 3

1. Foucault's late work on the ancients has received much criticism and insufficient serious consideration in terms of his overall project on the history of sexuality. For an extensive consideration of Foucault's writing on Greek and Roman cultural and sexual practices, see Paul Veyne, "The Final Foucault and His Ethics," and Foucault's own essay, "Writing the Self," both in *Foucault and his Interlocutors,* edited by Arnold I. Davidson.

2. As Foucault later explains, "Moderation was quite regularly represented among the qualities that belonged—or at least should belong—not just to anyone but particularly to those who had rank, status, and responsibility" (*History of Sexuality, Vol. 2: The Use of Pleasure* 61). Foucault explains that the man who was able to curtail his sensations was able to "[derive] pleasure from the moderation [he displayed]" (65).

3. LeRoy Smith claims that Willoughby is "the most sexually attractive of Austen's males" (77).

4. The youthful heroine insists that "Mr. Willoughby . . . is the only person who can have a right to shew that house," and hesitatingly remarks that the grounds "will one day be Mr. Willoughby's" (58–59). Marianne has already planned her marriage to the man whom she considers the eventual owner of the Allenham estate.

5. For an interesting consideration of female authority in the novel, see Tara Ghoshal Wallace, "*Sense and Sensibility* and the Problem of Feminine Authority" and Phoebe A. Smith's "*Sense and Sensibility* and 'The Lady's Law': The Failure of Benevolent Paternalism."

6. We learn that he has left his card while the Dashwood sisters were out (146). We discover that he received an invitation to attend a small dance sponsored by Sir John but did not attend (148), and we know that he does not return Marianne's letters. His character is certainly altered, and Elinor now relates "her suspicions of Willoughby's inconstancy" to her mother (149).

7. He retains a strong romantic sensibility for Marianne, and even the coldly rational Elinor realizes "that such a [romantic] regard had formerly existed" between him and her sister (155). The sisters' reaction to "Willoughby's" harsh letter provides us with further information concerning both his relationship to Marianne and his efforts to resolve the complex social forces that affect his self and gender. Elinor reacts quite strongly to the epistle. She could not "have supposed Willoughby capable of departing so far from the appearance of every honourable and delicate feeling—so far from the common decorum of a gentleman" (159). Critiquing his dishonorable, ungenteel language, Elinor reconstructs Willoughby through her expectation that he should write and behave as a socially proper gentleman. Marianne shatters her sister's perspective when she declares that "he is not so unworthy as you believe him" and informs her that "he has broken no faith with me" (161). Adamant that he did once reciprocate her amorous affection, the passionate heroine refuses to accuse Willoughby of conspiring against her. She claims that it is easier to believe that she has been deceived "by all the world, rather than by his own heart" (164). She even questions the potentially manipulative actions of his female companion at the previous evening's affair (165). Although Marianne's emotion overwhelms her, she also seems strangely aware of the many forces that have influenced Willoughby's actions. Wallace examines the multiple figures of feminine control in the novel and suggests that "there are so many women who inscribe their desires on Willoughby, who assert authority over him." Wallace concludes that Willoughby's "own desire, his very self, becomes muted and blurred" (*Sense and Sensibility* 157). Mrs. Smith, Elinor, Marianne, and others develop expectations for Willoughby. Paralleling the social discourses of masculinity that inform the construction of his self, he must resolve the requests of these authoritative women and his attraction and repulsion to their desires.

8. The Colonel's story, coupled with the news of Willoughby's marriage to Miss Grey, greatly alter the public perception of Brandon and Willoughby. Even though he explains to Elinor that his tale was meant only to alleviate her sister's suffering and not "to raise myself at the expense of others," the Colonel does garner a new level of respect after he tells his story (183). Marianne no longer avoids him, and the narrator reports that the romantic heroine "was obliged, or could oblige herself to speak" to the mature and rheumatic man (188). Mr. John Dashwood cautiously approves of Brandon's "[t]wo thousand a-year" living (195), and the Colonel again demonstrates his artistic sensibility by appreciating Elinor's screens (205). In addition, public attitudes toward Willoughby have significantly altered. Ultimately, the discourses and narratives that Sir John, the Palmers, and others constructed for a man like Willoughby have all failed. Sir John "could not have thought it possible" that a man "of whom he had always had such reason to think well" could ruthlessly neglect Marianne for another woman. After all, Sir John "did not believe there was a bolder rider in England." Mrs. Palmer "was determined to drop [Willoughby's] acquaintance immediately, and she was very thankful that she had never been acquainted with him at all" (187). Members of Willoughby's society recognize his inability to embrace fully the various demands they have placed upon him and chastise him for this "failure."

9. When her sickness becomes severe, and the Palmers realize they must vacate Cleveland for the safety of their child, Mrs. Jennings's cunningly acknowledges the need

for the Colonel to remain near the object of his affection. Mrs. Jennings also declares that "his stay at Cleveland was necessary to herself, that she should want him to play at piquet of an evening" (269). She attempts to reconfigure Brandon as a romantic and sentimental lover, but Mr. Palmer insists that the Colonel is simply a stable and knowledgeable man, "a person so well able to assist or advise Miss Dashwood in any emergence" (270). Mr. Palmer, like Brandon, has abandoned the role of the lover for the safety of a disciplined aesthetic of existence. Mr. Palmer cannot comprehend the Colonel's romantic reasons for remaining at Cleveland, but he has little difficulty understanding the utility of the mature Brandon in such a dire moment.

10. He adds: "To avoid a comparative poverty, which [Marianne's] affection and her society would have deprived of all its horrors, I have, by raising myself to affluence, lost every thing that could make it a blessing." Willoughby broaches his sustained love for Marianne, and the financial urgencies that forced his desperate actions; moreover, he is conscious of the decisions he had to make to limit his emotional sensibility and govern his desires. He can still recall the amorous passions enflamed by his time with Marianne. He admits: "To have resisted such attractions, to have withstood such tenderness!—Is there a man on earth who could have done it!" (281).

11. He tells Elinor not to feel sympathy for his present status, but for "my situation as it was *then*. . . . my head and heart full of your sister," when he "was forced to play the happy lover to another woman" (287). His self-consciousness reminds us of his training in the tradition of sensibility, but his remarks also suggest his earlier engagement in amorous emotions. Willoughby, in order to regulate his aesthetic of existence, has had to eschew the behavior of the male lover in favor of a well-disciplined masculinity. Marilyn Butler posits that "Willoughby's crime proves . . . not to have been rank villainy, but expensive self-indulgence so habitual that he must sacrifice everything, including domestic happiness, to it" (*Jane Austen and the War of Ideas* 194). Willoughby, indeed, has been self-indulgent. Austen's tale dramatizes how multiple and contradictory social desires prevent Willoughby from achieving a stable sexuality, but the narrator also emphasizes the causal effects of his decisions. Miss Dashwood listens patiently to the story of Willoughby's reconfigured masculinity and softened considerably in her attitude toward him, but she harshly reminds him, "You have made your own choice. It was not forced on you" (289). Elinor, through Austen's novelistic narration, explains the dynamics of his difficult situation:

> The world had made him extravagant and vain—Extravagance and vanity had made him cold-hearted and selfish. Vanity, while seeking its own guilty triumph at the expense of another, had involved him in a real attachment, which extravagance, or at least its offspring, necessity, had required to be sacrificed. Each faulty propensity in leading him to evil, had led him likewise to punishment. The attachment, from which against honour, against feeling, against every better interest he had outwardly torn himself, now, when no longer allowable, governed every thought; and the connection, for the sake of which he had, with little scruple, left her sister to misery, was likely to prove a source of unhappiness to himself of a far more incurable nature. (290–91)

Even the sense-saturated Elinor, sounding like a reflective Dr. Johnson, can identify the multilayered complexities of Willoughby's decisions and actions, and she is alert to the severe consequences that he must now embrace.

12. Alistair Duckworth argues that "Marianne's marriage to the rheumatic Colonel Brandon is a gross over-compensation for her misguided sensibility" (104).

13. Austen adds additional salt to his wounds by suggesting that "had he behaved with honour towards Marianne," Mrs. Smith would have offered him financial support, and "he might at once have been happy and rich" (334). The narrator suggests that had Willoughby reverted to chivalric rather than rational masculinity, he might have enjoyed financial security and a love relationship.

Notes to Chapter 4

1. For an interesting consideration of the long-standing popularity of *Pride and Prejudice* and its doting readers, see Joseph Litvak's "Delicacy and Disgust, Mourning and Melancholia, Privilege and Perversity: *Pride and Prejudice*" and Gene Koppel's "*Pride and Prejudice*: Conservative or Liberal Novel—Or Both? (A Gadmerian Approach)." Barbara Sherrod describes *Pride and Prejudice* as a "classic love story because it set the pattern for a modern popular love story, the story in which an independent-minded and fascinating woman is loved by a remote, powerful man" (68). For further consideration of the great attractiveness of Darcy, Elizabeth, and this "timeless" love story, see Lisa Hopkins, "Mr. Darcy's Body: Privileging the Female Gaze," Cheryl L. Nixon's "Balancing the Courtship Hero: Masculine Emotional Display in Film Adaptations of Austen's Novels," and Norma Rowen's "Reinscribing Cinderella: Jane Austen and the Fairy Tale."

2. Darcy is introduced as a "fine, tall person [with] handsome features, [and a] noble mien" and is appreciated for his appearance and "his having ten thousand a year" (7). He is a physically impressive man with many favorable attributes, and the other characters in the novel consistently reflect upon both his great wealth and his extensive accomplishments. When Charlotte Lucas discusses his purported pride with Elizabeth, the heroine's friend concludes that "his pride . . . does not offend *me* so much as pride often does, because there is an excuse for it. One cannot wonder that so very fine a young man, with family, fortune, every thing in his favour, should think highly of himself. If I may so express it, he has a *right* to be proud" (16). Charlotte ties Darcy's phenomenal individual accomplishments to his familial background and income, which James Heldman notes "is at least 300 times the per capita income in his day" ("How Wealthy" 39). Darcy's economic supremacy facilitates his personal flexibility and romantic grandeur, and according to Charlotte there is nothing wrong with owning up to your accomplishments. Charlotte's unnamed younger brother agrees: "If I were as rich as Mr. Darcy . . . I should not care how proud I was. I would keep a pack of foxhounds, and drink a bottle of wine every day" (16). Darcy is perceived as an appropriately confident man who functions as a role model for aspiring English boys.

3. Sherrod explains that Darcy's "love for Elizabeth makes him a better person [and] brings out the excellence of his character" (68).

4. John McAleer theorizes that Austen imagined a moral society as an effectively organized country estate that must be "administered by a caring landowner." McAleer adds that "a country estate was an embodiment of the natural moral order" and concludes that "[Austen] asked only that men would so conduct themselves that their behaviour would affirm the existence of a stable order energized by sound moral principles" (72).

5. Austen scholars have often discussed the importance of social class status in *Pride*

and Prejudice, but these critical treatments tend to revolve around the wealth of Darcy and the financial dilemmas of unmarried women. James Heldman, for example, points out that "[m]oney matters to everyone—to avid readers of Jane Austen as well as to normal people. It certainly mattered to Jane Austen herself. Her novels and her letters are liberally peppered with references to money. Characters are defined by their incomes and fortunes as much as they are by their appearances and their manners" ("How Wealthy" 38). And John McAleer explains that "each character in *Pride and Prejudice* adds to our knowledge of the workings of the social hierarchy" (74).

6. Austen's characterization of Bingley and Gardiner reflects this new cultural attitude, and their bourgeois ambition likewise recalls Godwin's post-Revolutionary critique of ancestral authority in his *Enquiry Concerning Political Justice* (1793). Godwin argues that "a generous blood, a gallant and fearless spirit, is by no means propagated from father to son" (I: 41). He insists that humans are equal and perfectible beings who maintain "the faculty of being continually made better and receiving perpetual improvement" (I: 92–93). Although neither Bingley nor Gardiner echoes Godwin's overt criticism of aristocratic heritage, they do embody his advocacy of individual amelioration.

7. Austen's portrayal of these ambitious male characters reminds us of Godwin's depiction of Barnabas Tyrrel in *Caleb Williams* (1794). Like Bingley and Gardiner, Tyrrel is a thriving member of the middle class who has raised himself in the social class system; Godwin even announces that he "might have passed for a true model of the English squire" (16). Bingley and Gardiner attempt to imitate the behavior of such an ersatz gentlemen, and while Austen, unlike Godwin, does not allow a villainous aristocrat to murder her aspiring men, she also does not allow her men of trade to assume aristocratic standing.

8. McAleer concludes that to Mr. Bingley "has fallen the task of acquiring a landed estate, the essential move that will establish him as a gentleman" (73).

9. When his sisters laugh at the report that the Bennets have an uncle who resides "somewhere near Cheapside," Bingley responds, "If they had uncles enough to fill *all* Cheapside . . . it would not make them one jot less agreeable" (30). As a man of trade himself, Bingley defends the domestic location of Mr. Gardiner, but Darcy instructs his friend that having relations in this mercantile center "must very materially lessen [the Bennet sisters'] chance of marrying men of any consideration in the world." Bingley makes "no answer" to Darcy's explanation, and his silence suggests his inability to understand fully the importance of class to complex social power structures and potential marital unions (31).

10. Juliet McMaster argues that "in Bingley we see the best of social mobility. He is good-humored and charming, and he never stands on ceremony" ("Class" 124). McMaster accurately identifies the attractive qualities of Bingley's character, but he is still a man in transition, and his social instability prevents him from experiencing utter happiness like Darcy.

11. Dennis Allen claims that "Jane and Bingley are prevented from the consummation of their love by diffidence, which makes each doubt that his or her love is reciprocated, and they are separated by Bingley's malleability, which makes him excessively dependent on Darcy's opinion." Allen concludes that "[t]heir reunion is brought about . . . by a reversal of Darcy's machinations, itself evidence that Bingley is still easily influenced" (436). Even at the novel's close, Darcy retains a definite degree of influence over his friend; Darcy managed to remove Bingley from Jane, and he now maneuvers to bring them together again.

12. For an interesting discussion of the marriage between Jane and Bingley, see Joel Weinsheimer's "Chance and the Hierarchy of Marriages in *Pride and Prejudice*," 18–19, Marvin Mudrick, *Jane Austen: Irony as Defense and Discovery* 105, and Bruce Stovel's "'A Contrariety of Emotion': Jane Austen's Ambivalent Lovers in *Pride and Prejudice*," 29.

13. For more discussion on the "worthiness" of Gardiner, see Monaghan, *Jane Austen: Structure and Social Vision*, 87; Juliet McMaster, "Class," 124; and Rachel Brownstein, "Jane Austen: Irony and Authority," 63.

14. Mrs. Reynolds, in her discussions with the Gardiners, claims that she "never had a cross word from [Darcy] in my life, and I have known him ever since he was four years old. . . . If I was to go through the world, I could not meet with a better." She speaks of Darcy as "the best landlord, and the best master . . . that ever lived" (218–19). David Monaghan indicates that "Darcy does not expect his employees to be groveling subordinates, but regards them as sensible human beings whose respect must be earned. Neither does he see them simply as instruments of labour, but rather as rational human beings who must be included in the community of the big house and introduced to Pemberley values" (83). Susan Morgan adds that "Darcy is an outstanding member of society, a landowner with both power and responsibility" (80). Mrs. Reynolds's comments may be the result of many years of intimacy with Darcy, but critics continue to laud the hero as a remarkable man.

15. Gardiner may model many of the masculine traits requested by Burke, but the tradesman also relies upon his reason, and he understands that in a modern post-chivalric nation men are not killed in duels. Moreover, when he joins Mr. Bennet in London, he agrees to assist his brother-in-law in his plan to "enquire at all the principal hotels in town," even though "Mr. Gardiner himself did not expect any success from this measure, but as his brother was eager in it, he meant to assist him in pursuing it" (260). Mr. Gardiner is a dutiful man who is willing to serve when needed, but he has nothing to prove. He is neither a youth who feels compelled to impress others with his valor and virility, nor a stern man of rigid tradition who must impose a strict procedural policy. He shows no inclination to "correct" idiotic people like Mr. Collins or Mrs. Bennet, and he, like Mr. Bennet, does not believe that the purpose of life is to "make sport for our neighbours, and laugh at them in our turn" (323). Gardiner is not interested in establishing unquestionable authority or raising himself at the expense of others. He is a respectable character because of his mature social affability that enables him to enhance his cultural role.

Notes to Chapter 5

1. In the early 1970s, a period that witnessed a severe reconfiguration of Austen as a politically invested writer, Duckworth and Butler turned to *Mansfield Park* to demonstrate Austen's anxiety about the stability of her society. Duckworth claims that in this novel Austen "is concerned with defining a proper relation between the individual and society" (37). Duckworth explains that such a relationship revolves around the individual's appreciation for the landed estate; he insists that individuals must discover and embrace their "proper" relation to society to "improve" the estate, cleansing it of modern perversions and returning it to an ancestral status. Duckworth concludes that "an estate is the appropriate home of what Burke terms the 'collected reason of the ages' or the 'wisdom of our ancestors'; and for Jane Austen as for Burke, historical prescription is an important basis for social and moral behavior" (58). Duckworth aligns Austen with Burke, suggesting that

Mansfield Park illustrates an ambition to recreate a nation rooted in ancestral wisdom, historical precedents, and traditional modes of behavior. Butler, likewise, reads the narrative as an explicitly anti-Jacobin text, claiming that "*Mansfield Park* is the most visibly ideological of Jane Austen's novels. . . . [in which] she can exploit to the full the artistic possibilities of the conservative case" (*War of Ideas* 219). Butler argues that "the theme of *Mansfield Park* is the contrast of man-centred or selfish habits of mind, with a temper that is sceptical of self and that refers beyond self to objective values" (*Jane Austen and the War of Ideas* 247). For Butler, Austen's novel advocates the sacrifice of self-importance for the good of the national community and its "shared" values.

2. Alma Zook investigates what she terms "the one explicitly astronomical reference in all of [Austen's] novels" and concludes that "Miss Austen gets it right." Zook indicates that the narrator's "reporting of the evening sky during this incident is sufficiently accurate and detailed," and Austen's precise description of this evening's sky suggests her concern with this event (29). Zook maintains that Austen's description of the night sky is accurate enough "that one may determine, to a fair degree of precision, the orientation of the drawing room at Mansfield Park in which this conversation takes place" (29).

3. Edmund appears to endorse Burke's revised version of the social contract as a "partnership [in which] all men have equal rights; but not to equal things." Burke adds that "he that has but five shillings in the partnership, has as good a right to it, as he that has five hundred pound has to his larger proportion" (110). Austen's hero, per Burke's theory, works to ensure that each member of society assumes a stable and efficient role in the nation.

4. Yuval-Davis effectively discusses the tripartite national significance of women, as she analyzes three discourses that "use" women to perpetuate national projects: (1) the people as power; (2) the eugenicist; and (3) the Malthusian. For an extensive discussion of these discourses, see Yuval-Davis 26–38.

5. For a detailed discussion of the Prince Regent's scandalous activity, see Sales 56–83.

6. This early encounter highlights Edmund's role as a supporter and protector of Fanny, and as Laura Mooneyham argues, his first act for his cousin "prepares us for the role Edmund will play in Fanny's education" (71). While we are far removed from his eventual marriage to the heroine, our hero quickly demonstrates his pastoral care for Fanny.

7. Pepper Worthington argues that "we are convinced Edmund Bertram will wear no lace on his shirts, no flowers in his lapels, no gold on his fingers, no make-up on his face." He maintains that Edmund is "a man of character . . . steady, predictable, the salt of the earth" (73).

8. Oliver MacDonagh notes that Edmund "presents the clergyman as social moulder," concluding that "it is not precisely social control which Edmund here envisages, but rather a form of social husbandry" (44).

9. Gary Kelly suggests that while "Mary Crawford . . . can only see the church as a field of play for the individual and the individualist," Edmund defends "the church as an important moral and therefore an important social institution . . . [echoing] the greatest British attacker of individualism and defender of traditional social institutions, that other Edmund, one of the greatest public speakers of the age, Edmund Burke" ("Reading Aloud" 133, 135). Tony Tanner maintains that Austen "clearly considered the role of the clergyman as being of special importance—less for the saving of souls . . . and more for the saving of society" (170).

10. For a specific discussion of the history of *Lovers' Vows*, see Pedley 311–12. Edmund's initial concerns with converting his father's house into a private theatre and allowing women to act are particularly important to Pedley's consideration of the scandalous dramatic production. Pedley specifically investigates the social opprobrium of female actors.

11. Duckworth notes that "despite all his reasoning, his agreement to act in the play marks his surrender to Mary Crawford's sexual attraction" (63). Mary later remembers his struggle to resist participating in the histrionic activities and proclaims, "His sturdy spirit to bend as it did! Oh! it was sweet beyond expression" (325). Depicting Edmund as a fallen hero in a sinister manner, Mary invokes the discourse of the heroic male reminiscent of Burke's writings but also notes her ability to tempt the "hero" into dangerous detours. She seems aware of Edmund's simultaneous attraction and repulsion to her and the opportunities she offers.

12. Following Edmund's disappointing evening at the ball, he departs for a week to Peterborough. Anticipating his son's eventual occupancy at Thornton Lacey, Sir Thomas informs Fanny that "As to Edmund, we must learn to do without him. This will be the last winter of his belonging to us, as he has done" (257). Predicting Edmund's permanent move from Mansfield, Sir Thomas presents his son as an adolescent male on the verge of manhood.

13. Sir Thomas's behavior is reminiscent of Imlay's Lord B——, who maintains that "the *tranquility of society depended upon the tyranny* which should be continually exercised over [women], otherwise a female *empire would destroy every thing that was beautiful, and which the talents of ages had accumulated*" (106).

14. For an impressive discussion of Edmund's strange feelings for Fanny at this point in the novel, see Claudia Johnson, *Jane Austen: Women, Politics, and the Novel,* 117.

15. We learn that Sir Thomas has proclaimed that his younger son "must be for ever divided from Miss Crawford" (413).

16. Austen uses the subjunctive mood to relate the alteration in her hero's attitude, revealing that this shift remains contrary to reality.

17. Critics, not surprisingly, have diverse views on the closing marriage of *Mansfield Park*. Laura Mooneyham notes the "relative passivity" that permeates the "scope allowed Edmund's and Fanny's romantic resolution." Mooneyham maintains that "Austen no doubt considered a love scene between Fanny and Edmund an unnecessary effusion" (105–6). Julia Prewitt Brown, on the other hand, claims that "the marriage of Fanny and Edmund is consciously invested with hope" (98). John Skinner reminds us that the strange marital union "further undermines expectations of orderly dénouement" (139). Austen tells us of "the joyful consent which met Edmund's application" for marriage (430), but Masami Usui correctly asserts that the "ending of Fanny's happy marriage . . . cannot be judged by the conventional value of marriage" (21). Moira Ferguson astutely mentions that when Edmund "decides [Fanny] will make him an appropriate wife, her parents' response is not mentioned. We assume they are neither told nor invited to the wedding" (125).

Notes to Chapter 6

1. Mary Evans places Austen's work in the context of England's post–French Revolution modernization and indicates that its "transformation . . . into an industrial capitalist

society involved the thorough integration of all aspects of social and material life into a form of order compatible with the demands of a society geared to the maximization of profit" (3). In this newly developing world, states must organize and employ any and all social resources, including their populations, effectively and strategically. Although the community of Highbury is not yet industrialized, *Emma* prefigures significant modifications in England's ancestral economic system, such as the rise of the trade class and the optimism of the yeomanry.

2. Austen dedicated the work to the Prince Regent, and it received the rave reviews of Walter Scott, England's most prolific and best-known author of the day. For a specific discussion of Austen's dedication and Scott's review, see B. C. Southam's Introduction to *Jane Austen: The Critical Heritage, Vol. I*. In the twentieth century, Trilling dubbed the novel's representation of England as "idyllic" (59), and Susan Morgan hailed it as "the great English novel of the early nineteenth century" (50).

3. Duckworth reads Austen's corpus as a body of conservative Tory texts that advocate social improvement via the improvement of the manor estate in her novels. He uses *Mansfield Park* as the basis for this argument and claims that *Emma* is also extremely concerned with improving the estate; however, he claims *Persuasion* is a failure because the estate is abandoned. It is worth noting that when Frank brings Harriet back to Hartfield after the encounter with the gypsies, Austen tells us that Emma quickly gave "notice of there being such a set of people in the neighbourhood to Mr. Knightley" (301).

4. The heroine's description of Donwell may have inspired Trilling's idyllic account of the world of *Emma*. He asserts that "there appears in *Emma* a tendency to conceive of a specifically English ideal of life" (53). He adds that "we cannot help feeling that 'English verdure, English culture, English comfort, seen under a sun bright without being oppressive' make an England perceived—if but for a moment—as an idyll" (57).

5. Foucault continues by pointing out that this modern individual is one "who lives, speaks, and works in accordance with the laws of an economics, a philology, and a biology . . . a being whose nature (that which determines it, contains it, and has traversed it from the beginning of time) is to know nature, and itself, in consequence, as a natural being" (*Order of Things* 310).

6. Foucault explains that "to man's experience a body has been given, a body which is his body—a fragment of ambiguous space, whose peculiar and irreducible spatiality is nevertheless articulated upon the space of things" (*Order of Things* 314).

7. It is interesting that while Knightley is tremendously critical of Frank throughout the story, our hero also envies his youthful counterpart. Late in the novel, Knightley informs Emma that "Frank Churchill is, indeed, the favourite of fortune. Every thing turns out for his good.—He meets with a young woman at a watering-place, gains her affection, cannot even weary her by negligent treatment—and had he and all his family sought round the world for a perfect wife for him, they could not have found her superior.—His aunt is in the way.—His aunt dies.—He has only to speak.—His friends are eager to promote his happiness.—He has used every body ill—and they are all delighted to forgive him.—He is a fortunate man indeed!" (388).

8. Johnson argues that "in moving to Hartfield, Knightley is sharing [Emma's] home, and in placing himself within her domain, Knightley gives his blessing to her rule" (*Jane Austen* 143).

9. Mrs. Arlbery later adds that in such a marriage, "The balance is always just, where

force is not used. The man has his reasons for chusing you; you have your reasons for suffering yourself to be chosen. What his are, you have no business to enquire; nor has he the smallest right to investigate yours" (780).

10. Knightley adds later that Mr. Martin was bitterly distressed by the rejection of his proposal, claiming that "a man cannot be more so" (90).

11. Mrs. Weston, interestingly enough, later directly confronts Mr. Knightley about his inexperience regarding intimate companions, reminding him that he is "so much used to [living] alone" that he "[does] not know the value of a companion" (32).

12. Although he refers to Harriet as a potential "silly wife" early in the novel, he later reports on her education and social development, announcing to Emma that she has become "an artless, amiable girl, with very good notions, very seriously good principles . . . placing her happiness in the affections and utility of domestic life" (431). Knightley discusses earlier signs of Harriet's social improvement. See specifically 293–95 and 298.

13. Prior to leaving for London, Knightley asks Emma if she has "any thing to send or say, besides the 'love,' which nobody carries" (348). While his comment is certainly conventional, it also suggests the hero's conception of love.

14. Knightley has made earlier mention of his knowledge of and intimacy with Emma from an early age. He tells Mrs. Weston that "Emma is spoiled by being the cleverest of her family. At ten years old, she had the misfortune of being able to answer questions which puzzled her sister at seventeen" (32).

Notes to Chapter 7

1. Nina Auerbach's groundbreaking essay, "O Brave New World: Evolution and Revolution in *Persuasion*," ushered in a new wave of criticism on this final completed Austen novel. Auerbach argued that *Persuasion* develops a new world that will be "guided by emotion and vision" and "governed by nature and by human desire." The men and women of the old landed interests "who cannot accommodate themselves to these laws . . . are threatened and deprived of power" by "the representatives of nature and feeling" (117). Many critics have followed Auerbach's lead in discussing how the novel imagines both the death of an old world and the development of a new world. Tony Tanner argues that "in this novel . . . institutions and codes and related values have undergone a radical transformation or devaluation. There *are* values, but many of them are new; and they are relocated or resisted" (216). Charles J. Rzepka returns specifically to Auerbach's articles and claims that "in *Persuasion*, the highest type of self-realization, for women as for men, seems to be comprised in the notion of active contribution, not in claims to individual rights and privileges, nor to freedom or self-assertion and self-expression, all of which can more aptly be said to characterize the values of Sir Walter and Elizabeth . . . than of Anne Elliot and Frederick Wentworth" (108). See also Timothy Fulford's "Romanticizing the Empire: The Naval Heroes of Southey, Coleridge, Austen, and Marryat."

2. Wentworth's naval background is very important to the maritime marriage that ends this novel. Tanner notes that "even though Anne and Wentworth are models of emotional stability and constancy, the emotions are by nature inherently potentially unstable" (246). Prewitt Brown adds that "Anne and Wentworth inherit the England of *Persuasion*, if only because they see it, and will experience it, as it really is: fragmented and uncertain. For the first time in Jane Austen, the future is not linked with the land" (146).

3. Roger Sales refers to Sir Walter as "an ageing dandy who spends a lot of time

admiring his face and figure in large looking-glasses. The family portraits watch him watching himself" (172).

4. Interestingly, he had earlier attempted to "free" himself from the Elliot tradition by marrying without the authorization of Sir Walter. Austen relates that "instead of pushing his fortune in the line marked out for the heir of the house of Elliot, he had purchased independence by uniting himself to a rich woman of inferior birth" (14).

5. Many critics have discussed this stubborn quality of Wentworth. Johnson claims that the hero's "steadfastness to the point of inflexibility actually aligns him with Sir Walter, and he must mitigate his self-will before reconciliation is possible" (*Jane Austen* 157). Michael Williams indicates that Wentworth "has a large and not unjustified self-confidence; he is always in search of sweeping and decisive action, always impatient of mere convention. He will where necessary defy authority, and he has an understanding that is as quick, emotionally, as it is in every other way" (163). LeRoy W. Smith simply dubs Wentworth "the most headstrong of Austen's heroes" (158). Smith adds that "Wentworth is not a fool or a hypocrite, but he is trapped by circumstances, sexual bias and masculine egotism. Before he can discover his own full nature or what a woman is, he must, like the female, exorcise the internalised patriarchal presence" (160).

6. Austen's novel is very much concerned with the financial successes of the navy during the Napoleonic Wars. For a detailed discussion of the financial prosperity enjoyed by many members of the British naval force, see Peter Smith's "Jane Austen's *Persuasion* and the Secret Conspiracy" and Monica F. Cohen's "Persuading the Navy Home: Austen and Married Women's Professional Property."

7. Austen carefully constructs Benwick's character. She relates that after the death of Fanny Harville, Benwick "considered his disposition as of the sort which must suffer heavily, uniting very strong feelings with quiet, serious, and retiring manners, and a decided taste for reading, and sedentary pursuits" (94–95). Austen also aligns Benwick with Byron and Scott through his tastes in poetry (98).

8. Prior to arriving in Bath, Wentworth travels "to see his brother in Shropshire," and we do not hear about Wentworth until Anne accidentally encounters Admiral Croft in Bath (128). Anne and the Admiral discuss the surprising news from Lyme that the melancholic Benwick and the recovering Louisa plan to marry. The Admiral attempts to explain Wentworth's response to this happening, suggesting that "Frederick is not a man to whine and complain; he has too much spirit for that. If the girl likes another man better, it is very fit she should have him" (163). Admiral Croft speaks of his brother-in-law as both a spirited and a rational man—one who will recover from this "disappointment" and one who apparently understands the rationale for Louisa's change of heart. The Admiral describes Wentworth as a strong individual who will overcome this setback, but we discover that the news of Benwick's relationship with Louisa actually fosters the hero's active pursuit of his desires for Anne.

9. Deleuze and Guattari believe that "sexuality is the production of a thousand sexes, which are so many uncontrollable becomings" (*Thousand Plateaus* 278). A sexual subject, according to Deleuze and Guattari, has the potential to experience a vast diversity of sexes, sexualities, and sexual sensations. The male figures of Austen's corpus are strongly discouraged from pursuing such profound multiplicity; in the decades following the unrest in France, the English nation requires sturdy and regulated men who can reestablish order.

10. He openly discusses the turmoil and pain of their recent trip to Lyme, concluding that "the day has produced some effects however—has had some consequences which

must be considered as the very reverse of frightful" (172). Wentworth's comment suggests his emerging understanding of the need to embrace unexpected events and surprising emotions. He is beginning to realize the significance of dynamic desires and malleability, and Anne reflects upon the alteration in Wentworth's behavior.

11. Austen relates how during this coastal expedition, "Captain Wentworth [had] looked round at [Anne] instantly in a way which shewed his noticing of it. He gave her a momentary glance,—a glance of brightness, which seemed to say, 'That man [Mr. Elliot] is struck with you,—and even I, at this moment, see something like Anne Elliot again'" (101).

12. Following the concert, Wentworth continues to struggle with his envy of Mr. Elliot, and when he encounters Anne in the company of the Harvilles and Musgroves she observes that "the same unfortunate persuasion, which had hastened him away from the concert room, still governed. He did not seem to want to be near enough for conversation." Wentworth remains apprehensive; he is frightened to reveal his powerful feelings for the heroine that could expose the latent multiplicity of his self and the potential malleability of his masculinity. When Anne discusses the travel plans of Mr. Elliot, "she felt that Captain Wentworth was looking at her; the consciousness of which vexed and embarrassed her, and made her regret that she had said so much" (209).

13. Anne charges that men are quicker to forget amorous emotions than women, instructing Harville that men "have always a profession, pursuits, business of some sort or other, to take you back into the world immediately, and continual occupation and change soon weaken impressions" (219). While Anne maintains a rather traditional view that women live a private life while men engage the public realm, Harville attempts to counter Anne's argument by employing a naval image. He declares, "if I could but make you comprehend what a man suffers when he takes a last look at his wife and children, and watches the boat that he has sent them off in, as long as it is in sight, and then turns away and says, 'God knows whether we ever meet again!'" (221). Harville's response reminds us of the transitory nautical existence that both he and Wentworth have lived over the past eight years and helps us imagine the emotion experienced by Wentworth during his time in the navy. We soon discover that Wentworth's various movements have not lessened his affection for the heroine.

14. Austen, on the final page of the story, specifically addresses Wentworth's compassionate assistance of Mrs. Smith "by putting her in the way of recovering her husband's property in the West Indies; by writing for her, acting for her, and seeing her through all the petty difficulties of the case, with the activity and exertion of a fearless man and a determined friend" (237).

Notes to Conclusion

1. Smith explained that "the annual labour of every nation is the fund which originally supplies it with all the necessaries and conveniences of life which it annually consumes, and which consist always, either in the immediate produce of that labour, or in what is purchased with that produce from other nations" (8). Smith adds that "the greatest improvement in the productive powers of labour, and the greater part of the skill, dexterity, and judgment with which it is any where directed, or applied, seem to have been the effects of the division of labour" (11).

2. I have argued elsewhere that America has historically turned to Austen as a potent

disciplinary force who has the power in both popular and academic culture to enforce conservative norms of heterosexuality. For a further discussion of this topic, see my article "The Potency of Jane, or the Disciplinary Function of Austen in America." Patricia Rozema's filmic adaptation of *Mansfield Park* (1999), the last of the Austen films released in the 1990s, posed a clear challenge to Morrow's conception of Austen. Jay Carr pronounced that Rozema's version of the fall of the Bertram family "continues Jane Austen's winning streak on film," and Kristine Huntley predicted that "yet another wave of Jane Austen mania is about to hit," but Rozema's film presented American popular culture with a notably distinct "Austen." The "Austen" of Rozema's *Mansfield Park* showed little inclination to inform us how to behave as stable socially proper sexualized subjects, and the movie left Americans wondering what happened to "Dear Aunt Jane." Eleanor Ringel Gillespie angrily asserted that Rozema revised the tale by giving it "a dash of lesbianism, a pinch of feminism and a dollop of social conscience." Desson Howe was also upset with this recent "perversion" of Austen's genteel world; Howe argued that "Rozema pushes the subtle Austen off the cliff of discretion. And discretion is the very essence of Austen's writing." Howe and Gillespie's comments reveal their expectation for an Austen who values the predictable simplicity of a mythical prior culture; like Morrow, Howe and Gillespie present Austen's stories as models of safety, manners, and propriety. Gillespie even concludes that "Rozema's at-arm's-length contemporary agenda may work as an intellectual exercise, but it robs the movie of any sense of anything being at stake."

And yet, Rozema's film actually heightens the social significance of Austen's corpus. The filmic adaptation captures the social complexity, sexual dynamism, and cultural instability of post-Revolutionary England, but as Johnson notes, these are features of Austen's corpus that admirers prefer to ignore. Johnson explains that "Rozema's movie is controversial because a powerful nostalgia motivates many assumptions about Austen, who is imagined to have celebrated a life that unfolded before the advent of the ills of modernity—such as doubt, war and, more recently, feminism and multiculturalism" ("This Is a *Mansfield Park*"). Although Austen's texts capture a moment of severe crisis in the history of the modern English nation, contemporary American culture continues to maintain an anachronistic view of Austen as a wise counselor who can provide us with guidelines for living a civilized and well-mannered life, replete with sexual regulations and gendered propriety. Rozema's film awakens American society to the reality that Austen never sought to offer an instruction manual for social/sexual stability. Austen's works do not provide us with characters who serve as paragons of the appropriate male and female subject; nor do her tales necessarily inform us how to live as stable and singular sexualized creatures. Austen's novels detail the responses of men and women to post-Revolutionary society's desires for their sexualities, and her narratives document how men and women curtail and manage their desires to ensure both their individual security and their involvement in the modern nation. Austen never attempts to draw us a map to a promised land of social stability; her works, indeed, suggest that such a sphere does not exist. She does, however, point the way to the sea, and while the sea holds no promises of security, it allows individuals the opportunity to embrace their own diversity as well as the complexity of others. It is at the sea where men and women can transcend the limits of their modern finitude and explore new desires without becoming reterritorialized.

WORKS CITED

◄◉►

Allen, Dennis W. "No Love for Lydia: The Fate of Desire in *Pride and Prejudice*." *Texas Studies in Literature and Language* 27 (1985): 425–43.

Allestree, Richard. *The Gentleman's Calling*. London: Robert Pawlet, 1676.

———. *The Ladies Calling: In Two Parts*. Oxford: Printed at the Theatre, 1673.

———. *The Whole Duty of Man: Laid Down, in a Plain and Familiar Way for the Use of All, But Especially the Meanest Reader*. London: Timothy Garthwait, 1661.

Anderson, Beatrice. "The Unmasking of Lady Susan." In *Jane Austen's Beginnings: The Juvenilia and* Lady Susan, edited by. J. David Grey, 193–203. Ann Arbor, MI: UMI Research Press, 1989.

Anderson, Benedict. *Imagined Communities: Reflections on the Origin and Spread of Nationalism*. 1983. Rev. ed. London: Verso, 1991.

Anonymous. *The Lady's Preceptor; or, A Letter to a Young Lady of Distinction upon Politeness*. London: J. Watts, 1743.

Armstrong, Nancy. *Desire and Domestic Fiction: A Political History of the Novel*. New York: Oxford University Press, 1987.

Auerbach, Nina. "O Brave New World: Evolution and Revolution in *Persuasion*." *ELH* 39 (1972): 112–28.

Austen, Jane. *Catharine and Other Writings*. Edited by Margaret Anne Doody and Douglas Murray. Oxford: Oxford University Press, 1993.

———. *Emma*. 1816. Edited by James Kinsley. Oxford: Oxford University Press, 1991.

———. *Mansfield Park*. 1814. Edited by James Kinsley. Oxford: Oxford University Press, 1991.

———. *Northanger Abbey, Lady Susan, The Watsons, and Sanditon*. Edited by John Davie. Oxford: Oxford University Press, 1991.

———. *Persuasion*. 1818. Edited by John Davie. Oxford: Oxford University Press, 1991.

———. *Pride and Prejudice*. 1813. Edited by James Kinsley. Oxford: Oxford University Press, 1991.

———. *Sense and Sensibility*. 1811. Edited by James Kinsley. Oxford: Oxford University Press, 1991.

Austen-Leigh, James Edward. *A Memoir of Jane Austen*. 1870. Edited by R.W. Chapman. Oxford: Oxford University Press, 1926.

Baidou, Alain. "Gilles Deleuze, The Fold: *Leibniz and the Baroque.*" *Gilles Deleuze and the Theatre of Philosophy.* Ed. Constantin V. Boundas and Dorothea Olkowski. New York: Routledge, 1994. 51–69.

Barker-Benfield, G. J. "Mary Wollstonecraft: Eighteenth-Century Commonwealthwoman." *Journal of the History of Ideas* 50 (1989): 95–115.

Beer, Frances. Introduction to *The Juvenilia of Jane Austen and Charlotte Brontë,* edited by Frances Beer, 7–30. Harmondsworth: Penguin Books, 1986.

Bogue, Ronald. *Deleuze and Guattari.* London: Routledge, 1989.

Boothby, Sir Brooke. *A Letter to the Right Honourable Edmund Burke.* London, 1791.

Boundas, Constantin V. "Deleuze: Serialization and Subject-Formation." *Gilles Deleuze and the Theatre of Philosophy.* Ed. Constantin V. Boundas and Dorothea Olkowski. New York: Routledge, 1994. 99–116.

Bly, Robert. *Iron John: A Book About Men.* Reading, MA: Addison-Wesley, 1990.

Brooks, Gary R., and Glenn E. Good. Introduction to *The New Handbook of Psychotherapy and Counseling with Men: A Comprehensive Guide to Settings, Problems and Treatment Approaches, Vol. I,* edited by Gary R. Brooks and Glenn E. Good. San Francisco: Jossey-Bass, 2001.

Brown, Julia Prewitt. *Jane Austen's Novels: Social Change and Literary Form.* Cambridge: Harvard University Press, 1979.

Brownstein, Rachel M. "Jane Austen: Irony and Authority." *Women's Studies* 15 (1988): 57–70.

Burke, Edmund. *Reflections on the Revolution in France, 1790–1794, Vol. 8.* 1794. In *The Writings and Speeches of Edmund Burke,* edited by. L. G. Mitchell, 53–293. Oxford: Clarendon Press, 1989.

Burney, Frances. *Camilla; Or a Picture of Youth.* 1796. Edited by Edward A. Bloom and Lillian D. Bloom. Oxford: Oxford University Press, 1972.

———. *Evelina, or, The History of a Young Lady's Entrance into the World.* 1778. Ed. Edward A. Bloom. Oxford: Oxford University Press.

Butler, Marilyn. *Jane Austen and the War of Ideas.* Oxford: Clarendon Press, 1975.

Canby, Henry Seidel. "The War and Jane Austen." *The Saturday Review of Literature* (December 5, 1942): 26.

Carr, Jay. "*Mansfield:* Jane Austen Shines Again." *Boston Globe* (November 24, 1999): C5.

Castle, Terry. Introduction to *Northanger Abbey, Lady Susan, The Watsons, and Senditon.* Ed. John Davie. Oxford: Oxford University Press, 1991. vii–xxxii.

———. "Sister-Sister." *The London Review of Books* 17 (August 3, 1995): 3–6.

Chaber, Lois A. "Transgressive Youth: Lady Mary, Jane Austen, and the Juvenilia Press." *Eighteenth-Century Fiction* 8 (1995): 81–88.

Chandler, Alice. *A Dream of Order: The Medieval Ideal in Nineteenth-Century English Literature.* Lincoln: University of Nebraska Press, 1970.

Chesterfield, Earl of. *Letters to His Son on the Fine Art of Becoming A Man of the World and a Gentleman.* 2 Vols. 1746–47. Washington: M. Walter Dunne, 1901.

Claeys, Gregory. "Republicanism versus Commercial Society: Paine, Burke and the French Revolution Debate." *History of European Ideas* 11 (1989): 313–24.

Cohen, Monica F. "Persuading the Navy Home: Austen and Married Women's Professional Property." *Novel* 29, no. 3 (1996): 346–66.

Colley, Linda. *Britons: Forging the Nation, 1707–1837.* New Haven, CT: Yale University Press, 1992.

Connell, R. W. *Masculinities.* Berkeley: University of California Press, 1995.

Crafton, Lisa Plummer. *The French Revolution Debate in English Literature and Culture.*

Westport, CT: Greenwood, Press, 1997.

Davidoff, Leonore, and Catherine Hall. *Family Fortunes: Men and Women of the English Middle Class, 1780–1850.* Chicago: University of Chicago Press, 1987.

De Bruyn, Frans. "Edmund Burke's Natural Aristocrat: The 'Man of Taste' as a Political Ideal." *Eighteenth-Century Life* 11 (1987): 41–60.

Deane, Seamus. *The French Revolution and Enlightenment in England, 1798–1832.* Cambridge, MA: Harvard University Press, 1988.

Deleuze, Gilles. "Control and Becoming." In *Negotiations, 1972–1990.* Translated by Martin Joughin, 169–76. New York: Columbia University Press, 1995.

———. *The Fold: Leibniz and the Baroque.* Translated by Tom Conley. Minneapolis: University of Minnesota Press, 1993.

———. *Foucault.* 1986. Translated by Seán Hand. Minneapolis: University of Minnesota Press, 1988.

———. "A Letter to a Harsh Critic." In *Negotiations, 1972–1990.* Translated by Martin Joughin, 3–12. New York: Columbia University Press, 1995.

———. "On Philosophy." In *Negotiations, 1972–1990.* Translated by Martin Joughin, 135–55. New York: Columbia University Press, 1995.

———. *Proust and Signs.* 1964. Translated by Richard Howard. New York: George Braziller, 1972.

Deleuze, Gilles, and Félix Guattari. *Anti-Oedipus: Capitalism and Schizophrenia.* Translated by Robert Hurley, Mark Seem, and Helen R. Lane. Minneapolis: University of Minnesota Press, 1983.

———. *A Thousand Plateaus: Capitalism & Schizophrenia.* Translated by Brian Massumi. Minneapolis: University of Minnesota Press, 1987.

———. *What Is Philosophy?* Translated by Hugh Tomlinson and Graham Burchell. New York: Columbia University Press, 1991.

D'Israeli, Isaac. *Vaurien: Or, Sketches of the Times: Exhibiting Views of the Philosophies, Religions, Politics, Literature, and Manners of the Age.* 2 Vols. London: T. Cadell, 1797.

Doody, Margaret A. Introduction to *Catharine and Other Writings,* edited by Margaret Anne Doody and Douglas Murray, ix–xxxviii. Oxford: Oxford University Press, 1993.

Doody, Margaret Anne, and Douglas Murray, eds. *Catharine and Other Writings.* Oxford: Oxford University Press, 1993.

Drabble, Margaret. Foreword to *Jane Austen's Beginnings: The Juvenilia and* Lady Susan, edited by J. David Grey, xiii–xiv. Ann Arbor, MI: UMI Research Press, 1989.

Duara, Prasenjit. "Historicizing National Identity, or Who Imagines What and When." In *Becoming National: A Reader,* edited by Geoff Eley and Ronald Grigor Suny, 151–77. New York: Oxford University Press, 1996.

Duckworth, Alistair M. *The Improvement of the Estate: A Study of Jane Austen's Novels.* Baltimore: The Johns Hopkins University Press, 1971.

Epstein, Julia. "Jane Austen's Juvenilia and the Female Epistolary Tradition." *Papers on Language and Literature: A Journal for Scholars and Critics of Language and Literature* 21 (1985): 399–416.

Essex, John. *The Young Ladies Conduct: or, Rules for education, under several heads; with instructions upon dress, both before and after marriage; and advice to young wives.* London: John Broterton, 1722.

Evans, Mary. *Jane Austen and the State.* London: Tavistock Publications, 1987.

Ferguson, Moira. "*Mansfield Park:* Slavery, Colonialism, and Gender." *The Oxford Liter-*

ary Review 13 (1991): 118–39.

Fogel, Gerald I. "Introduction: Being a Man." In *The Psychology of Men: New Psycho-analytic Perspectives,* edited by Gerald I. Fogel, Frederick M. Lane, and Robert S. Liebert, 3–22. New York: Basic Books, 1986.

Foucault, Michel. "The Ethics of the Concern of the Self as a Practice of Freedom." In *Ethics, Subjectivity, and Truth: The Essential Works of Michel Foucault, 1954–1984,* edited by Paul Rabinow, 281–301. New York: The New Press, 1994.

———. *The History of Sexuality, Vol. 1: An Introduction.* Translated by Robert Hurley. New York: Vintage Books, 1978.

———. *The History of Sexuality, Vol. 2: The Use of Pleasure.* Translated by Robert Hurley. New York: Pantheon Books, 1985.

———. *The History of Sexuality, Vol. 3: The Care of the Self.* Translated by Robert Hurley. New York: Vintage Books, 1986.

———. "Omnes et Singulation": Toward a Critique of Political Reason." In *Power: The Essential Works of Michel Foucault, 1954–1984,* edited by Paul Rabinow, 298–325. New York: The New Press, 1994.

———. "On the Genealogy of Ethics: An Overview of Work in Progress." In *Ethics, Subjectivity, and Truth: The Essential Works of Michel Foucault, 1954–1984,* edited by Paul Rabinow, 253–80. New York: The New Press, 1994.

———. *The Order of Things: An Archaeology of the Human Sciences.* New York: Vintage Books, 1970.

———. "Sexual Choice, Sexual Act." In *Ethics, Subjectivity, and Truth: The Essential Works of Michel Foucault, 1954–1984,* edited by Paul Rabinow, 141–56. New York: The New Press, 1994.

———. "The Social Triumph of the Sexual Will." In *Ethics, Subjectivity, and Truth: The Essential Works of Michel Foucault, 1954–1984,* edited by Paul Rabinow, 157–62. New York: The New Press, 1994.

———. "Writing the Self." In *Foucault and His Interlocutors,* edited by Arnold I. Davidson, 234–47. Chicago: The University of Chicago Press, 1997.

Freud, Sigmund. *Sexuality and the Psychology of Love.* Translated by James Strachey. New York: Collier Books, 1925.

Fritzer, Penelope Joan. *Jane Austen and Eighteenth-Century Courtesy Books.* Westport, CT: Greenwood Press, 1997.

Fulford, Tim. *Romanticism and Masculinity: Gender, Politics and Poetics in the Writings of Burke, Coleridge, Cobbett, Wordsworth, De Quincey, and Hazlitt.* London: Palgrave Publishers, 1999.

———. "Romanticizing the Empire: The Naval Heroes of Southey, Coleridge, Austen, and Marryat." *Modern Language Quarterly* 60, no. 2 (1999): 161–96.

———. "Sighing for a Soldier: Jane Austen and Military Pride and Prejudice." *Nineteenth-Century Literature* 57, no. 2 (2002): 153–78.

Furniss, Tom. *Edmund Burke's Aesthetic Ideology: Language, Gender, and Political Economy in Revolution.* Cambridge: Cambridge University Press, 1993.

Gardiner, Judith Kegan, ed. *Masculinity Studies and Feminist Theory: New Directions.* New York: Columbia University Press, 2002.

———. "Theorizing Age with Gender: Bly's Boys, Feminism, and Maturity Masculinity." In *Masculinity Studies and Feminist Theory: New Directions,* edited by Judith Kegan Gardiner, 90–118. New York: Columbia University Press, 2002.

Gilbert, Sandra, and Susan Gubar. *The Madwoman in the Attic: The Woman Writer and the Nineteenth-Century Literary Imagination.* New Haven, CT: Yale University Press, 1979.

Gillespie, Eleanor Ringel. "Jane Austen 'updated'—too bad." *The Atlanta Journal and Constitution* (December 24, 1999): 3.

Gilroy, Paul. "One Nation under a Groove: The Cultural Politics of 'Race' and Racism in Britain." In *Becoming National: A Reader,* edited by Geoff Eley and Ronald Grigor Suny, 352–69. New York: Oxford University Press, 1996.

Gisborne, Thomas. *An Enquiry into the Duties of Men in the Higher and Middle Classes of Society in Great Britain.* 2 volumes. 1794. 5th ed. London: A Strahan, 1800.

Gleadle, Kathryn. "British Women and Radical Politics in the Late Nonconformist Enlightenment, c. 1780–1830." *Women, Privilege, and Power.* Ed. Amanda Vickery. Stanford: Stanford University Press, 2001. 123–51.

Godwin, William. *Caleb Williams.* 1794. Edited by David McCracken. London: Oxford University Press, 1970.

———. *Enquiry Concerning Political Justice and Its Influence on Morals and Happiness.* 3 volumes. 1793. Edited by F. E. L. Priestley. Toronto: The University of Toronto Press, 1946.

Goodman, Ellen. "Jane Austen's Sensibility Makes Sense Today." *Boston Globe* (December 17, 1995): A23.

Gouge, William. *Of Domesticall Duties.* 1622. Amsterdam: Walter J. Johnson, Inc., 1976.

Gray, John. *Men Are from Mars, Women Are from Venus: A Practical Guide for Improving Communication and Getting What You Want in Your Relationships.* New York: Harper Collins Publishers, 1992.

Gregory, John. *A Father's Legacy to His Daughters.* 1774. New York: Garland Publishing, 1974.

Grey, J. David, ed. *Jane Austen's Beginnings: The Juvenilia and* Lady Susan. Ann Arbor, MI: UMI Research Press, 1989.

Grunwald, Henry. "Jane Austen's Civil Society." *The Wall Street Journal* (October 2, 1996): A16.

Guest, Harriet. *Small Change: Women, Learning, Patriotism, 1750–1810.* Chicago: University of Chicago Press, 2000.

Halperin, John. "Introduction: Jane Austen's Nineteenth-Century Critics: Walter Scott to Henry James." In *Jane Austen: Bicentenary Essays,* edited by John Halperin, 3–42. Cambridge: Cambridge University Press, 1975.

———. "Unengaged Laughter: Jane Austen's Juvenilia." In *Jane Austen's Beginnings: The Juvenilia and Lady Susan.* Ed. J. David Grey. Ann Arbor: UMI Research Press, 1989. 29–44.

Hamilton, Elizabeth. *Memoirs of Modern Philosophers: A Novel.* 1800. 3 Vols. New York: Garland Publishing, 1974.

Hardy, John. *Jane Austen's Heroines: Intimacy in Human Relationships.* London: Routledge & Kegan Paul, 1984.

Harris, Jocelyn. *Jane Austen's Art of Memory.* Cambridge: Cambridge University Press, 1989.

Hawkridge, Audrey. *Jane and Her Gentlemen: Jane Austen and the Men in Her Life and Novels.* London: Peter Owen Publishers, 2000.

Hays, Mary. *Appeal to the Men of Great Britain on Behalf of Women.* 1798. New York: Garland Publishers, 1974.

———. *Memoirs of Emma Courtney.* 1796. Edited by Eleanor Ty. Oxford: Oxford University Press, 1996.

————. *The Victim of Prejudice.* 1799. Edited by Eleanor Ty. Peterborough, Ontario: Broadview Press, 1998.

Heldman, James. "How Wealthy Is Mr. Darcy—*Really?*: Pounds and Dollars in the World of *Pride and Prejudice.*" *Persuasions* 12 (1990): 38–49.

Hobson, Harold. "War Hasn't Touched Jane Austen." *Christian Science Monitor* (December, 19, 1942): 6.

Hoeveler, Diane. "Vindicating *Northanger Abbey:* Mary Wollstonecraft, Jane Austen, and Gothic Feminism." In *Jane Austen and Discourses of Feminism,* edited by Devoney Looser, 117–35. New York: St. Martin's Press, 1995.

Holcroft, Thomas. *Anna St. Ives.* 1792. Edited by Peter Faulkner. London: Oxford University Press, 1970.

Hopkins, Lisa. "Mr. Darcy's Body: Privileging the Female Gaze." In *Jane Austen in Hollywood,* edited by Linda Troost and Sayre Greenfield, 111–21. Lexington: The University Press of Kentucky, 1998.

Horwitz, Barbara. "Lady Susan: The Wicked Mother in Jane Austen's Work." In *Jane Austen's Beginnings: The Juvenilia and Lady Susan,* edited by J. David Grey, 181–91. Ann Arbor, MI: UMI Research Press, 1989.

Howe, Desson. "*Mansfield Park:* Austen Dour." *Washington Post* (November 26, 1999): N45.

Huntley, Kristine. "The Friendly Jane Austen: A Well-Mannered Introduction to a Lady of Sense and Sensibility." *The Booklist* (November 15, 1999): 595.

Hroch, Miroslav. "From National Movement to Fully-Formed Nation: The Nation-Building Process in Europe." *Becoming National: A Reader.* Ed. Geoff Eley and Ronald Grigor Suny. Oxford: Oxford University Press, 1996. 60–77.

Imlay, Gilbert. *The Emigrants.* 1793. Gainesville, FL: Scholars' Facsimiles & Reprints, 1964.

Inchbald, Elizabeth. *Nature and Art.* 1796. Edited by Shawn L. Maurer. London: Pickering & Chatto, 1997.

————. *A Simple Story.* 1791. Edited by J. M. S. Tompkins. London: Oxford University Press, 1967.

"Jane Extended." *Time* (January 19, 1959): 92.

Jerinic, Maria. "In Defense of the Gothic: Rereading *Northanger Abbey.*" In *Jane Austen and Discourses of Feminism,* edited by Devoney Looser, 137–49. New York: St. Martin's Press, 1995.

Johnson, Claudia. "Austen Cults and Cultures." In *The Cambridge Companion to Jane Austen,* edited by Edward Copeland and Juliet McMaster, 211–26. Cambridge: Cambridge University Press, 1997.

————. "The Divine Miss Jane: Jane Austen, Janeites and the Discipline of Novel Studies." In *Reception Study: From Literary Theory to Cultural Studies,* edited by James L. Machor and Philip Goldstein, 119–32. New York: Routledge, 2001.

————. Editorial Response to "Sister-Sister." *London Review of Books* 17 (October 5, 1995): 4.

————. *Equivocal Beings: Politics, Gender, and Sentimentality in the 1790s— Wollstonecraft, Radcliffe, Burney, Austen.* Chicago: The University of Chicago Press, 1995.

————. *Jane Austen: Women, Politics, and the Novel.* Chicago: The University of Chicago Press, 1988.

————. "'The Kingdom at Sixes and Sevens': Politics and the Juvenilia." In *Jane Austen's Beginnings: The Juvenilia and Lady Susan,* edited by J. David Grey, 45–58. Ann

Arbor, MI: UMI Research Press, 1989.

———. "This Is a *Mansfield Park* Worth Visiting." *The Los Angeles Times* (December 20, 1999): 3.

Kadish, Doris Y. *Politicizing Gender: Narrative Strategies in the Aftermath of the French Revolution.* New Brunswick, NJ: Rutgers University Press, 1991.

Kaplan, Deborah. *Jane Austen among Women.* Baltimore: The Johns Hopkins University Press, 1992.

———. "Mass Marketing Jane Austen: Men, Women, and Courtship in Two of the Recent Films." *Persuasions* 18 (December 16, 1996): 171–81.

Kelly, Gary. "Reading Aloud in *Mansfield Park.*" In *Jane Austen: Modern Critical Views,* edited by Harold Bloom, 129–46. New York: Chelsea House Publishers, 1986.

———. *Revolutionary Feminism: The Mind and Career of Mary Wollstonecraft.* New York: St. Martin's Press, 1992.

Kestner, Joseph A. "Jane Austen: Revolutionizing Masculinities." *Persuasions* 16 (1994): 147–60.

Kidron, Hedva Ben-Israel. *English Historians on the French Revolution.* London: Cambridge University Press, 1968.

Kimmel, Michael. *The Gendered Society.* New York: Oxford University Press, 2000.

———. *Manhood in America: A Cultural History.* New York: Free Press, 1996.

———. *The Politics of Manhood: Profeminist Men Respond to the Mythopoetic Men's Movement (And the Mythopoetic Leaders Answer).* Philadelphia: Temple University Press, 1995.

Kimmel, Michael, and Michael Kaufman. "Weekend Warriors: The New Men's Movement." In *Theorizing Masculinities,* edited by Harry Brod and Michael Kaufman, 259–88. London: Sage Publications, 1994.

King, Sophia. *Waldorf: Or, the Dangers of Philosophy.* 2 volumes. 1798. New York: Garland Publishing, 1974.

Kirkham, Margaret. *Jane Austen, Feminism and Fiction.* Sussex: The Harvester Press, 1983.

Knuth, Deborah J. "'We Fainted Alternately on a Sofa': Female Friendship in Jane Austen's Juvenilia." *Persuasions* 9 (1987): 64–71.

Koppel, Gene. "*Pride and Prejudice:* Conservative or Liberal Novel—Or Both? (A Gadmerian Approach)." *Persuasions* 11 (1989): 132–39.

Kramp, Michael. "The Potency of Jane, or the Disciplinary Function of Austen in America." *Studies in Popular Culture* 22, no. 2 (1999): 19–32.

Lewis, Matthew. *The Monk.* 1796. Edited by Howard Anderson. Oxford: Oxford University Press, 1973.

Litvak, Joseph. "Charming Men, Charming History." *Genders* 24 (1996): 248–74.

———. "Delicacy and Disgust, Mourning and Melancholia, Privilege and Perversity: *Pride and Prejudice.*" *Qui Parle* 6 (1992): 35–51.

Looser, Devoney. "Jane Austen 'Responds' to the Men's Movement." *Persuasions* 18 (December 16, 1996): 159–70.

Loveridge, Mark. "*Northanger Abbey;* or, Nature and Probability." *Nineteenth-Century Literature* 56 (1991): 1–29.

Macaulay, Catherine. *Letters on Education . . . with Observations on Metaphysical and Metaphysical Subjects.* London, 1790. New York: Garland Publishing, 1974.

———. *On Burke's Reflections on the French Revolution.* 1790. Poole: Woodstock Books, 1997.

MacDonagh, Oliver. "The Church in *Mansfield Park:* A Serious Call?" *Sydney Studies in English* 12 (1986–87): 36–55.

Marantz Cohen, Paula. "Jane Austen's Rejection of Rousseau: A Novelistic and Feminist Initiation." *Papers on Language and Literature* 30 (1994): 215–34.

Mason, Philip. *The English Gentleman: The Rise and Fall of an Ideal.* New York: William Morrow and Company, 1982.

McAleer, John. "The Comedy of Social Distinctions in *Pride and Prejudice.*" *Persuasions* 11 (1989): 70–76.

McCartney, Bill, Stephen Griffith, Bill Deckard, and Promise Keepers. *What Makes a Man?: 12 Promises That Will Change Your Life.* Colorado Springs: Navpress, 1992.

McClintock, Anne. "'No Longer in a Future Heaven': Nationalism, Gender, and Race." In *Becoming National: A Reader,* edited by Geoff Eley and Ronald Grigor Suny, 260–84. New York: Oxford University Press, 1996.

McKellar, Hugh. "*Lady Susan:* Sport or Cinderella?" In *Jane Austen's Beginnings: The Juvenilia and* Lady Susan, edited by J. David Grey, 205–14. Ann Arbor, MI: UMI Research Press, 1989.

McLaren, Angus. *The Trials of Masculinity: Policing Sexual Boundaries, 1870–1930.* Chicago: University of Chicago Press, 1997.

McMaster, Juliet. "Class." In *The Cambridge Companion to Jane Austen,* edited by Edward Copeland and Juliet McMaster, 115–30. Cambridge: Cambridge University Press, 1997.

Messner, Michael A. *Politics of Masculinities: Men in Movements.* Thousand Oaks, CA: Sage Publications, 1997.

Miller. D. A. *Jane Austen, or the Secret of Style.* Princeton, NJ: Princeton University Press, 2003.

Mitchell, L. G. Introduction. *Reflections on the Revolution in France,* edited by L. G. Mitchell. Oxford: Oxford University Press, 1993. vii–xix.

Moir, Anne, and Bill Moir. *Why Men Don't Iron: The Fascinating and Unalterable Differences Between Men and Women.* New York: Kensington Publishing, 1999.

Monaghan, David. *Jane Austen: Structure and Social Vision.* New York: Barnes and Noble, 1980.

Mooneyham, Laura G. *Romance, Language and Education in Jane Austen's Novels.* New York: St. Martin's Press, 1988.

More, Hannah. *Strictures on the Modern System of Female Education.* 2 Vols. 1799. Bristol: Thoemmes Press, 1995.

Morgan, Susan. *In the Meantime: Character and Perception in Jane Austen's Fiction.* Chicago: The University of Chicago Press, 1980.

Morrow, Laurie. "Mannerly Novels for an Ill-Mannered Age." *The World & I* 11 (1996): 261–74.

Mudrick, Marvin. *Jane Austen: Irony as Defense and Discovery.* Princeton, NJ: Princeton University Press, 1952.

Nagel, Joane. "Nation." In *Handbook of Studies on Men & Masculinities,* edited by Michael S. Kimmel, Jeff Hearn, and R. W. Connell, 397–413. Thousand Oaks, CA: Sage Publications, 2005.

Nixon, Cheryl L. "Balancing the Courtship Hero: Masculine Emotional Display in Film Adaptations of Austen's Novels." In *Jane Austen in Hollywood,* edited by Linda Troost and Sayre Greenfield, 22–43. Lexington: The University Press of Kentucky, 1998.

Ollivier, Alfred P. "Jane Austen's Male Characters." M.A. thesis, Boston College, 1950.

Paine, Thomas. *Rights of Man.* 1791–92. In *Rights of Man, Common Sense, and Other Political Writings,* edited by Mark Philip. Oxford: Oxford University Press, 1995.

Pedley, Colin. "'Terrific and Unprincipled Compositions': The Reception of *Lovers' Vows* and *Mansfield Park.*" *Philological Quarterly* 74 (1995): 297–316.

Poovey, Mary. *The Proper Lady and the Woman Writer: Ideology as Style in the Works of Mary Wollstonecraft, Mary Shelley, and Jane Austen.* Chicago: The University of Chicago Press, 1984.

Price, Richard. *A Discourse on the Love of Our Country.* Oxford: Woodstock Books, 1992.

Priestley, Joseph. *Letters to Burke.* 1791. Washington, DC: Woodstock Books, 1997.

Radcliffe, Ann. *The Italian.* 1797. Edited by Frederick Garber. London: Oxford University Press, 1968.

———. *The Romance of the Forest.* 1791. Edited by Chloe Chard. Oxford: Oxford University Press, 1999.

———. *A Sicilian Romance.* 1790. Edited by Alison Milbank. Oxford: Oxford University Press, 1993.

Radcliffe, Mary Anne. *The Female Advocate.* 1799. New York: Garland Publishing, 1974.

Renan, Ernest. "What Is a Nation?" In *Becoming National: A Reader,* edited by Geoff Eley and Ronald Grigor Suny, 42–55. New York: Oxford University Press, 1996.

Rowen, Norma. "Reinscribing Cinderella: Jane Austen and the Fairy Tale." In *Functions of the Fantastic: Selected Essays from the Thirteenth International Conference on the Fantastic in the Arts,* edited by Joe Sanders, 29–36. Westport, CT: Greenwood Press, 1992.

Rzepka, Charles J. "Making It in a Brave New World: Marriage, Profession, and Anti-Romantic *Ekstasis* in Austen's *Persuasion.*" *Studies in the Novel* 26 (1994): 99–115.

Sales, Roger. *Jane Austen and the Representations of Regency England.* London: Routledge, 1994.

Sapiro, Virginia. *A Vindication of Political Virtue: The Political Theory of Mary Wollstonecraft.* Chicago: The University of Chicago Press, 1992.

Scott, Sir Walter. *Waverley; or, 'Tis Sixty Years Since.* 1814. Edited by Claire Lamont. Oxford: Clarendon Press, 1981.

Sedgwick, Eve Kosofsky. "Jane Austen and the Masturbating Girl." In *Close Reading: The Reader,* edited by Frank Lentricchia and Andrew DuBois, 301–320. Durham, NC: Duke University Press, 2003.

Shaftesbury, Earl Anthony. *Characteristics of Men, Manners, Opinions, Times.* 1711. Edited by John M. Robertson. Vols. I–II. Indianapolis: The Bobbs-Merrill Company, 1964.

Sherrod, Barbara. "*Pride and Prejudice:* A Classic Love Story." *Persuasions* 11 (1989): 66–69.

Shoemaker, Robert B. *Gender in English Society, 1650–1850: The Emergence of Separate Spheres?* London: Longman, 1998.

Silverman, Kaja. *Male Subjectivity at the Margins.* New York: Routledge, 1992.

"Single Irish Female." *Stranger* 29 July 1999:85.

Skinner, Gillian. *Sensibility and Economics in the Novel, 1740–1900: The Price of a Tear.* New York: St. Martin's Press, 1999.

Skinner, John. "Exploring Space: The Constellations of *Mansfield Park.*" *Eighteenth Century Fiction* 4 (1992): 125–48.

Smith, Adam. *An Inquiry into the Nature and Causes of the Wealth of Nations.* Oxford:

Oxford University Press, 1993.

Smith, Charlotte. *Desmond*. 1792. Edited by Antje Blank and Janet Todd. London: Pickering & Chatto, 1997.

―――. *The Young Philosopher: A Novel*. 1798. 4 Vols. New York: Garland Publishing, 1974.

Smith, LeRoy W. *Jane Austen and the Drama of Woman*. New York: Macmillan, 1983.

Smith, Peter. "Jane Austen's *Persuasion* and the Secret Conspiracy." *Cambridge Quarterly* 24 (1995): 279–303.

―――. "Politics and Religion in Jane Austen's *Emma*." *Cambridge Quarterly* 26 (1997): 219–41.

Smith, Phoebe A. "*Sense and Sensibility* and 'The Lady's Law': The Failure of Benevolent Paternalism." *The CEA Critic* 55 (1993): 3–25.

Solomon-Godeau, Abigail. "Male Trouble." In *Constructing Masculinity*, edited by Maurice Berger, Brian Wallis, and Simon Watson, 69–76. London: Routledge, 1995.

Southam, B. C. Introduction to *Jane Austen: The Critical Heritage, 1811–1870, Vol. 1*, edited by B. C. Southam. London: Routledge & Kegan Paul, 1968. 1–3.

―――. Introduction to *Jane Austen: The Critical Heritage 1870–1940, Vol. 2*, edited by B. C. Southam, 1–158. London: Routledge & Kegan Paul, 1987.

Stanlis, Peter J. *Edmund Burke: The Enlightenment and Revolution*. New Brunswick, NJ: Transaction Publishers, 1991.

Stovel, Bruce. "'A Contrariety of Emotion': Jane Austen's Ambivalent Lovers in *Pride and Prejudice*." *International Fiction Review* 14, no. 1 (1987): 27–33.

Tanner, Tony. *Jane Austen*. London: Macmillan, 1986.

Tracy, Laura. "Relational Competence: Jane Austen's *Persuasion*." *Persuasions* 18 (December 16, 1996): 154–58.

Trilling, Lionel. "Emma." *Encounter* 8 (1957): 49–59.

Tuite, Clara. *Romantic Austen: Sexual Politics and the Literary Canon*. Cambridge: Cambridge University Press, 2002.

Turan, Kenneth. "*Pride and Prejudice*: An Informal History of the Garson-Olivier Motion Picture." *Persuasions* 11 (1989): 140–43.

Ty, Eleanor. *Unsex'd Revolutionaries: Five Women Novelists of the 1790s*. Toronto: University of Toronto Press, 1993.

Tyler, Natalie. *The Friendly Jane Austen: A Well-Mannered Introduction to a Lady of Sense and Sensibility*. New York: Viking, 1999.

Usui, Masami. "Fanny's Awakening to Herself in Quest for Privacy in Jane Austen's *Mansfield Park*." *Studies in Culture and the Humanities* 2 (1993): 1–28.

Van Sant, Ann Jessie. *Eighteenth-Century Sensibility and the Novel: The Senses in Social Context*. Cambridge: Cambridge University Press, 1993.

Veyne, Paul. "The Final Foucault and His Ethics." In *Foucault and His Interlocutors*, edited by Arnold I. Davidson, 225–33. Chicago: The University of Chicago Press, 1997.

Vickery, Amanda, ed. *Women, Privilege, and Power: British Politics, 1750 to the Present*. Stanford, CA: Stanford University Press, 2001.

Wallace, Tara Ghoshal. "*Northanger Abbey* and the Limits of Parody." *Studies in the Novel* 20 (1988): 262–73.

―――. "*Sense and Sensibility* and the Problem of Feminine Authority." *Eighteenth-Century Fiction* 4 (1992): 149–63.

Watt, Ian. Introduction to *Jane Austen: A Collection of Critical Essays*, edited by Ian Watt, 1–14. Englewood Cliffs, NJ: Prentice-Hall, 1963.

Weinsheimer, Joel. "Chance and the Hierarchy of Marriages in *Pride and Prejudice*." In *Jane Austen: Modern Critical Views*, edited by Harold Bloom, 13–25. New York: Chelsea House Publishers, 1986.

West, Jane. *The Advantages of Education: Or, the History of Maria Williams*. 1793. 2 Vols. New York: Garland Publishing, 1974.

———. *A Gossip's Story, and a Legendary Tale*. 1797. 2 Vols. New York: Garland Publishing, 1974.

———. *Letters Addressed to a Young Man on His First Entrance into Life*. 1801. 2 Vols. Boston: Samuel H. Parker, 1803.

———. *A Tale of the Times*. 1799. 3 Vols. New York: Garland Publishing, 1974.

White, Stephen K. *Edmund Burke: Modernity, Politics, and Aesthetics*. Thousand Oaks, CA: Sage Publications, 1994.

Wiegman, Robyn. *American Anatomies: Theorizing Race and Gender*. Durham, NC: Duke University Press, 1995.

———. "Unmaking: Men and Masculinity in Feminist Theory." In *Masculinity Studies and Feminist Theory: New Directions*, edited by Judith Kegan Gardiner, 31–59. New York: Columbia University Press, 2002.

Williams, Michael. *Jane Austen: Six Novels and Their Methods*. New York: St. Martin's Press, 1986.

Wiltshire, John. *Jane Austen and the Body: "The Picture of Health."* Cambridge: Cambridge University Press, 1992.

Wollstonecraft, Mary. *A Vindication of the Rights of Men*. London, 1790. In *The Works of Mary Wollstonecraft*, Vol. 5, edited by Janet Todd and Marilyn Butler, 1–60. New York: New York University Press, 1989.

———. *A Vindication of the Rights of Woman*. London, 1792. In *The Works of Mary Wollstonecraft*, Vol. 5, edited by Janet Todd and Marilyn Butler, 61–266. New York: New York University Press, 1989.

Woolf, Virginia. "Jane Austen." In *The Common Reader*, 191–206. New York: Harcourt, Brace & Company, 1925.

Worthington, Pepper. "Jane Austen's Image of Female Character and Personality in *Mansfield Park*." *Mount Olive Review: Images of Women in Literature* 6 (1992): 61–76.

Wright, Andrew H. "*Persuasion*." In *Jane Austen: A Collection of Critical Essays*, edited by Ian Watt, 145–53. Englewood Cliffs, NJ: Prentice-Hall, 1963.

Yuval-Davis, Nira. *Gender & Nation*. London: Sage Publications, 1997.

Zaw, Susan Khin. "'Appealing to the head *and* heart': Wollstonecraft and Burke on *taste, morals* and *human nature*." In *Femininity and Masculinity in Eighteenth-Century Art and Culture*, edited by Gill Perry and Michael Rossington, 123–41. Manchester: Manchester University Press, 1994.

Zook, Alma C. "Star-gazing at Mansfield Park." *Persuasions* 8 (1986): 29–33.

INDEX

◄○►

Adams, Rachel, 155n14

The Advantages of Education (West), 67, 69

Allen, Dennis, 173n11

Allestree, Richard, 23, 31–32. See also *The Gentleman's Calling; The Whole Duty of Man*

anti-Jacobins, 21; critique of Jacobin figures, 59; philosophical advisor figure, 43–45, 54; political and novelistic tradition, 27–28, 43, 175n1

American Anatomies (Wiegman), 8

American Revolution, 19, 159n14

Anderson, Beatrice, 165n13

Anderson, Benedict, 156n1

Anna St. Ives (Holcroft), 61

Appeal to the Men of Great Britain (Hays), 31

Armstrong, Nancy, 122, 157n7, 158n8

Auerbach, Nina, 178n1

Austen, Jane: authority on love and marriage, 3–4, 153n3; critical emphasis on love and marriage, 4–5; critical emphasis on women, 4, 143, 153n3, 154n9; critical treatments of men, 4–5, 155–56n15; enduring cultural appeal of narratives, ix, xi–xiii, 3, 147–48, 151n1, 181n2; heteronormativity of scholarship, 4, 153n3, 153–54n6, 181n2; icon status of male characters, 6, 156n17; mid-1990s cultural revival, ix–xii, 7–8, 147–48, 152n4, 181n2; post–World War II reception, 151–52n1, 152n4; prominence in queer culture, 154n7; role of 1790s in critical treatments of, 157n2. *See also specific works;* Jane Austen Society of North America (JASNA); Janeitism

Austen-Leigh, James Edward, 151–52n1

Badiou, Alain, 155n12

Barker-Benfield, G. J., 26, 160n24

Beer, Francis, 161–62n5

Bentham, Jeremy, 45

Blair, Hugh, 166n23

Bly, Robert, ix–xii, 5, 148, 152n2; Wild Man, 148

Bogue, Ronald, 153n2

Booth, Wayne, 153n4

Boothby, Sir Brooke, 26, 28–29

Boundas, Constantin V., 155n12

Brooks, Gary R., 148

Brown, Julia Prewitt, 112, 119, 139, 176n17, 179n2

Brown, Patricia P., 153n4

Brownstein, Rachel, 174n13

Burke, Edmund, 11–12, 21, 32, 63, 77, 159n14; on chivalry, 22–26, 31, 74–75, 81, 90, 129, 159n17, 160n26; ancestral cultural vision, 24–28, 44, 76, 84, 105, 126, 159n17; on aristocratic principles and social responsibility; 22–23, 41, 45, 63, 74, 77, 89, 112, 159n15, 159n16,